THE
HEALTHY
BEEF
COOKBOOK

Steaks, Salads, Stir-fry, and More—
Over 130 Luscious Lean Beef
Recipes for Every Occasion

National Cattlemen's Beef Association
American Dietetic Association

Richard Chamberlain
Betsy Hornick, MS, RD

John Wiley & Sons, Inc.

Recipe development, photography, and beef culinary information were funded by beef producers through the Cattlemen's Beef Board. The checkoff program was established as part of the 1985 Farm Bill and assesses $1 per head on the sale of domestic and imported cattle and beef products to fund research and educate American consumers about beef. The Cattlemen's Beef Board administers the checkoff program, subject to USDA approval, and contracts with industry organizations to carry out science-based nutrition education and communications, as well as other promotion, education, and research projects. National Cattlemen's Beef Association serves as one of the Beef Board's contractors for checkoff-funded programs.

This book is printed on acid-free paper. ∞

Published by John Wiley & Sons, Inc., Hoboken, New Jersey
Published simultaneously in Canada

Design and composition by Navta Associates, Inc.

Photography credits: Photography: Hans Rott, Hans Rott Photography; art direction: Susan Lamb Parenti, TreAmici Marketing; photography assistants: Jennifer Marx, David Miezal; food styling: Lois Szydlowski, Lee Mooney; food styling assistants: Kathy Takemura, Elaine Funk, Lisa Lecat-Knych; prop stylist: Karen Johnson; image conversion work: Design Two, Ltd., and Great Lakes Graphics.

For general information about our other products and services, please contact our Customer Care Department within the United States at (800) 762-2974, outside the United States at (317) 572-3993 or fax (317) 572-4002.

Wiley also publishes its books in a variety of electronic formats. Some content that appears in print may not be available in electronic books. For more information about Wiley products, visit our web site at www.wiley.com.

Library of Congress Cataloging-in-Publication Data:

The healthy beef cookbook : steaks, salads, stir-fry, and more : over 130 luscious lean beef recipes for every occasion / American Dietetic Association and National Cattlemen's Beef Association.
     p. cm.
   Includes bibliographical references and index.
   ISBN-13 978-0-471-73881-7 (paper : alk. paper)
   ISBN-10 0-471-73881-6 (paper : alk. paper)
  1. Cookery (Beef) I. American Dietetic Association. II. National Cattlemen's Beef Association (U.S.)
   TX749.5.B43H37 2006
   641.6'62—dc22
                                                                                              2005005770

Printed in the United States of America

10 9 8 7 6 5 4

Contents

Foreword

Beef is an American tradition; it is a part of our heritage. Often the featured entrée item, beef can be enjoyed at any meal and prepared in many different ways. In fact, the beauty of beef is its versatility. It can be a key ingredient in a food as simple as chili, grilled to perfection as a steak, or elegantly prepared as a holiday roast. This quality alone makes it easy to see why beef is so much a part of our diet, but a lesser known and even more positive attribute of beef is its nutrient-dense profile. It supplies protein and many vitamins and minerals, including B vitamins, zinc, selenium, phosphorous, and iron, making it a good source of nutrients that can sometimes be difficult to obtain in the diet. Taken together, these qualities make it easy to justify beef's place in a healthy diet.

To help meet our society's increasing demand that healthy foods be both savory and satisfying, the beef industry has renewed its commitment to providing lean, tender, and flavorful cuts of beef. Consequently, there are now twenty-nine cuts of beef to choose from that meet the government's labeling guidelines for *lean*, meaning the total fat and saturated fat are minimal.

A common misperception is that beef is too high in fat to be eaten regularly. My research, along with other published studies, has confirmed that not all fats are created equal. In fact, a portion of the saturated fat in beef has been shown to have no effect on blood cholesterol levels. Another fact that many people find surprising is that nearly half of beef's fat is monounsaturated, the primary type of fat found in olive oil. Two servings (3 ounces per serving) of lean beef per day can easily be included in a heart-healthy diet that provides less than the recommended 10 percent of calories from saturated fat. For individuals on a cholesterol-lowering diet that restricts saturated fat to less than 7 percent of calories, 5 ounces of lean beef can be included in the diet daily.

With the growing selection of lean beef cuts in the marketplace, many of today's home cooks need cooking guidance to achieve tender, moist, and tasty results. The *Healthy Beef Cookbook* fills the gap between understanding the health benefits of choosing lean cuts of beef and knowing how to apply the right cooking techniques so your dining experience is not only healthy, but delicious.

With more than 130 recipes in various categories, *The Healthy Beef Cookbook* should be part of your cookbook library. It melds the culinary skills of a renowned chef with the nutrition expertise of a registered dietitian and is backed by two industry leaders in their fields—the nutrition experts of the American Dietetic Association (ADA) and the beef experts of the National Cattlemen's Beef Association (NCBA). The outcome of this collaboration is a fabulous collection of recipes that features lean beef, along with informative sections on beef nutrition and cookery. For those of you who have veered off the beef path, here is a reliable resource to help you welcome beef back to your healthy diet. If you are cooking with higher-fat cuts of beef, this cookbook will show you how to switch to leaner cuts and continue to enjoy the wonderful taste and nutritional qualities of beef with fewer calories and fat.

Here's to a delicious and healthy eating experience with beef!

P. M. Kris-Etherton, PhD, RD
Distinguished Professor
Director, Diet Study Center
Penn State University

Acknowledgments

This cookbook could not have been completed without the expertise and dedication of many people. Special thanks to:

- Mary K. Young, MS, RD, Betty Anne Redson, Caroline Margolis, RD, Dave Zino, Debra Baughman, Michaele Musel, Kristen Reisinger, Judy Van de Mark, Sara Armstrong Reddington, Alyson C. Wahl, MS, RD, Elizabeth Matlin, and Susan Parenti for their contributions to the content and organization of the book.

- Lee Mooney, Jeanene Reddick, Julie Morris, Nina Boratto, and Margaret Martin for helping develop and test recipes in the Culinary Center test kitchen.

- Diana Faulhaber, Jason Muzinic, Mary Beth Whalen, and Michael Weitz at the American Dietetic Association for their guidance and support.

- Thomas W. Miller, Teryn Johnson, and Hope Breeman at John Wiley & Sons for seeing the value of this cookbook and helping to make it a reality.

- ADA members and reviewers who spent hours reviewing for accuracy and clarity, especially: Amy Burris Burrow, RD, Kristen Albani, MS, RD, Geeta Sikand, MA, RD, FADA, CDE, Bridget Klawitter, PhD, RD, FADA, Mikelle McCoin, Melissa Ohlson, MS, RD, Mylissa Trowbridge, MS, RD, and Georgia Clark-Albert, MS, RD.

- The countless consumers and dietitians who participated in focus groups to help determine the content and layout of this cookbook.

Introduction

When you detect the aroma of beef cooking on a grill, your mouth immediately begins to water. You frequently crave the savory flavor of a rich, succulent steak or a delicious, juicy burger. At the same time, you make a conscious effort to serve healthy meals and you may be concerned that beef is too high in fat to eat regularly.

Well, you'll be happy to learn that lean beef fits easily in a healthful diet—not just once in awhile, but even several times a week. Consider these facts:

- There are at least twenty-nine cuts of lean beef that meet government guidelines for "lean." In fact, the total fat content of each of these twenty-nine cuts of lean beef falls between a skinless chicken breast and skinless chicken thigh when you compare the amounts of fat in 3-ounce cooked portions.

- As part of a low-fat diet, choosing lean beef, just like skinless chicken, can be effective in lowering blood cholesterol levels.

- Lean beef is naturally nutrient-rich. A 3-ounce serving meets government guidelines as an *excellent* source of five essential nutrients: protein, zinc, vitamin B_{12}, selenium, and phosphorus.

And it qualifies as a *good* source of niacin, vitamin B$_6$, iron, and riboflavin.

This cookbook is packed with everything you need to know about enjoying lean beef as part of your overall healthy lifestyle. Here is what you'll find:

- *An array of fresh and healthy recipes featuring lean beef.* With more than 130 recipes, you'll find ideas that will appeal to a range of tastes, kitchen know-how, and meal situations. Whether you like to prepare quick and easy meals, such as one-dish soups, sandwiches, or stir-fry, or you're looking for meal ideas for special occasions, you'll find creative new ways to cook with lean beef as well as leaner versions of classic beef favorites.

- *Simple, straightforward instructions using readily available ingredients.* Each recipe has been developed and tested by a team of food experts from the checkoff-funded Beef and Veal Culinary Center managed by NCBA so it comes out right every time. Richard Chamberlain, owner and executive chef of Chamberlain's Steak and Chop House in Dallas, Texas, contributed his own favorite recipes and put his creative and tasty touches on many of the other recipes. Throughout, he shares secrets for bringing out the flavor in lean beef. Most recipes require no more than eight to ten ingredients, and estimated preparation and cooking times are provided.

- *Enticing photos and serving ideas.* No doubt you'll want to prepare the recipes featured in the mouth-watering photos. These also show serving ideas for presenting meals in an attractive and appetizing way. An added bonus: many of the recipes feature a balanced variety of foods along with beef, including vegetables, fruits, grains, and dairy products. A nutritionally balanced meal is just a recipe away!

- *Nutrition information for each recipe.* Most recipes have no more than 15 grams of total fat and 5 grams of saturated fat per serving, amounts that are no more than one-quarter of the average daily allowances for fat and saturated fat (based on a 2,000-calorie diet). And you'll find key nutrition facts per serving for each recipe, including calories, total fat, saturated fat, monounsaturated fat, cholesterol, sodium, carbohydrates, fiber, protein, niacin, vitamin B$_6$, vitamin B$_{12}$, iron, selenium, and zinc. The recipes also identify the nutrients supplied at levels defined by government labeling regulations as "good" or "excellent."

We hope this book helps you cook confidently with lean beef and enjoy great taste and good health!

About the Recipes

The nutritional analysis for each recipe is based on the food items listed in the ingredient list, except ingredients labeled as "optional" or "for toppings," which are not included. When more than one ingredient choice is listed, the first ingredient is used for the analysis. If a range for the amount is given, the nutritional analysis is based on the lowest amount. Foods offered as "serve with" suggestions are not included in the analysis unless otherwise stated. The nutrition information for beef is based on USDA data for "separable lean-only," which means visible fat is trimmed from around the edges and within the meat (not including the small flecks of fat called marbling).

Protein, plus vitamins and minerals that are 10 percent to 19 percent of the Daily Value, or recommended amount, per serving, are considered a "good" source of that nutrient. Those that are more than 20 percent of the Daily Value per serving are considered an "excellent" source. These "good" and "excellent" source designations are based on government labeling guidelines and are specified with each recipe.

Many beef cuts can be used interchangeably in the recipes. Use Appendix D to select alternate cuts of lean beef for the recipes in this book. Appendix E is a useful guide for matching cuts of beef that you may have on hand with various recipes in this book. It also shows other common names of cuts of beef you may find in your supermarket.

1

GREAT GRILLING WITH BEEF

5

Tenderloin Steaks with Arugula Salad and Sweet and Spicy Beets

The vibrant colors of this steak salad let you know it's naturally nutrient-rich.

Total preparation and cooking time: 1 hour
Makes 4 servings.

2   cups diced peeled beets
1   cup orange juice
2   tablespoons honey
⅛ to ¼ teaspoon ground red pepper
2   tablespoons red wine vinegar
1½ tablespoons olive oil
¼   teaspoon salt
2   cloves garlic, minced
2   teaspoons cumin seeds
4   beef tenderloin steaks, cut 1 inch thick (about 4 ounces each)
    Salt, as desired
1   can (15 ounces) Mandarin orange segments, drained
6   cups arugula
    Freshly grated orange peel (optional)

1. Combine beets, orange juice, honey, and pepper in small saucepan; bring to a boil. Reduce heat; simmer 40 to 45 minutes or until beets are tender. Drain beets, reserving cooking liquid; cool.

2. Heat beet-cooking liquid over medium-high heat until reduced to ¼ cup; cool slightly. Whisk in vinegar, oil, and ¼ teaspoon salt; set aside to use as dressing.

3. Press garlic and cumin seeds evenly onto beef steaks. Place steaks on grid over medium, ash-covered coals. Grill, uncovered, 13 to 15 minutes for medium-rare to medium doneness, turning occasionally. Season with salt, as desired.

4. Toss beets, orange segments, and arugula in large bowl; drizzle with dressing. Serve with steaks. Garnish with orange peel, if desired.

COOK'S TIPS

- To broil, place steaks on rack in broiler pan so surface of beef is 2 to 3 inches from heat. Broil 13 to 16 minutes for medium-rare to medium doneness, turning once.
- Baby spinach can also serve as a tasty substitute for arugula.

• • • • • • • • • • •
BEEF SMARTS

A 3-ounce cooked portion of beef is about the size of a deck of cards or a computer mouse. Uncooked, this same portion (boneless) is about 4 ounces. See pages 236–237 for examples.

Nutrition information per serving

Calories: 353
Fat: 13 g
   Saturated fat: 3 g
   Monounsaturated fat: 7 g
Cholesterol: 67 mg
Sodium: 361 mg
Carbohydrate: 33 g
Fiber: 2.6 g
Protein: 28 g
Niacin: 8.3 mg
Vitamin B_6: 0.7 mg
Vitamin B_{12}: 1.4 mcg
Iron: 3.7 mg
Selenium: 30.8 mcg
Zinc: 5.6 mg

This recipe is an excellent source of protein, niacin, vitamin B_6, vitamin B_{12}, iron, selenium, and zinc, and a good source of fiber.

Balsamic-Dijon Steak with Asparagus

Total preparation and
cooking time: 25 minutes
Marinating time: 15 minutes
to 2 hours
Makes 4 servings.

• • • • • • • • • • • •
BEEF SMARTS

A 3-ounce serving of
lean beef contributes
less than 10 percent
of calories to a 2,000-
calorie diet, yet it sup-
plies more than 10
percent of the Daily
Value for protein, iron,
zinc, vitamin B_{12}, niacin,
vitamin B_6, riboflavin,
selenium, and
phosphorus.

**Nutrition information
per serving**

Calories: 369
Fat: 14 g
    Saturated fat: 4 g
    Monounsaturated fat: 4 g
Cholesterol: 138 mg
Sodium: 641 mg
Carbohydrate: 7 g
Fiber: 2.5 g
Protein: 52 g
Niacin: 6.4 mg
Vitamin B_6: 0.7 mg
Vitamin B_{12}: 4.9 mcg
Iron: 5.5 mg
Selenium: 47.0 mcg
Zinc: 12 mg

**This recipe is an excellent
source of protein, niacin,
vitamin B_6, vitamin B_{12}, iron,
selenium, and zinc, and a
good source of fiber.**

This quick and easy recipe packs a flavor punch that will please the entire family.

MARINADE
⅔ cup prepared balsamic vinaigrette
2   tablespoons Dijon-style mustard

4   beef sirloin tip side steaks, cut 1 inch thick (about 8 ounces each)
1   pound fresh asparagus
½   cup water
½   teaspoon salt
⅛   teaspoon pepper

1. Combine marinade ingredients in small bowl. Remove and reserve 2 tablespoons. Place beef steaks and remaining marinade in food-safe plastic bag; turn steaks to coat. Close bag securely and marinate in refrigerator 15 minutes to 2 hours.

2. Place asparagus in shallow microwave-safe dish; add water. Cover and microwave on HIGH 3 to 6 minutes or until crisp-tender. Drain asparagus. Add reserved 2 tablespoons marinade to asparagus; toss to coat. Set aside.

3. Remove steaks from marinade; discard marinade. Place steaks on grid over medium, ash-covered coals. Grill, covered, 12 to 14 minutes for medium-rare doneness, turning once. (Do not overcook.)

4. During last 3 minutes of grilling, arrange asparagus on grid around steaks; grill 2 to 3 minutes, turning once. Season steaks and asparagus with salt and pepper.

Beef Kabobs with Roasted Red Pepper Coulis

A coulis is a thick sauce or puree. Used as a dipping sauce, this Roasted Red Pepper Coulis enhances the savory flavor of grilled beef.

Total preparation and cooking time: 35 minutes
Makes 6 servings.

ROASTED RED PEPPER COULIS

1	tablespoon olive oil
1	medium onion, finely chopped
2	cloves garlic, minced
2	jars (7 ounces each) roasted red peppers, rinsed, drained, finely chopped
½	cup dry white wine
2	tablespoons tomato paste
¾	teaspoon dried thyme leaves, crushed, or 2 teaspoons minced fresh thyme
1	cup ready-to-serve beef broth
2	teaspoons cornstarch

1½	pounds boneless beef top sirloin steak, cut 1 inch thick
2	teaspoons coarse-grind black pepper
¾	teaspoon salt
¾	teaspoon sweet paprika
1	clove garlic, minced

1. To prepare Roasted Red Pepper Coulis, heat oil in large nonstick skillet over medium heat until hot. Add onion and garlic; cook and stir 2 to 3 minutes or until onion is tender.

2. Add red peppers, wine, tomato paste, and thyme, stirring until blended. Combine broth and cornstarch in small bowl, mixing until smooth. Stir into pepper mixture; bring to a boil. Reduce heat to medium-low; simmer 10 to 12 minutes or until slightly thickened, stirring occasionally. Keep warm.

3. Meanwhile, cut beef steak into 1¼-inch pieces. Combine pepper, salt, paprika, and garlic in large bowl. Add beef; toss to coat. Thread beef pieces evenly onto six 12-inch metal skewers, leaving small space between pieces.

4. Place kabobs on grid over medium, ash-covered coals. Grill, uncovered, about 8 to 10 minutes for medium-rare to medium doneness, turning once. Serve with dipping sauce.

COOK'S TIP
To broil, place kabobs on rack in broiler pan so surface of beef is 3 to 4 inches from heat. Broil about 9 to 11 minutes for medium-rare to medium doneness, turning once.

Nutrition information per serving

Calories: 220
Fat: 8 g
  Saturated fat: 2 g
  Monounsaturated fat: 4 g
Cholesterol: 50 mg
Sodium: 608 mg
Carbohydrate: 7 g
Fiber: 1.2 g
Protein: 28 g
Niacin: 7.6 mg
Vitamin B_6: 0.6 mg
Vitamin B_{12}: 1.4 mcg
Iron: 2.3 mg
Selenium: 31.7 mcg
Zinc: 4.9 mg

This recipe is an excellent source of protein, niacin, vitamin B_6, vitamin B_{12}, selenium, and zinc, and a good source of iron.

Spicy Five-Pepper T-Bone Steaks

T-bone steaks rubbed with five-pepper seasoning are grilled and served with a spicy, peppery sauce for the ultimate peppercorn steak experience.

Total preparation and cooking time: 1 hour
Makes 4 servings.

FIVE-PEPPER SEASONING
- 3 tablespoons coarsely ground mixed peppercorns (black, white, green, and pink)
- 2 teaspoons kosher or table salt
- 1/8 teaspoon ground red pepper

SPICY PEPPERCORN STEAK SAUCE
- 2 teaspoons vegetable oil
- 1/4 cup chopped onion
- 1 teaspoon minced garlic
- 1 cup ketchup
- 1/2 cup ready-to-serve beef broth
- 1/3 cup raisins
- 3 tablespoons balsamic vinegar
- 1 tablespoon molasses
- 1 tablespoon soy sauce
- Additional ready-to-serve beef broth (optional)

- 2 beef T-bone steaks, cut 3/4 inch thick (about 12 ounces each)

1. Combine Five-Pepper Seasoning ingredients in small bowl; mix well. Reserve 2 teaspoons for Spicy Peppercorn Steak Sauce. Set aside remaining mixture for seasoning beef steaks.

2. To prepare Spicy Peppercorn Steak Sauce, heat oil in small saucepan over medium heat until hot. Add onion and garlic; cook and stir 1 to 2 minutes or until tender but not browned. Stir in ketchup, broth, raisins, vinegar, molasses, soy sauce, and reserved 2 teaspoons Five-Pepper Seasoning; bring to a boil. Reduce heat; simmer gently 10 minutes to blend flavors, stirring occasionally. (Sauce will thicken slightly.)

3. Place sauce in blender or food processor container. Cover; pulse on and off for slightly chunky texture. (For a thinner sauce, additional broth may be added 1 tablespoon at a time; pulse on and off after each addition.) Return sauce to saucepan; keep warm until ready to serve.

CHEF RICHARD'S TIP

Top chefs use only freshly ground pepper for seasoning. Try it and notice the difference in flavor.

Nutrition information per serving

Calories: 335
Fat: 11 g
    Saturated fat: 3 g
    Monounsaturated fat: 5 g
Cholesterol: 48 mg
Sodium: 1,984 mg
Carbohydrate: 35 g
Fiber: 3.1 g
Protein: 26 g
Niacin: 5.1 mg
Vitamin B_6: 0.5 mg
Vitamin B_{12}: 1.9 mcg
Iron: 4.5 mg
Selenium: 9.8 mcg
Zinc: 4.6 mg

This recipe is an excellent source of protein, niacin, vitamin B_6, vitamin B_{12}, iron, and zinc, and a good source of fiber and selenium.

4. Press remaining Five-Pepper Seasoning evenly onto beef steaks. Place steaks on grid over medium, ash-covered coals. Grill, uncovered, 10 to 12 minutes for medium-rare to medium doneness, turning occasionally.

5. Remove bones; carve steaks crosswise into slices. Serve with sauce.

COOK'S TIPS

Mixed peppercorns are sold in specialty food markets and some supermarkets. If a four-peppercorn mix is not available, a three-peppercorn mix may be substituted. Or make your own mix by combining equal amounts of whole black, white, green, and pink peppercorns.

To easily grind whole peppercorns, use a pepper mill or coffee grinder (used only for seasonings). They can also be crushed in a food-safe plastic bag. Place the peppercorns in the bag, squeeze out the air, and seal. Use the bottom of a custard cup, a rolling pin, or the bottom of a heavy pan to crush the peppercorns.

Spicy Peppercorn Steak Sauce may be prepared ahead and frozen in an airtight container for up to 2 months. To reheat, heat from frozen in a saucepan over medium heat until hot, stirring occasionally.

Serve this classic steak with simple sides such as steamed broccoli and roasted new potatoes.

Tenderloin Steaks with Espresso-Bourbon Sauce

No need to take the family to a steakhouse. This recipe brings steak-house quality and flavor right to your table.

ESPRESSO-BOURBON SAUCE

¼ cup bourbon
¼ cup maple syrup
¼ cup reduced-sodium soy sauce
1 tablespoon fresh lemon juice
2 teaspoons instant espresso coffee powder
⅛ teaspoon pepper

4 beef tenderloin steaks, cut 1 inch thick (about 4 ounces each)
Salt and pepper, as desired

1. Combine Espresso-Bourbon Sauce ingredients, except pepper, in small saucepan; bring to a boil. Reduce heat to medium-low; simmer, uncovered, 12 to 15 minutes or until sauce is thickened and reduced by about half, stirring occasionally. Stir in pepper. Keep warm.

2. Place steaks on grid over medium, ash-covered coals. Grill, uncovered, 13 to 15 minutes for medium-rare to medium doneness, turning occasionally. Season with salt and pepper, as desired. Serve with sauce.

COOK'S TIPS

- To broil, place steaks on rack in broiler pan so surface of beef is 2 to 3 inches from heat. Broil 13 to 16 minutes for medium-rare to medium doneness, turning once.
- Serve with steamed asparagus and multigrain rolls.

Total preparation and cooking time: 35 minutes
Makes 4 servings.

• • • • • • • • • • •
BEEF SMARTS
Use this rule of thumb to remember many of the lean cuts of beef: "loin" or "round" in the name always means *lean*. Other lean cuts are listed in the chart on page 226.

Nutrition information per serving

Calories: 250
Fat: 7 g
  Saturated fat: 3 g
  Monounsaturated fat: 3 g
Cholesterol: 67 mg
Sodium: 659 mg
Carbohydrate: 15 g
Fiber: 0.0 g
Protein: 26 g
Niacin: 7.5 mg
Vitamin B_6: 0.5 mg
Vitamin B_{12}: 1.4 mcg
Iron: 1.9 mg
Selenium: 30 mcg
Zinc: 5.4 mg

This recipe is an excellent source or protein, niacin, vitamin B_6, vitamin B_{12}, selenium, and zinc, and a good source of iron.

Grilled Beef Tri-Tip Roast with Caramelized Three-Onion Sauce

Total preparation and cooking time: 1 hour

Makes 6 to 8 servings.

Three kinds of onions make the distinctive sauce for this grilled roast.

CARAMELIZED THREE-ONION SAUCE

2 tablespoons olive oil
1 thinly sliced large red onion
1 thinly sliced large yellow onion
2 bunches green onions, green part only, thinly sliced
¾ cup balsamic vinegar
¼ cup packed brown sugar
  Salt and pepper, as desired

¼ cup Ancho Steak Seasoning (recipe follows)
1 beef tri-tip roast (1½ to 2 pounds)

1. To prepare Caramelized Three-Onion Sauce, heat oil in large non-stick skillet over medium heat until hot. Add red, yellow, and green onions; cook and stir 8 to 10 minutes or until onions are tender and beginning to brown. Reduce heat to low; cook 12 minutes or until onions are caramelized, stirring occasionally. Increase heat to medium-high. Stir in vinegar; cook 4 minutes or until reduced by half, stirring occasionally. Stir in sugar; season with salt and pepper, as desired. Reduce heat to low; cook 5 minutes or until liquid evaporates and onion mixture thickens.

2. Meanwhile, press Ancho Steak Seasoning evenly onto beef roast. Place roast on grid over medium, ash-covered coals. Grill, covered, 25 to 35 minutes for medium-rare to medium doneness, turning occasionally. Remove roast when instant-read thermometer inserted into center of thickest part of beef registers 140°F for medium-rare, 155°F for medium. Let stand 10 minutes.

Nutrition information per serving

Calories: 291
Fat: 12 g
  Saturated fat: 3 g
  Monounsaturated fat: 7 g
Cholesterol: 60 mg
Sodium: 1,330 mg
Carbohydrate: 23 g
Fiber: 2.0 g
Protein: 24 g
Niacin: 6.7 mg
Vitamin B_6: 0.6 mg
Vitamin B_{12}: 1.3 mcg
Iron: 2.5 mg
Selenium: 27 mcg
Zinc: 4.4 mg

This recipe is an excellent source of protein, niacin, vitamin B_6, vitamin B_{12}, selenium, and zinc, and a good source of iron.

COOK'S TIPS

- To thinly slice onions, peel and trim root ends. Stand each onion on its root end; slice through the center, top to bottom. Lay flat and thinly slice each half to produce thin, semicircular julienne slices.
- Serve with a cooling pasta and vegetable salad to counteract the effects of the spicy Ancho rub.

(Temperature will continue to rise about 5°F to reach 145°F for medium-rare, 160°F for medium.)

3. Carve roast across the grain into thin slices. Serve with Caramelized Three-Onion Sauce.

ANCHO STEAK SEASONING   Makes about ¾ cup.
- ¼ cup kosher salt or table salt
- 3 tablespoons ground ancho chili powder
- 2 tablespoons ground cumin
- 2 tablespoons dried granulated garlic
- 2 tablespoons coarse-grind black pepper
- 2 tablespoons sugar
- 1 tablespoon ground thyme

1. Combine all ingredients in a small bowl; store in airtight container. Shake well before using.

Mojo Beef Kabobs

Total preparation and
  cooking time: 40 minutes
Makes 4 servings.

Mojo sauce is a classic Cuban combination of lime, garlic, and oregano. It is also great with whole grilled steaks, such as flank, or top loin steaks.

MOJO SAUCE

¼	cup fresh orange juice
¼	cup fresh lime juice
3	tablespoons finely chopped fresh oregano
3	tablespoons olive oil
2	tablespoons finely chopped fresh parsley
1	teaspoon ground cumin
1	teaspoon minced garlic
¾	teaspoon salt

1	pound boneless beef top sirloin steak, cut 1 inch thick
1	teaspoon coarse-grind black pepper
1	large lime, cut into 8 wedges
1	small red onion, cut into 8 thin wedges
1	container grape or cherry tomatoes (about 10 ounces)

1. Whisk Mojo Sauce ingredients in small bowl. Set aside.

2. Cut beef steak into 1¼-inch pieces; season with pepper.

3. Alternately thread beef with lime and onion wedges evenly onto four 12-inch metal skewers. Thread tomatoes evenly onto four 12-inch metal skewers.

4. Place kabobs on grid over medium, ash-covered coals. Grill tomato kabobs, uncovered, about 2 to 4 minutes or until slightly softened, turning occasionally. Grill beef kabobs, uncovered, about 8 to 10 minutes for medium-rare to medium doneness, turning occasionally.

5. Serve kabobs drizzled with sauce.

HEALTHY LIVING TIP

Be adventurous and expand your tastes to get the nutrients your body craves. Your taste buds will appreciate the new flavors, and your body will reap the benefits of good nutrition.

Nutrition information per serving

Calories: 285
Fat: 15 g
  Saturated fat: 3 g
  Monounsaturated fat: 10 g
Cholesterol: 50 mg
Sodium: 500 mg
Carbohydrate: 10 g
Fiber: 1.8 g
Protein: 27 g
Niacin: 8.2 mg
Vitamin B_6: 0.6 mg
Vitamin B_{12}: 1.4 mcg
Iron: 2.6 mg
Selenium: 31.9 mcg
Zinc: 5.1 mg

This recipe is an excellent source of protein, niacin, vitamin B_6, vitamin B_{12}, selenium, and zinc, and a good source of iron.

COOK'S TIPS

- If using eight 12-inch bamboo skewers, soak them in water for at least 10 minutes before grilling.
- When cutting onion into wedges for kabobs, leave root end intact so wedges hold together during skewering.
- To make lime wedges, cut lime crosswise in half. Cut each half into quarters, forming wedges.
- Serve with tricolor couscous, which combines the flavors of spinach, tomato, and basil with regular couscous. Add black beans for a fiber boost.

Chamberlain's Steak Rub

Total preparation time:
5 minutes
Makes about 1 cup rub.

This amazing rub tastes great on all the beef steaks and roasts recommended for grilling in this cookbook. Cooking times vary with the specific beef cut used.

¼ cup kosher salt or 3 tablespoons table salt
2 tablespoons sugar
2 tablespoons granulated garlic
2 tablespoons chipotle chili powder
1 tablespoon dry mustard
1 tablespoon ground cumin
1 tablespoon chili powder
1 tablespoon coarse-grind black pepper
1½ teaspoons dried oregano leaves, crushed

1. Combine all ingredients in small bowl; blend well. Store in airtight container until ready to use.

2. Use 1 to 2 teaspoons rub for each 8-ounce beef steak and 2 to 4 teaspoons rub per pound of beef roast. Press evenly onto steak or onto all surfaces of beef roast before cooking.

> **COOK'S TIP**
> Chipotle peppers are dried, smoked jalapeño peppers. They have a very dark brown, wrinkled skin, and strong smoky aroma and are sold canned in adobo sauce or ground into a powder. Chipotle chili powder is available in the spice or ethnic section of supermarkets or in specialty food markets.

Curried Flank Steak with Fruit and Almond Basmati Rice

Basmati rice is considered an aromatic rice. These varieties have a natural nutlike flavor and a fine texture.

CURRY-YOGURT MARINADE

1	cup plain nonfat yogurt
1	tablespoon minced fresh ginger
2	teaspoons honey
1	clove garlic, minced
¾	teaspoon curry powder
½	teaspoon salt
¼	teaspoon pepper

1	beef flank steak (about 1½ pounds)
	Fruit and Almond Basmati Rice (recipe follows)
1	tablespoon chopped fresh mint

1. Combine Curry-Yogurt Marinade ingredients in medium bowl. Remove and reserve ½ cup in refrigerator for sauce. Place beef steak and remaining marinade in food-safe plastic bag; turn steak to coat. Close bag securely and marinate in refrigerator 6 hours or as long as overnight.

2. Remove steak from marinade; discard marinade. Place steak on grid over medium, ash-covered coals. Grill, uncovered, 17 to 21 minutes for medium-rare to medium doneness, turning occasionally.

3. Carve steak across the grain into thin slices. Serve with rice. Drizzle beef with reserved sauce; sprinkle mint over beef and rice.

FRUIT AND ALMOND BASMATI RICE

1	cup uncooked basmati rice
¾	cup mixed dried fruit, chopped
¼	cup slivered almonds, toasted

1. Prepare rice according to package directions, omitting butter or oil. Add dried fruit and almonds during stand time.

COOK'S TIP

To toast almonds, spread in single layer on metal baking sheet. Bake in 350°F oven 3 to 5 minutes or until lightly browned, stirring occasionally. (Watch carefully to prevent burning.) Set aside to cool.

Total preparation and cooking time: 40 minutes

Marinating time: 6 hours or overnight

Makes 6 servings.

Nutrition information per serving

Calories: 394
Fat: 9 g
    Saturated fat: 3 g
    Monounsaturated fat: 4 g
Cholesterol: 42 mg
Sodium: 236 mg
Carbohydrate: 51 g
Fiber: 2.6 g
Protein: 28 g
Niacin: 8.1 mg
Vitamin B_6: 0.5 mg
Vitamin B_{12}: 1.4 mcg
Iron: 3.0 mg
Selenium: 27.4 mcg
Zinc: 4.5 mg

This recipe is an excellent source of protein, niacin, vitamin B_6, vitamin B_{12}, selenium, and zinc, and a good source of fiber and iron.

Garlic-Yogurt Marinated Eye Round Steaks

Total preparation and
cooking time: 35 minutes

Marinating time: 6 hours or
overnight

Makes 4 servings.

Fresh lemon juice, parsley, and garlic work together perfectly in this tangy marinade and sauce.

GARLIC-YOGURT MARINADE AND SAUCE

1	cup plain nonfat yogurt
¼	cup chopped fresh parsley
2	tablespoons fresh lemon juice
1	tablespoon sweet paprika
1	tablespoon minced garlic
1	teaspoon salt

4	beef eye round steaks, cut 1 inch thick (about 8 ounces each)
¼	cup mayonnaise
	Salt, as desired

COOK'S TIP

For a complete meal, serve with a cracked wheat salad such as tabbouleh and leafy greens.

1. Combine Garlic-Yogurt Marinade ingredients in small bowl; mix well. Divide mixture in half. Place beef steaks and half of the mixture in food-safe plastic bag; turn steaks to coat. Close bag securely and marinate in refrigerator 6 hours or as long as overnight. Stir mayonnaise into remaining half of mixture for sauce; cover and refrigerate.

2. Remove steaks from marinade; discard marinade. Place steaks on grid over medium, ash-covered coals. Grill, uncovered, 19 to 23 minutes for medium-rare doneness, turning occasionally. (Do not overcook.) Season steaks with salt, as desired. Serve with sauce.

**Nutrition information
per serving**

Calories: 365
Fat: 13 g
   Saturated fat: 4 g
   Monounsaturated fat: 3 g
Cholesterol: 112 mg
Sodium: 650 mg
Carbohydrate: 7 g
Fiber: 0.6 g
Protein: 53 g
Niacin: 9.3 mg
Vitamin B_6: 0.7 mg
Vitamin B_{12}: 2.8 mcg
Iron: 4.7 mg
Selenium: 60.1 mcg
Zinc: 8.7 mg

This recipe is an excellent source of protein, niacin, vitamin B_6, vitamin B_{12}, iron, selenium, and zinc.

Southern Spiced T-Bone Steaks with Chipotle Mashed Potatoes

Buttery in color and flavor, Yukon Gold potatoes are excellent for mashing.

SEASONING

1	tablespoon kosher or table salt
1	tablespoon packed brown sugar
1	teaspoon ground cumin
½	teaspoon chili powder
½	teaspoon paprika
½	teaspoon black pepper
¼	teaspoon garlic powder
¼	teaspoon onion powder
⅛	teaspoon ground allspice

4   beef T-bone steaks, cut ¾ inch thick (about 12 ounces each)

CHIPOTLE MASHED POTATOES

3	pounds Yukon Gold potatoes, peeled, cut into 1½-inch pieces
1	tablespoon kosher or table salt
¾	cup reduced-fat milk
3	tablespoons butter (optional)
1	canned chipotle pepper in adobo sauce, minced
¼	teaspoon ground white pepper
	Salt, as desired

1. Combine seasoning ingredients; press evenly onto beef steaks. Cover and refrigerate 15 minutes.

2. To prepare Chipotle Mashed Potatoes, place potatoes and salt in stockpot. Add enough water to cover potatoes; bring to a boil. Reduce heat; cover and cook 20 to 25 minutes or until potatoes are just tender. Drain well. Place milk and butter, if desired, in small microwave-safe bowl. Microwave on HIGH 1½ to 2 minutes or until milk is warm and butter melts. Add milk mixture and chipotle pepper to potatoes. Mash potatoes with electric mixer or manual potato masher until smooth. Season with white pepper and salt, as desired. Keep warm.

3. Meanwhile place steaks on grid over medium, ash-covered coals. Grill, uncovered, 10 to 12 minutes for medium-rare to medium doneness, turning occasionally.

4. Carve steaks into slices. Serve with mashed potatoes.

Total preparation and cooking time: 1 hour
Makes 8 servings.

HEALTHY LIVING TIP
• • • • •

Enjoy your steak twice as much. Eat a reasonable portion today, and enjoy the leftovers again tomorrow on a salad or in a sandwich.

Nutrition information per serving

Calories: 334
Fat: 9 g
    Saturated fat: 3 g
    Monounsaturated fat: 4 g
Cholesterol: 50 mg
Sodium: 1,672 mg
Carbohydrate: 33 g
Fiber: 2.3 g
Protein: 28 g
Niacin: 4.0 mg
Vitamin B$_6$: 0.4 mg
Vitamin B$_{12}$: 2.0 mcg
Iron: 4.8 mg
Selenium: 9.2 mcg
Zinc: 4.4 mg

This recipe is an excellent source of protein, niacin, vitamin B$_6$, vitamin B$_{12}$, iron, and zinc, and a good source of selenium.

Grilled Steak with Spicy Mango Salsa

Fresh ingredients abound in this delicious grilled steak recipe.

Total preparation and cooking time: 1 hour

Marinating time: 6 hours or overnight

Makes 4 servings.

MARINADE

¼	cup fresh lime juice
2	tablespoons minced green onion
2	tablespoons water
1	tablespoon vegetable oil
2	teaspoons minced fresh ginger
2	cloves garlic, minced
¼	teaspoon salt
1	beef top round steak, cut ¾ inch thick (about 1 pound)

MANGO SALSA

1½	cups finely diced fresh mango
2	tablespoons minced green onion
1	tablespoon fresh lime juice
1	tablespoon minced fresh cilantro
1	red serrano or red jalapeño pepper, seeded, finely chopped
4	cups hot cooked couscous
2	cups sugar snap peas, steamed
	Salt and black pepper, as desired

COOK'S TIP

When handling chili peppers, wear clean latex gloves to protect your hands from the burning oils. Avoid touching your eyes, nose, or mouth.

Nutrition information per serving

Calories: 435
Fat: 7 g
 Saturated fat: 2 g
 Monounsaturated fat: 3 g
Cholesterol: 61 mg
Sodium: 130 mg
Carbohydrate: 56 g
Fiber: 6.0 g
Protein: 36 g
Niacin: 7.8 mg
Vitamin B_6: 0.6 mg
Vitamin B_{12}: 1.5 mcg
Iron: 4.3 mg
Selenium: 76.4 mcg
Zinc: 5.3 mg

This recipe is an excellent source of fiber, protein, niacin, vitamin B_6, vitamin B_{12}, iron, selenium, and zinc.

1. Combine marinade ingredients in medium bowl. Place beef steak and marinade in food-safe plastic bag; turn steak to coat. Close bag securely and marinate in refrigerator 6 hours or as long as overnight, turning occasionally.

2. Just before grilling steak, combine Mango Salsa ingredients in medium bowl. Cover and refrigerate until ready to serve.

3. Remove steak from marinade; discard marinade. Place steak on grid over medium, ash-covered coals. Grill, uncovered, 8 to 9 minutes for medium-rare doneness, turning occasionally. (Do not overcook.)

4. Carve steak into thin slices. Season with salt and black pepper, as desired. Serve with salsa, couscous, and sugar snap peas.

Southwest Burgers with Corn Relish

Total preparation and
  cooking time: 40 minutes
Makes 4 servings.

This bunless burger is full of spicy Southwest flavor.

CORN RELISH

1	cup frozen corn, defrosted
½	cup chopped seeded tomato
½	cup chopped seeded cucumber
3	tablespoons sliced green onions
1½	tablespoons cider vinegar
2	teaspoons olive oil
1	teaspoon sugar
½	teaspoon ground cumin
¼	teaspoon salt

1	pound ground beef (95% lean)
¼	cup chopped onion
½	teaspoon ground cumin
½	teaspoon salt
¼	teaspoon pepper

1. Combine Corn Relish ingredients in medium bowl; set aside.

2. Combine ground beef, onion, cumin, salt, and pepper in large bowl, mixing lightly but thoroughly. Shape into four ½-inch-thick patties.

3. Place patties on grid over medium, ash-covered coals. Grill, uncovered, 11 to 13 minutes to medium (160°F) doneness, until no longer pink in center and juices show no pink color, turning occasionally. Serve with relish.

Nutrition information per serving

Calories: 225
Fat: 8 g
  Saturated fat: 3 g
  Monounsaturated fat: 4 g
Cholesterol: 65 mg
Sodium: 352 mg
Carbohydrate: 14 g
Fiber: 2.1 g
Protein: 24 g
Niacin: 6.0 mg
Vitamin B_6: 0.5 mg
Vitamin B_{12}: 2.1 mcg
Iron: 3.1 mg
Selenium: 18.9 mcg
Zinc: 5.8 mg

This recipe is an excellent source of protein, niacin, vitamin B_6, vitamin B_{12}, selenium, and zinc, and a good source of iron.

COOK'S TIP

To broil, place patties on rack in broiler pan so surface of beef is 3 to 4 inches from heat. Broil 10 to 12 minutes to medium (160°F) doneness, until no longer pink in center and juices show no pink color, turning once.

Grilled Italian Steak and Pasta

The simplicity of grilled steak paired with garden-fresh vegetables and herbs is what makes this recipe a summertime classic.

Total preparation and cooking time: 30 minutes
Makes 4 servings.

- 2 tablespoons olive oil
- 1 cup chopped onion
- 2 cloves garlic, minced
- 3 cups grape tomatoes, cut in half
- ¾ teaspoon salt, divided
- ½ teaspoon ground black pepper, divided
- ¼ cup fresh basil, thinly sliced
- 2 cups uncooked bow tie or gemelli pasta
- 1 teaspoon coarse-grind or cracked black pepper
- 1 boneless beef top sirloin steak, cut ¾ inch thick (about 1 pound)
- ½ cup crumbled goat cheese

1. Heat oil in large saucepan over medium heat until hot. Add onion and garlic; cook and stir 3 to 5 minutes or until tender. Add tomatoes, ½ teaspoon salt and ¼ teaspoon ground pepper; cook about 5 minutes or until tomatoes start to soften, stirring occasionally. Stir in basil; cover and remove from heat. Set aside.

2. Meanwhile, cook pasta in salted water according to package directions; drain and return to pan. Stir in tomato mixture and remaining ¼ teaspoon salt and ¼ teaspoon ground pepper. Keep warm.

3. Press coarse-grind pepper evenly onto beef steak. Place steak on grid over medium, ash-covered coals. Grill, uncovered, 13 to 16 minutes for medium-rare to medium doneness, turning occasionally.

4. Carve steak into thin slices. Sprinkle cheese over pasta; serve with steak.

HEALTHY LIVING TIP

No single food or food group provides every nutrient you need. Mix up your menu with a variety of nutrient-rich foods from all five food groups.

COOK'S TIPS

- To broil, place steak on rack in broiler pan so surface of beef is 2 to 3 inches from heat. Broil 9 to 12 minutes for medium-rare to medium doneness, turning once.
- Toss pasta with sautéed arugula or spinach for added flavor.

Nutrition information per serving

Calories: 425
Fat: 14 g
    Saturated fat: 5 g
    Monounsaturated fat: 6 g
Cholesterol: 56 mg
Sodium: 556 mg
Carbohydrate: 39 g
Fiber: 3.4 g
Protein: 35 g
Niacin: 10.1 mg
Vitamin B_6: 0.8 mg
Vitamin B_{12}: 1.5 mcg
Iron: 4.2 mg
Selenium: 54.2 mcg
Zinc: 5.7 mg

This recipe is an excellent source of protein, niacin, vitamin B_6, vitamin B_{12}, iron, selenium, and zinc, and a good source of fiber.

Dijon-Wine Steak Kabobs with Mushroom Wild Rice

Originated in Asia, the shiitake mushroom is now grown in the United States.

1   pound boneless beef round tip steak, cut 1 inch thick

MARINADE

2   tablespoons water
2   tablespoons red wine vinegar
2   tablespoons coarse-grain Dijon-style mustard
2   cloves garlic, minced
2   teaspoons vegetable oil
½   teaspoon coarse-grind black pepper

½   small red onion, cut into ¾-inch wedges
1   small yellow summer squash, cut lengthwise in half then crosswise into 1-inch slices
1   small red or green bell pepper, cut into 1-inch pieces
     Mushroom Wild Rice (recipe follows)

1. Cut beef steak into 1¼-inch pieces. Combine marinade ingredients in small bowl. Place beef and marinade in food-safe plastic bag; turn to coat. Close bag securely and marinate in refrigerator 6 hours or as long as overnight, turning occasionally.

2. Soak eight 9-inch bamboo skewers in water 10 minutes; drain. Remove beef from marinade; discard marinade. Alternately thread beef, onion, squash, and bell pepper evenly onto skewers. Place kabobs on grid over medium, ash-covered coals. Grill, uncovered, 8 to 10 minutes for medium-rare to medium doneness, turning occasionally.

3. Serve kabobs over Mushroom Wild Rice.

MUSHROOM WILD RICE

2   teaspoons vegetable oil
2   cups thinly sliced assorted wild mushrooms (oyster, cremini, and shiitake)
1   package (6 ounces) long-grain and wild rice blend

1. Heat 2 teaspoons oil in large nonstick skillet over medium heat until hot. Add mushrooms; cook and stir until tender. Remove and keep warm. Meanwhile, cook rice according to package directions, omitting salt and butter. When rice is done, stir in mushrooms.

Total preparation and cooking time: 30 minutes

Marinating time: 6 hours or overnight

Makes 4 servings.

Nutrition information per serving

Calories: 350
Fat: 9 g
    Saturated fat: 2 g
    Monounsaturated fat: 4 g
Cholesterol: 69 mg
Sodium: 737 mg
Carbohydrate: 36 g
Fiber: 1.7 g
Protein: 31 g
Niacin: 4.7 mg
Vitamin B_6: 0.5 mg
Vitamin B_{12}: 2.5 mcg
Iron: 4.1 mg
Selenium: 26.8 mcg
Zinc: 6.3 mg

This recipe is an excellent source of protein, niacin, vitamin B_6, vitamin B_{12}, iron, selenium, and zinc.

Beef Tostadas with Grilled Vegetable Salsa

Total preparation and cooking time: 30 minutes
Makes 6 servings.

Experience the taste of this Mexican-inspired open-faced sandwich!

ANCHO CHILI RUB

1	tablespoon ground ancho chili powder
2	teaspoons brown sugar
2	teaspoons ground cumin
2	teaspoons minced garlic
1	teaspoon dried oregano leaves, crushed
¾	teaspoon salt

3	beef shoulder center steaks (Ranch Steaks), cut ¾ inch thick (about 8 ounces each)
1	red bell pepper, cut lengthwise in half, seeded, stemmed
1	yellow bell pepper, cut lengthwise in half, seeded, stemmed
1	small onion, cut into ½-inch-thick slices
	Cooking spray

VEGETABLE SALSA

1	can (15 ounces) black beans, rinsed, drained
¼	cup chopped fresh cilantro
3	tablespoons fresh lime juice
1	tablespoon olive oil
1	teaspoon minced garlic
½	teaspoon salt
¼	teaspoon black pepper

12	corn tortillas
	Prepared tomatillo salsa, as desired
6	tablespoons crumbled queso fresco

1. Combine Ancho Chili Rub ingredients in small bowl; press evenly onto beef steaks. Spray bell peppers and onion with nonstick cooking spray.

2. Place steaks in center of grid over medium, ash-covered coals; arrange bell peppers and onion around steaks. Grill steaks, covered, 9 to 11 minutes for medium-rare to medium doneness, turning once. Remove; keep warm. Grill bell peppers and onion, about 10 to 12 minutes or until tender, turning occasionally.

Nutrition information per serving

Calories: 343
Fat: 11 g
  Saturated fat: 3 g
  Monounsaturated fat: 5 g
Cholesterol: 62 mg
Sodium: 844 mg
Carbohydrate: 29 g
Fiber: 5.0 g
Protein: 31 g
Niacin: 3.4 mg
Vitamin B_6: 0.4 mg
Vitamin B_{12}: 2.7 mcg
Iron: 5.4 mg
Selenium: 26.0 mcg
Zinc: 5.8 mg

This recipe is an excellent source of fiber, protein, vitamin B_6, vitamin B_{12}, iron, selenium, and zinc, and a good source of niacin.

3. To prepare Vegetable Salsa, chop grilled bell peppers and onion; place in medium bowl. Add beans, cilantro, lime juice, oil, garlic, salt, and pepper; toss gently. Set aside.

4. Grill corn tortillas 30 seconds on each side. Carve steaks into thin slices; serve on tortillas with Vegetable Salsa, tomatillo salsa, as desired, and queso fresco.

COOK'S TIPS

- Four beef tenderloin steaks cut 1 inch thick (about 4 to 6 ounces each) may be substituted for beef shoulder center steaks. Grill steaks, uncovered, 13 to 15 minutes for medium-rare to medium doneness, turning occasionally.
- Substitute feta cheese in place of queso fresco for a Greek flair.
- This recipe can be served rolled up in a soft corn tortilla, or make it as a salad, served with baked tortillas.

Beef Sirloin with Grilled Tomato Pesto

Total preparation and cooking time: 40 minutes
Makes 4 servings.

Fresh tomato pesto is the perfect summer complement to steak, and with the grill already on, grilling tomatoes is easy!

2	cloves garlic, minced
2	teaspoons coarse-grind black pepper
1	boneless beef top sirloin steak, cut ¾ inch thick (about 1 pound)
3	large plum tomatoes, cut lengthwise in half

TOMATO PESTO

2	cups lightly packed fresh basil
¼	cup grated Parmesan cheese
3	cloves garlic
1	tablespoon olive oil
½	teaspoon salt
¼	teaspoon black pepper

1	tablespoon butter
3	cups hot cooked polenta
2	cups hot cooked peas

1. Combine 2 cloves garlic and coarse-grind pepper in small bowl; press evenly onto beef steak. Place steak in center of grid over medium, ash-covered coals; arrange tomatoes around steak. Grill tomatoes, uncovered, 6 to 8 minutes, turning once. Grill steak 13 to 16 minutes for medium-rare to medium doneness, turning occasionally. Remove; keep warm.

2. To prepare Tomato Pesto, place grilled tomatoes, basil, cheese, garlic, oil, salt, and ground pepper in food processor or blender container. Cover; process until smooth.

3. Stir butter into polenta. Carve steak into slices. Serve with polenta, peas, and Tomato Pesto.

COOK'S TIPS

- To broil, place steak and tomatoes on rack in broiler pan so surface of beef is 2 to 3 inches from heat. Broil tomatoes 6 to 8 minutes, turning once. Broil steak 9 to 12 minutes for medium-rare to medium doneness, turning once.
- Add extra flavor by using extra-virgin olive oil and sprinkling fresh-grated Parmesan cheese onto the polenta.

Nutrition information per serving

Calories: 735
Fat: 13 g
 Saturated fat: 5 g
 Monounsaturated fat: 6 g
Cholesterol: 62 mg
Sodium: 426 mg
Carbohydrate: 113 g
Fiber: 13.8 g
Protein: 41 g
Niacin: 8.1 mg
Vitamin B_6: 0.7 mg
Vitamin B_{12}: 1.6 mcg
Iron: 4.9 mg
Selenium: 33.0 mcg
Zinc: 5.4 mg

This recipe is an excellent source of fiber, protein, niacin, vitamin B_6, vitamin B_{12}, iron, selenium, and zinc.

Steaks with Cowboy Coffee Rub and Spicy Pico de Gallo

Total preparation and cooking time: 25 minutes
Makes 6 servings.

Cowboys began their day with a hearty breakfast and a strong cup of coffee. Why not end your day the same way?

SPICY PICO DE GALLO

1	cup chopped red onion
1	cup chopped seeded tomatoes
½	cup coarsely chopped fresh cilantro
1½	teaspoons minced pickled jalapeño pepper slices
1	tablespoon fresh lemon juice
¼	teaspoon salt

COWBOY COFFEE RUB

1	tablespoon freshly ground coffee beans
1½	teaspoons kosher salt or table salt
1½	teaspoons brown sugar
1	teaspoon coarse-grind black pepper
3	beef shoulder center steaks (Ranch Steaks), cut ¾ inch thick (about 8 ounces each)

1. Combine Spicy Pico de Gallo ingredients in medium bowl; mix well. Set aside.

2. Combine Cowboy Coffee Rub ingredients in small bowl. Press evenly onto beef steaks. Place steaks on grid over medium, ash-covered coals. Grill, covered, 9 to 11 minutes for medium-rare to medium doneness, turning once.

3. Carve steaks into slices. Serve with Spicy Pico de Gallo.

HEALTHY LIVING TIP

Being physically active leads to more muscle, which uses up more calories compared to body fat. The bonus: the more muscle you have, the more calories you burn.

Nutrition information per serving

Calories: 173
Fat: 5 g
    Saturated fat: 2 g
    Monounsaturated fat: 3 g
Cholesterol: 57 mg
Sodium: 686 mg
Carbohydrate: 6 g
Fiber: 0.9 g
Protein: 24 g
Niacin: 3.6 mg
Vitamin B_6: 0.3 mg
Vitamin B_{12}: 2.6 mcg
Iron: 3.0 mg
Selenium: 25.8 mcg
Zinc: 5.5 mg

This recipe is an excellent source of protein, vitamin B_{12}, selenium, and zinc, and a good source of niacin, vitamin B_6, and iron.

COOK'S TIPS

- Four beef tenderloin steaks cut 1 inch thick (4 to 6 ounces each) may be substituted for beef shoulder center steaks (Ranch Steaks). Grill steaks, uncovered, 13 to 15 minutes for medium-rare to medium doneness, turning occasionally.
- Serve with mixed steamed or sautéed summer vegetables such as zucchini, summer squash, and green beans.

Grilled Brazilian Beef with Chimichurri

Chimichurri sauce is most commonly served with grilled meats. In South America it is as popular as ketchup is in the United States.

Total preparation and cooking time: 35 minutes
Makes 4 servings.

CHIMICHURRI SAUCE

1	clove garlic
¼	cup packed fresh parsley
¼	cup packed fresh cilantro
2	tablespoons olive oil
1	tablespoon sherry wine vinegar
¼	teaspoon salt
⅛	teaspoon crushed red pepper
½	teaspoon black pepper
¼	teaspoon ground red pepper
2	boneless beef top loin (strip) steaks, cut ¾ inch thick (about 8 ounces each)
	Salt, as desired

1. To prepare Chimichurri Sauce, place garlic in food processor bowl. Cover; process until finely chopped. Add parsley and cilantro; process until finely chopped. Add oil, vinegar, salt, and crushed red pepper; process until well blended. Set aside.

2. Combine black pepper and ground red pepper; press evenly onto beef steaks. Place steaks on grid over medium, ash-covered coals. Grill, uncovered, 10 to 12 minutes for medium-rare to medium doneness, turning occasionally.

3. Carve steak into slices. Season with salt, as desired. Serve with sauce.

COOK'S TIPS

- Make Chimichurri Sauce up to 1 day ahead. Prepare as directed. Cover and refrigerate. Bring to room temperature before serving.
- Serve with a rice and black bean salad and fresh tomato slices; both are complemented by the fresh flavor of the Chimichurri Sauce.

Nutrition information per serving

Calories: 223
Fat: 12 g
    Saturated fat: 3 g
    Monounsaturated fat: 7 g
Cholesterol: 50 mg
Sodium: 204 mg
Carbohydrate: 2 g
Fiber: 0.6 g
Protein: 26 g
Niacin: 7.8 mg
Vitamin B_6: 0.6 mg
Vitamin B_{12}: 1.4 mcg
Iron: 2.2 mg
Selenium: 31.7 mcg
Zinc: 5.0 mg

This recipe is an excellent source of protein, niacin, vitamin B_6, vitamin B_{12}, selenium, and zinc, and a good source of iron.

Steak with Ginger Plum Barbecue Sauce

This versatile sauce does double duty as a marinade in this Asian-inspired grilled steak recipe.

MARINADE

½   cup prepared plum sauce
2   tablespoons minced fresh ginger
2   tablespoons fresh lemon juice
2   tablespoons soy sauce
2   tablespoons ketchup
1   tablespoon minced garlic
1   tablespoon brown sugar
¼   teaspoon ground red pepper

1   beef top round steak, cut ¾ inch thick (about 1 pound)
1   tablespoon vegetable oil
2   cups thinly sliced carrots
3   cups fresh pea pods, strings removed
1   clove garlic, minced
    Salt and black pepper, as desired
3   cups hot cooked jasmine rice, prepared without butter or salt
    Chopped fresh cilantro (optional)

1. Combine marinade ingredients in small bowl. Place beef steak and ½ cup marinade in food-safe plastic bag; turn steak to coat. Close bag securely and marinate in refrigerator 6 hours or as long as overnight, turning occasionally. Cover and reserve remaining marinade in refrigerator.

2. Remove steak from marinade; discard marinade. Place steak on grid over medium, ash-covered coals. Grill, uncovered, 8 to 9 minutes for medium-rare doneness, turning occasionally and basting with some of the reserved marinade during last 2 to 3 minutes of grilling. Remove; keep warm.

3. Heat oil in large nonstick skillet over medium-high heat until hot. Add carrots; stir-fry 5 minutes. Add pea pods and garlic; stir-fry 2 minutes.

Total preparation and cooking time: 35 minutes
Marinating time: 6 hours or overnight
Makes 4 servings.

Nutrition information per serving

Calories: 496
Fat: 9 g
   Saturated fat: 2 g
   Monounsaturated fat: 4 g
Cholesterol: 61mg
Sodium: 531 mg
Carbohydrate: 66 g
Fiber: 6.2 g
Protein: 36 g
Niacin: 8.4 mg
Vitamin B_6: 0.8 mg
Vitamin B_{12}: 1.5 mcg
Iron: 6.9 mg
Selenium: 43.0 mcg
Zinc: 6.1 mg

This recipe is an excellent source of fiber, protein, niacin, vitamin B_6, vitamin B_{12}, iron, selenium, and zinc.

Steak with Ginger Plum
Barbecue Sauce
(continued)

4. Carve steak into thin slices. Season with salt and black pepper, as desired. Place remaining marinade in small saucepan; heat until warm. Serve with steak, vegetables, and rice. Garnish with cilantro, if desired.

COOK'S TIPS

○ To broil, place steak on rack in broiler pan so surface of beef is 2 to 3 inches from heat. Broil 12 to 13 minutes for medium-rare doneness, turning once.

○ To easily remove pea pod strings, slightly cut corner of pod with paring knife and peel back string.

SENSATIONAL MAIN-DISH BEEF SALADS

2

Beef and Heirloom Tomato Salad with Balsamic Syrup

Heirloom tomatoes, prized for their unique shapes and colors, are grown from seeds that have been passed down from generation to generation. Many believe the flavors of heirloom tomatoes cannot be duplicated with today's modern farming methods.

BALSAMIC SYRUP

1	cup balsamic vinegar
½	teaspoon salt
¼	teaspoon pepper
1½	tablespoons olive oil

1½	teaspoons chopped fresh thyme
1½	teaspoons minced garlic
2	beef shoulder center steaks (Ranch Steaks), cut ¾ inch thick (about 8 ounces each)
	Cooking spray
4	cups arugula, torn into pieces
6	small heirloom tomatoes (2 each red, green, and yellow), sliced
½	teaspoon salt
¼	teaspoon pepper
¼	cup Parmesan cheese shavings

1. To prepare Balsamic Syrup, bring vinegar to a boil in medium saucepan; reduce heat and simmer 20 minutes or until reduced to about ⅓ cup (consistency will be syrupy). Remove from heat; cool. Season with salt and pepper. Whisk in oil.

2. Meanwhile, press thyme and garlic evenly onto beef steaks. Spray large nonstick skillet with cooking spray; heat over medium heat until hot. Place steaks in skillet; cook 9 to 12 minutes for medium-rare to medium doneness, turning twice. Carve steaks into thin slices. Arrange arugula and tomatoes on serving platter; drizzle with Balsamic Syrup. Top with steak slices; sprinkle with salt, pepper, and cheese shavings.

HEALTHY LIVING TIP

Always wash your hands between food preparation tasks, such as handling raw meats or poultry, and then cutting vegetables or fruits.

Nutrition information per serving

Calories: 263
Fat: 12 g
  Saturated fat: 3 g
  Monounsaturated fat: 7 g
Cholesterol: 60 mg
Sodium: 638 mg
Carbohydrate: 11 g
Fiber: 2.1 g
Protein: 27 g
Niacin: 3.9 mg
Vitamin B_6: 0.4 mg
Vitamin B_{12}: 2.7 mcg
Iron: 3.8 mg
Selenium: 26.9 mcg
Zinc: 5.9 mg

This recipe is an excellent source of protein, vitamin B_6, vitamin B_{12}, iron, selenium, and zinc, and a good source of niacin.

COOK'S TIP

Look for heirloom tomatoes at a farmer's market or in your local grocery store.

Provençal Beef Salad

Total preparation and
cooking time: 35 minutes

Makes 4 servings.

This delightful salad is based on the cuisine of Provence, a southern province of France, using the traditional flavors of olive oil, tomatoes, and garlic.

8 ounces small new potatoes, cut in half
8 ounces haricots verts or green beans, trimmed
   Salt and pepper, as desired
1 pound beef tenderloin roast

DRESSING
3 tablespoons olive oil
1 tablespoon sherry wine vinegar
1 tablespoon chopped fresh parsley
2 teaspoons minced shallot
1 teaspoon Dijon-style mustard
½ teaspoon salt
¼ teaspoon pepper

4 cups mixed baby salad greens
1 cup grape tomatoes
¼ cup thinly sliced red onion
16 pitted niçoise olives (optional)

COOK'S TIPS
- To grill, place kabobs on grid over medium, ash-covered coals. Grill, uncovered, about 8 to 10 minutes for medium-rare to medium doneness, turning occasionally.
- One pound beef top sirloin steak may be substituted for beef tenderloin.

1. Fill large saucepan with water one-half to three-quarters full; bring to boil. Add potatoes to boiling water; cook 2 to 3 minutes. Add beans; continue cooking 5 minutes. Drain; season with salt and pepper, as desired. Set aside.

2. Cut beef tenderloin into 1¼-inch pieces. Thread beef pieces onto four 12-inch metal skewers, leaving small space between pieces. Place kabobs on rack in broiler pan so surface of beef is 3 to 4 inches from heat. Broil about 8 to 10 minutes for medium-rare to medium doneness, turning once. Remove beef from skewers; keep warm.

3. Meanwhile, whisk dressing ingredients in small bowl until blended. Toss beef, potatoes, and beans with 2 tablespoons dressing in large bowl. Add greens, tomatoes, onion, and olives, if desired; toss. Serve with remaining dressing.

Nutrition information per serving

Calories: 307
Fat: 14 g
  Saturated fat: 4 g
  Monounsaturated fat: 8 g
Cholesterol: 67 mg
Sodium: 392 mg
Carbohydrate: 16 g
Fiber: 4.8 g
Protein: 28 g
Niacin: 8.5 mg
Vitamin B_6: 0.6 mg
Vitamin B_{12}: 1.4 mcg
Iron: 3.2 mg
Selenium: 29.8 mcg
Zinc: 5.1 mg

This recipe is an excellent source of protein, niacin, vitamin B_6, vitamin B_{12}, selenium, and zinc, and a good source of fiber and iron.

COOK'S TIP
Haricots verts (the French term for green beans) are young, slender green beans with tender pods. They are available in bulk or packages in the produce department of many large supermarkets.

Thai Beef Noodle Salad

If you're feeling adventurous, try using Japanese udon noodles, found in your local Asian market, instead of the spaghetti.

1 pound beef top round steak, cut ¾ inch thick

MARINADE
6 tablespoons orange juice
3 tablespoons rice wine vinegar
3 tablespoons reduced-sodium soy sauce
2 tablespoons minced fresh ginger
2 cloves garlic, minced
2 teaspoons dark sesame oil
1½ teaspoons chili paste

7 ounces uncooked spaghetti
2 teaspoons vegetable oil
1 cup shredded carrots
1 medium red bell pepper, cut into ⅛-inch strips
½ cup sliced green onions
    Salt and black pepper, as desired
¼ cup peanuts, chopped

1. Cut beef steak lengthwise in half, then crosswise into ⅛-inch-thick strips. Combine marinade ingredients in small bowl. Place beef and ¼ cup marinade in food-safe plastic bag; turn beef to coat. Close bag securely and marinate in refrigerator 1 to 2 hours. Reserve remaining marinade for dressing.

2. Cook spaghetti according to package directions; drain and place in serving bowl. Add reserved marinade and toss; set aside.

3. Meanwhile, heat 1 teaspoon oil in large nonstick skillet over medium-high heat until hot. Add carrots, bell pepper, and green onions; stir-fry 1 to 2 minutes or until crisp-tender. Remove from skillet; add to noodles. Set aside to cool.

4. Remove beef from marinade; discard marinade. Heat 1 teaspoon oil in same skillet until hot. Add half of the beef; stir-fry 1 to 2 minutes or until outside surface of beef is no longer pink. (Do not overcook.) Remove from skillet; keep warm. Repeat with remaining beef. Season with salt and pepper, as desired.

5. Add beef to noodle mixture. Top with peanuts.

Total preparation and cooking time: 30 minutes
Marinating time: 1 to 2 hours
Makes 4 servings.

COOK'S TIP
In this recipe, take advantage of the natural tenderizing enzymes found in fresh ginger. Powdered ginger doesn't have the same effect.

Nutrition information per serving

Calories: 440
Fat: 12 g
    Saturated fat: 3 g
    Monounsaturated fat: 5 g
Cholesterol: 61 mg
Sodium: 461 mg
Carbohydrate: 45 g
Fiber: 4.3 g
Protein: 36 g
Niacin: 8.8 mg
Vitamin B_6: 0.6 mg
Vitamin B_{12}: 1.5 mcg
Iron: 4.6 mg
Selenium: 59.8 mcg
Zinc: 5.9 mg

This recipe is an excellent source of protein, niacin, vitamin B_6, vitamin B_{12}, iron, selenium, and zinc, and a good source of fiber.

Tenderloin, Cranberry, and Pear Salad with Honey Mustard Dressing

The fresh pears in this wonderful salad add quite a bit of fiber to each serving.

4	beef tenderloin steaks, cut ¾ inch thick (about 4 ounces each)
½	teaspoon coarse-grind black pepper

HONEY MUSTARD DRESSING

½	cup prepared honey mustard
2 to 3	tablespoons water
1½	teaspoons olive oil
1	teaspoon white wine vinegar
¼	teaspoon coarse-grind black pepper
⅛	teaspoon salt

1	package (5 ounces) mixed baby salad greens
1	medium red or green pear, cored, cut into 16 wedges
¼	cup dried cranberries
¼	cup coarsely chopped pecans, toasted
¼	cup crumbled goat cheese (optional)
	Salt, as desired

Total preparation and cooking time: 25 minutes
Makes 4 servings.

• • • • • • • • • • •
BEEF SMARTS
Lean beef fits easily into low-fat meal plans designed to decrease blood cholesterol levels. Half of the fat in beef is monounsaturated fat, the same type of fat found in olive oil and championed for its heart-healthy properties.

1. Season beef steaks with pepper. Heat large nonstick skillet over medium heat until hot. Place steaks in skillet; cook 7 to 9 minutes for medium-rare to medium doneness, turning occasionally.

2. Meanwhile, whisk Honey Mustard Dressing ingredients in small bowl until well blended. Set aside. Divide greens evenly among 4 plates. Top evenly with pear wedges and dried cranberries.

3. Carve steaks into thin slices; season with salt as desired. Divide steak slices evenly over each salad. Top each salad evenly with dressing, pecans, and goat cheese, if desired.

Nutrition information per serving

Calories: 321
Fat: 14 g
  Saturated fat: 3 g
  Monounsaturated fat: 7 g
Cholesterol: 67 mg
Sodium: 434 mg
Carbohydrate: 21 g
Fiber: 3.3 g
Protein: 26 g
Niacin: 7.6 mg
Vitamin B_6: 0.6 mg
Vitamin B_{12}: 1.4 mcg
Iron: 2.4 mg
Selenium: 30.0 mcg
Zinc: 5.1 mg

This recipe is an excellent source of protein, niacin, vitamin B_6, vitamin B_{12}, selenium, and zinc, and a good source of fiber and iron.

COOK'S TIP
To toast pecans, spread in single layer on metal baking sheet. Bake in 350°F oven 3 to 5 minutes or until lightly browned, stirring occasionally. (Watch carefully to prevent burning.) Set aside to cool.

Beef and Spinach Salad with Roasted Tomato Vinaigrette

Total preparation and cooking time: 30 minutes
Makes 4 servings.

Roasting the tomatoes allows them to caramelize, which brings out their natural sweet flavor.

Cooking spray
3 large plum tomatoes, cut into ¼-inch thick slices
5 cloves garlic, minced
3 tablespoons olive oil, divided
2 cups cubed French bread (¾-inch)
   Dash kosher or table salt
2 tablespoons thinly sliced fresh basil
2 tablespoons balsamic vinegar
½ teaspoon salt
¼ teaspoon ground black pepper
¾ teaspoon coarse-grind black pepper
2 boneless beef top loin (strip) steaks, cut ¾ inch thick (about 8 ounces each)
   Salt, as desired
6 cups fresh baby spinach
   Fresh Parmesan cheese shavings (optional)

1. Heat oven to 400°F. Spray 2 metal baking sheets with cooking spray. Place tomatoes in single layer on one of the baking pans. Combine garlic and 2 tablespoons oil in small bowl. Brush half of the garlic mixture over tomatoes. Roast in 400°F oven for 10 minutes; set aside.

2. Toss bread cubes with remaining garlic mixture in small bowl. Place in single layer on second baking sheet. Sprinkle with kosher salt. Bake in 400°F oven for 8 minutes or until lightly browned; set aside as croutons.

3. Place roasted tomatoes, basil, vinegar, 1 tablespoon oil, salt, and ground pepper in blender container. Cover; process until pureed; set aside as vinaigrette.

4. Press coarse-grind pepper evenly onto beef steaks. Heat large non-stick skillet over medium heat until hot. Place steaks in skillet; cook 10 to 12 minutes for medium-rare to medium doneness, turning once.

5. Carve steak into thin slices. Season with salt, as desired. Arrange on spinach. Top with croutons. Garnish with cheese shavings, if desired. Drizzle vinaigrette over salad.

Nutrition information per serving

Calories: 304
Fat: 15 g
   Saturated fat: 4 g
   Monounsaturated fat: 9 g
Cholesterol: 56 mg
Sodium: 462 mg
Carbohydrate: 13 g
Fiber: 2.1 g
Protein: 28 g
Niacin: 8.3 mg
Vitamin B_6: 0.6 mg
Vitamin B_{12}: 1.4 mcg
Iron: 3.5 mg
Selenium: 35 mcg
Zinc: 4.9 mg

This recipe is an excellent source of protein, niacin, vitamin B_6, vitamin B_{12}, selenium, and zinc, and a good source of iron.

Pizza on the Side Salad

Whole wheat pitas crisp up nicely in the oven, making a wonderful alternative to croutons.

Total preparation and cooking time: 35 minutes
Makes 4 servings.

VINAIGRETTE

⅓ cup sun-dried tomatoes, not packed in oil, chopped
¼ cup water
1 tablespoon balsamic vinegar
1 tablespoon olive oil
1 clove garlic, minced
¾ teaspoon salt
½ teaspoon pepper

2 whole wheat pita breads, split in half horizontally
¼ cup diced fresh mozzarella cheese (about 1½ ounces)
¼ cup fresh basil, thinly sliced
12 thin tomato slices
1 clove garlic, minced
2 boneless beef top loin (strip) steaks, cut ¾ inch thick (about 8 ounces each)
4 cups chopped romaine lettuce
Salt and pepper, as desired

1. Heat oven to 350°F. Whisk vinaigrette ingredients in small bowl until blended; set aside.

2. Place pita bread rounds in single layers on 2 metal baking sheets. Bake in 350°F oven 5 minutes or until toasted. Remove from oven; sprinkle evenly with cheese. Top evenly with basil and tomatoes; set aside.

3. Press garlic evenly onto beef steaks. Heat large nonstick skillet over medium heat until hot. Place steaks in skillet; cook 10 to 12 minutes for medium-rare to medium doneness, turning once.

4. Carve steaks into thin slices. Toss with lettuce and vinaigrette. Season with salt and pepper, as desired. Evenly divide salad mixture onto plates. Serve with pita bread "pizza."

Nutrition information per serving

Calories: 296
Fat: 12 g
    Saturated fat: 4 g
    Monounsaturated fat: 5 g
Cholesterol: 65 mg
Sodium: 681 mg
Carbohydrate: 16 g
Fiber: 3.7 g
Protein: 30 g
Niacin: 8.7 mg
Vitamin B_6: 0.7 mg
Vitamin B_{12}: 1.4 mcg
Iron: 3.5 mg
Selenium: 37 mcg
Zinc: 5.2 mg

This recipe is an excellent source of protein, niacin, vitamin B_6, vitamin B_{12}, selenium, and zinc, and a good source of fiber and iron.

COOK'S TIP
To thinly slice fresh basil, stack several basil leaves. Roll stack lengthwise into cylinder. Cut cylinder crosswise into thin slices with sharp knife.

Farmer's Market Vegetable, Beef, and Brown Rice Salad

Total preparation and
  cooking time: 50 minutes
Marinating time: 6 hours or
  overnight
Makes 4 servings.

HEALTHY LIVING **TIP**
• • • • •

For optimal flavor and nutrition, use the freshest ingredients possible in your cooking.

Nutrition information per serving

Calories: 514
Fat: 15 g
  Saturated fat: 3 g
  Monounsaturated fat: 8 g
Cholesterol: 61 mg
Sodium: 593 mg
Carbohydrate: 60 g
Fiber: 7.3 g
Protein: 36 g
Niacin: 8.6 mg
Vitamin B$_6$: 1.1 mg
Vitamin B$_{12}$: 1.5 mcg
Iron: 5.9 mg
Selenium: 50.8 mcg
Zinc: 7.0 mg

This recipe is an excellent source of fiber, protein, niacin, vitamin B$_6$, vitamin B$_{12}$, iron, selenium, and zinc.

Brown rice has a nutty flavor and is full of fiber and vitamins, making it a healthy foundation for this garden-fresh salad.

MARINADE
¼ cup olive oil
2 tablespoons fresh lemon juice
1 tablespoon minced garlic
1 tablespoon honey
2 teaspoons fresh chopped thyme
2 teaspoons chopped fresh oregano
¼ teaspoon salt
⅛ teaspoon pepper

1 beef top round steak, cut ¾ inch thick (about 1 pound)
1 teaspoon olive oil
2 cups asparagus (2-inch pieces)
1 medium yellow squash, cut lengthwise in half, then crosswise into ¼-inch-thick slices
3 cups hot cooked brown rice
1 cup diced, seeded tomatoes
1 cup canned garbanzo beans, rinsed, drained
¼ cup fresh basil, thinly sliced
½ teaspoon salt

COOK'S TIP
To grill, place steak on grid over medium, ash-covered coals. Grill, uncovered, 8 to 9 minutes for medium-rare doneness, turning occasionally.

1. Combine marinade ingredients in small bowl. Place beef steak and ¼ cup marinade in food-safe plastic bag; turn steak to coat. Close bag securely and marinate in refrigerator 6 hours or as long as overnight. Reserve remaining marinade in refrigerator for dressing.

2. Remove steak from marinade; discard marinade. Place steak on rack in broiler pan so surface of beef is 2 to 3 inches from heat. Broil 12 to 13 minutes for medium-rare doneness, turning once. Remove; keep warm.

3. Heat oil in large nonstick skillet over medium-high heat until hot. Add asparagus and squash; cook and stir 7 to 8 minutes or until tender. Toss with rice, tomatoes, beans, basil, salt, and reserved marinade in large bowl.

4. Carve steak into thin slices. Serve over rice salad.

Southwest Beef and Warm Vegetable Salad

Total preparation and cooking time: 55 minutes
Makes 6 servings.

Chipotle peppers are smoked jalapeño peppers, typically found in the international foods section of your local supermarket. These flavorful peppers add a spicy dimension to this warm salad.

DRESSING
2	tablespoons fresh lime juice
2	tablespoons olive oil
2	teaspoons brown sugar
1¼	teaspoons chipotle peppers in adobo sauce, minced
¼	teaspoon ground cumin
¼	teaspoon salt

	Cooking spray
2	cups frozen corn
1	large zucchini, cut lengthwise in half, then crosswise into ¼-inch-thick slices
2	cups chopped red bell peppers
1	cup coarsely chopped onion
½	teaspoon minced garlic
¼	cup chopped fresh cilantro
½	teaspoon salt
¼	teaspoon black pepper

RUB
1	tablespoon minced garlic
2	teaspoons brown sugar
1½	teaspoons chili powder
1	teaspoon ground cumin
1	teaspoon freshly grated lime peel
½	teaspoon salt

3	beef shoulder center steaks (Ranch Steaks), cut ¾ inch thick (about 8 ounces each)
	Salt and pepper, as desired
	Crunchy Tortilla Strips (page 61)

1. Whisk dressing ingredients in small bowl until blended; set aside.

2. Spray large nonstick skillet with cooking spray; heat over medium-high heat until hot. Add corn, zucchini, bell peppers, onion, and

Nutrition information per serving

Calories: 310
Fat: 11 g
  Saturated fat: 2 g
  Monounsaturated fat: 6 g
Cholesterol: 57 mg
Sodium: 576 mg
Carbohydrate: 29 g
Fiber: 3.7 g
Protein: 26 g
Niacin: 4.8 mg
Vitamin B_6: 0.7 mg
Vitamin B_{12}: 2.6 mcg
Iron: 4.0 mg
Selenium: 27.0 mcg
Zinc: 6.2 mg

This recipe is an excellent source of protein, niacin, vitamin B_6, vitamin B_{12}, iron, selenium, and zinc, and a good source of fiber.

garlic; cook 10 to 13 minutes or until tender, stirring frequently. Stir in cilantro, salt, and pepper. Remove and set aside.

3. Combine rub ingredients in small bowl; press evenly onto beef steaks. Heat same skillet over medium heat until hot. Place steaks in skillet; cook 9 to 12 minutes for medium-rare to medium doneness, turning twice.

4. Carve steaks into thin slices. Season with salt and pepper, as desired. Drizzle dressing over steak and vegetables. Top with Crunchy Tortilla Strips.

COOK'S TIP
To grill, place steak on grid over medium, ash-covered coals. Grill, covered, 9 to 11 minutes for medium-rare to medium doneness, turning once.

Sirloin with Sugar Snap Pea and Pasta Salad with Gremolata Dressing

A gremolata is made with fresh parsley, garlic, and lemon peel. This fresh-tasting dressing is an outstanding accompaniment to beef and pasta.

Total preparation and cooking time: 1 hour
Makes 4 servings.

Water
2   cups fresh sugar snap peas
2   cups cooked gemelli or corkscrew pasta
1   cup grape or teardrop tomatoes, cut in halves

GREMOLATA DRESSING
¼   cup fresh lemon juice
2   tablespoons olive oil
2   tablespoons chopped fresh parsley
2   cloves garlic, minced
2   teaspoons freshly grated lemon peel
¼   teaspoon salt
⅛   teaspoon pepper

3   cloves garlic, minced
1   teaspoon pepper
1   boneless beef top sirloin steak, cut ¾ inch thick (about 1 pound)
    Salt, as desired
    Freshly grated lemon peel
    Chopped fresh parsley (optional)

1. Bring water to boil in large saucepan. Add peas; cook 2 to 3 minutes until crisp-tender. Drain; rinse under cold water. Combine peas, pasta, and tomatoes in large bowl. Set aside.

2. Whisk Gremolata Dressing ingredients in small bowl until well blended. Toss 2 tablespoons dressing with pasta mixture. Set aside.

3. Combine garlic and pepper; press evenly onto beef steak. Place steak on rack in broiler pan so surface of beef is 2 to 3 inches from heat. Broil 9 to 12 minutes for medium-rare to medium doneness, turning once.

4. Carve steak into thin slices; season with salt, as desired. Add steak slices and remaining dressing to pasta mixture; toss to coat evenly. Garnish with lemon peel and parsley, if desired.

Nutrition information per serving

Calories: 369
Fat: 12 g
   Saturated fat: 3 g
   Monounsaturated fat: 7 g
Cholesterol: 50 mg
Sodium: 216 mg
Carbohydrate: 31 g
Fiber: 4.2 g
Protein: 32 g
Niacin: 10.0 mg
Vitamin B_6: 0.7 mg
Vitamin B_{12}: 1.4 mcg
Iron: 4.4 mg
Selenium: 46.5 mcg
Zinc: 5.3 mg

This recipe is an excellent source of protein, niacin, vitamin B_6, vitamin B_{12}, iron, selenium, and zinc, and a good source of fiber.

Beef and Lemony Lentil Salad

Total preparation and cooking time: 1 hour
Makes 4 servings.

Lentils are full of fiber and cook more quickly than other legumes. Uncooked lentils can be stored in an airtight container in a cool dry place for up to a year.

2	teaspoons olive oil
1	cup chopped carrots
1	cup finely chopped onion
2	teaspoons minced garlic
1	can (14 to 14½ ounces) ready-to-serve vegetable broth
1	cup uncooked lentils, rinsed, picked over
1	cup water
1	teaspoon ground cumin
	Cooking spray
2	beef shoulder center steaks (Ranch Steaks), cut ¾ inch thick (about 8 ounces each)
	Salt, as desired
¼	cup chopped fresh parsley
2	tablespoons fresh lemon juice
1	teaspoon freshly grated lemon peel
¾	teaspoon salt
½	teaspoon pepper
½	cup chopped tomato
	Chopped fresh parsley (optional)

COOK'S TIP

Substitute 1 teaspoon cumin seeds, crushed, for the ground cumin, if desired.

1. Heat oil in large nonstick skillet over medium heat until hot. Add carrots, onion, and garlic; cook and stir 3 to 5 minutes or until onion is tender. Stir in broth, lentils, and water; bring to a boil. Reduce heat; cover and simmer 25 to 30 minutes or until lentils are tender. Set aside to cool. (There will be a small amount of liquid in skillet that lentils will absorb during stand time.)

2. Meanwhile, press cumin evenly onto beef steaks. Spray large nonstick skillet with cooking spray; heat over medium heat until hot. Place steaks in skillet; cook 9 to 12 minutes for medium-rare to medium doneness, turning twice. Carve steaks into thin slices; season with salt, as desired.

3. Add parsley, lemon juice, lemon peel, salt, and pepper to lentils; toss gently. Spoon lentils onto serving platter. Arrange steak slices over lentils; top with tomato. Garnish with parsley, if desired.

Nutrition information per serving

Calories: 379
Fat: 9 g
 Saturated fat: 2 g
 Monounsaturated fat: 4 g
Cholesterol: 57 mg
Sodium: 983 mg
Carbohydrate: 39 g
Fiber: 13.2 g
Protein: 37 g
Niacin: 5.0 mg
Vitamin B_6: 0.6 mg
Vitamin B_{12}: 2.6 mcg
Iron: 8.1 mg
Selenium: 29.9 mcg
Zinc: 7.4 mg

This recipe is an excellent source of fiber, protein, niacin, vitamin B_6, vitamin B_{12}, iron, selenium, and zinc.

Beef and Wild Rice with Belgian Endive Salad

For a special presentation, serve this salad on a bed of leaf lettuce or endive spears and sprinkle with additional chopped fresh oregano.

1   pound boneless beef top round steak, cut ¾ inch thick

MARINADE

⅔   cup orange juice
2   tablespoons finely chopped shallot
2   tablespoons sherry wine vinegar
2   teaspoons freshly grated orange peel
½   teaspoon pepper

DRESSING

2   teaspoons olive oil
2   teaspoons finely chopped fresh oregano
¼   teaspoon salt

1   teaspoon olive oil
2   cups thinly sliced red onions
3   cups cooked long-grain and wild rice blend (prepared without seasoning packet)
2   cups thinly sliced Belgian endive
¼   cup pitted, sliced kalamata olives
½   teaspoon salt
½   teaspoon pepper
1   can (15 ounces) mandarin orange segments, drained

1. Cut beef steak lengthwise in half, then crosswise into ⅛-inch-thick strips. Combine marinade ingredients in large bowl. Remove and reserve ¼ cup for dressing. Add beef to remaining marinade in bowl, tossing to coat. Cover and marinate in refrigerator 30 minutes to 2 hours.

2. To prepare dressing, add oil, oregano, and salt to reserved marinade. Whisk until blended; cover and refrigerate.

3. Heat ½ teaspoon oil in large nonstick skillet over medium heat until hot. Add onions; cook and stir 7 to 8 minutes or until crisp-tender and starting to brown on edges. Remove from skillet. Set aside.

Total preparation and cooking time: 40 minutes

Marinating time: 30 minutes to 2 hours

Makes 4 servings.

Nutrition information per serving

Calories: 392
Fat: 9 g
 Saturated fat: 2 g
 Monounsaturated fat: 5 g
Cholesterol: 61 mg
Sodium: 1,042 mg
Carbohydrate: 45 g
Fiber: 3.3 g
Protein: 32 g
Niacin: 6.5 mg
Vitamin B_6: 0.5 mg
Vitamin B_{12}: 1.5 mcg
Iron: 4.2 mg
Selenium: 33.6 mcg
Zinc: 5.4 mg

This recipe is an excellent source of protein, niacin, vitamin B_6, vitamin B_{12}, iron, selenium, and zinc, and a good source of fiber.

Beef and Wild Rice with
Belgian Endive Salad
(continued)

4. Remove beef from marinade; discard marinade. In same skillet, heat remaining ½ teaspoon oil until hot. Add half of the beef; stir-fry 1 to 2 minutes or until outside surface of beef is no longer pink. (Do not overcook.) Remove from skillet with slotted spoon. Repeat with remaining beef.

5. Toss rice, beef, onions, endive, and olives with dressing in serving bowl until well mixed. Season with salt and pepper. Top with orange segments.

COOK'S TIP
One (6-ounce) package of long-grain and wild rice yields about 3 cups cooked rice.

Cracked Wheat and Beef Salad

Cracked wheat gives a terrific nutty flavor to this salad and is an excellent source of fiber. It is the whole wheat berry that has been broken into coarse, medium, or fine granules.

MARINADE

1	cup fresh lemon juice
½	cup finely chopped fresh parsley
¼	cup olive oil
1	tablespoon minced garlic
1	teaspoon ground cumin
½	teaspoon salt
½	teaspoon pepper

1	beef flank steak (about 1½ pounds)
3	cups water
1½	cups coarse cracked wheat, rinsed, drained
½	teaspoon salt
3	cups chopped seeded tomatoes
½	cup finely chopped fresh parsley
¼	cup finely chopped fresh mint

Total preparation and cooking time: 1 hour
Marinating time: 6 hours or overnight
Makes 6 servings.

COOK'S TIP

To finely chop fresh mint and other leafy herbs, stack several leaves. Roll stack lengthwise into cylinder. Cut cylinder crosswise at close intervals with sharp knife into thin slivers. Chop slivers into fine pieces.

HEALTHY LIVING TIP

Put fiber on the menu with a whole-grain side dish, such as brown rice, quinoa, barley, cracked wheat, or whole wheat pasta. Boost fiber even more by adding some chopped vegetables or fruits, legumes, and chopped nuts.

1. Combine marinade ingredients in medium bowl. Place beef steak in food-safe plastic bag. Pour half of the marinade over steak; turn steak to coat. Close bag securely and marinate in refrigerator 6 hours or as long as overnight. Reserve remaining marinade in refrigerator for dressing.

2. Bring water to a boil in medium saucepan. Stir in cracked wheat and salt. Reduce heat; cover and simmer 20 minutes or until wheat is tender and water is absorbed. (If necessary, pour off any excess water.) Spread on metal baking sheet to cool.

3. Meanwhile, remove steak from marinade; discard marinade. Place steak on grid over medium, ash-covered coals. Grill, uncovered, 17 to 21 minutes for medium-rare to medium doneness, turning occasionally.

4. Carve steak across the grain into thin slices. Toss cracked wheat with tomatoes, parsley, mint, and reserved marinade. Serve with steak slices.

Nutrition information per serving

Calories: 351
Fat: 14 g
    Saturated fat: 4 g
    Monounsaturated fat: 8 g
Cholesterol: 42 mg
Sodium: 387 mg
Carbohydrate: 29 g
Fiber: 5.4 g
Protein: 29 g
Niacin: 9.4 mg
Vitamin B_6: 0.7 mg
Vitamin B_{12}: 1.4 mcg
Iron: 4.1 mg
Selenium: 48.5 mcg
Zinc: 5.5 mg

This recipe is an excellent source of fiber, protein, niacin, vitamin B_6, vitamin B_{12}, iron, selenium, and zinc.

Beef, Mango, and Barley Salad

Mango adds a potent punch to this salad, both with its sweetness and with a boost of vitamin C.

Total preparation and cooking time: 1½ hours
Makes 6 to 8 servings.

HEALTHY LIVING TIP

Think of your plate as a palette, then add color with a range of fruits and vegetables. These naturally nutrient-rich foods are loaded with vitamins, minerals, fiber, and phyto-nutrients.

2	medium red bell peppers, cut into 1½-inch pieces
	Cooking spray
1½	teaspoons sweet paprika, divided
1	beef tri-tip roast (about 1½ to 2 pounds)
1	cup uncooked quick-cooking barley
½	teaspoon salt
¼	teaspoon black pepper
⅓	cup fresh lime juice
1	teaspoon olive oil
2	medium mangoes, cut into ½-inch pieces
⅓	cup chopped green onions
¼	cup chopped fresh cilantro
4	large Boston lettuce leaves (optional)

1. Heat oven to 425°F. Place bell peppers on metal baking sheet; spray with nonstick cooking spray. Set aside.

2. Press 1 teaspoon paprika evenly onto all surfaces of beef roast. Place roast on rack in shallow roasting pan. Do not add water or cover. Roast in 425°F oven 30 to 40 minutes for medium-rare, 40 to 45 minutes for medium doneness. Roast bell peppers in oven with beef about 30 minutes or until tender. Set peppers aside to cool.

3. Remove roast when instant-read thermometer, inserted into center of thickest part, registers 135°F for medium-rare, 150°F for medium. Transfer roast to carving board; tent loosely with aluminum foil. Let stand 15 minutes. (Temperature will continue to rise about 10°F to reach 145°F for medium-rare, 160°F for medium.)

4. Meanwhile, cook barley according to package directions. Set aside to cool slightly.

5. Cut beef into ½-inch pieces; season with salt and black pepper. Whisk lime juice, oil, and ½ teaspoon paprika in small bowl until blended. Toss with beef, barley, roasted peppers, mangoes, green onions, and cilantro in large bowl. Serve in Boston lettuce leaves, if desired.

COOK'S TIP
To quickly cool barley and prevent it from clumping, spread on a metal baking sheet.

Nutrition information per serving

Calories: 309
Fat: 9 g
   Saturated fat: 3 g
   Monounsaturated fat: 4 g
Cholesterol: 60 mg
Sodium: 246 mg
Carbohydrate: 35 g
Fiber: 4.3 g
Protein: 26 g
Niacin: 8.4 mg
Vitamin B_6: 0.8 mg
Vitamin B_{12}: 1.3 mcg
Iron: 2.3 mg
Selenium: 27 mcg
Zinc: 4.7 mg

This recipe is an excellent source of protein, niacin, vitamin B_6, vitamin B_{12}, selenium, and zinc, and a good source of fiber and iron.

Caribbean Jerk Tri-Tip with Basil Lime Salad

Total preparation and
   cooking time: 1¼ hours
Marinating time: 30 minutes
   to 2 hours
Makes 8 servings.

Most of the ingredients in this recipe are prepared spices and condiments that lend authentic island flavor to this tropical beef salad.

MARINADE

6 to 7 green onions, white and green parts cut into 1-inch pieces

3	tablespoons fresh lime juice
3	tablespoons balsamic vinegar
2	tablespoons ground allspice
2	tablespoons Asian hot chili sauce or Sriracha sauce
2	tablespoons soy sauce
1	tablespoon grated fresh ginger
1	tablespoon vegetable oil
1	teaspoon kosher or table salt
½	teaspoon ground cinnamon
½	teaspoon black pepper
⅛	teaspoon ground nutmeg
1	beef tri-tip roast (about 2 pounds)

DRESSING

2	tablespoons light mayonnaise
¼	cup sugar
¼	cup fresh lime juice
2	tablespoons water
2	teaspoons grated fresh ginger
2	teaspoons Asian hot chili sauce or Sriracha sauce
2	teaspoons anchovy paste (optional)

SALAD

1	package (10 ounces) romaine lettuce
1	medium cucumber, cut lengthwise in half, seeded, then cut crosswise into ¼-inch-thick slices
2	medium red bell peppers, cut into ¼-inch strips
1	medium red onion, cut into thin wedges
1	cup loosely packed fresh basil, chopped
½	cup loosely packed fresh mint, chopped
⅛	teaspoon kosher or table salt
⅛	teaspoon black pepper

Nutrition information per serving

Calories: 267
Fat: 9 g
   Saturated fat: 3 g
   Monounsaturated fat: 4 g
Cholesterol: 60 mg
Sodium: 505 mg
Carbohydrate: 24 g
Fiber: 3.6 g
Protein: 25 g
Niacin: 7.1 mg
Vitamin B_6: 0.7 mg
Vitamin B_{12}: 1.3 mcg
Iron: 3.7 mg
Selenium: 26.8 mcg
Zinc: 4.6 mg

This recipe is an excellent source of protein, niacin, vitamin B_6, vitamin B_{12}, iron, selenium, and zinc, and a good source of fiber.

1. To prepare marinade, place green onions in food processor container. Cover; process 10 seconds or until chopped. Add remaining marinade ingredients. Cover; process 30 seconds or until smooth. Place beef roast and marinade in food-safe plastic bag; turn roast to coat. Close bag securely and marinate in refrigerator 30 minutes or as long as 2 hours.

2. Meanwhile, prepare dressing. Place mayonnaise in small bowl; gradually whisk in remaining dressing ingredients until blended. Cover and refrigerate.

3. Combine salad ingredients in large bowl. Cover and refrigerate.

4. Remove roast from marinade; discard marinade. Place roast on grid over medium, ash-covered coals. Grill, covered, 25 to 35 minutes for medium-rare to medium doneness, turning occasionally. Remove roast when instant-read thermometer, inserted into center of thickest part, registers 140°F for medium-rare, 155°F for medium. Transfer roast to carving board; tent loosely with aluminum foil. Let stand 10 minutes. (Temperature will continue to rise about 5°F to reach 145°F for medium-rare, 160°F for medium.)

5. Add dressing to salad; toss lightly. Carve roast across the grain into thin slices. Serve with salad.

CHEF RICHARD'S TIP

Convenient, prepared salad greens streamline meal preparation, making it quicker and easier.

COOK'S TIPS

- Sriracha, a Vietnamese hot sauce made from sun-ripened chilies that are ground into a smooth paste and combined with vinegar, garlic, and other seasonings, is often used in Asian recipes to impart a delicious, spicy heat. It's available in Asian markets and the Asian section of most supermarkets.
- Anchovy paste is a mixture of anchovies, vinegar, and spices and is sold in tubes. It's available in Italian or other Mediterranean markets and some supermarkets.

Summertime Steak Salad

Looking for a steak salad that encompasses the fresh crispness of summer? Well, here you have it! Freshly grilled steak, crisp cucumber, green bell peppers, and ripe baby pear tomatoes are combined to make an unforgettable summer meal.

Total preparation and
  cooking time: 30 minutes
Marinating time: 6 hours or
  overnight
Makes 4 servings.

1   beef shoulder steak, cut 1 inch thick (about 1 pound)
1   can (5½ ounces) spicy 100% vegetable juice

SPICY TOMATO DRESSING
1   can (5½ ounces) spicy 100% vegetable juice
½   cup chopped tomato
¼   cup finely chopped green bell pepper
1   tablespoon red wine vinegar
1   tablespoon chopped fresh cilantro
2   teaspoons olive oil
1   clove garlic, minced

8   cups mixed greens or 1 package (10 ounces) romaine and leaf lettuce mixture
1   cup baby pear or grape tomatoes, halved
1   cup cucumber, cut in half lengthwise, then into thin slices
1   cup chopped green bell pepper
    Salt and black pepper, as desired
    Crunchy Tortilla Strips (recipe follows)

1. Place beef steak and 1 can vegetable juice in food-safe plastic bag; turn steak to coat. Close bag securely and marinate in refrigerator 6 hours or as long as overnight.
2. Whisk Spicy Tomato Dressing ingredients in small bowl until blended; refrigerate. Combine lettuce, baby pear tomatoes, cucumber, and green bell pepper; refrigerate.
3. Remove steak from marinade; discard marinade. Place steak on grid over medium, ash-covered coals. Grill steak, uncovered, 16 to 20 minutes for medium-rare to medium doneness, turning occasionally. Carve steak into thin slices. Season with salt and pepper, as desired.
4. Meanwhile, prepare Crunchy Tortilla Strips. Add steak to salad mixture. Drizzle with dressing and top with tortilla strips.

CRUNCHY TORTILLA STRIPS
1. Cut 2 corn tortillas in half, then crosswise into ¼-inch-wide strips. Place strips in single layer on baking sheet. Spray tortilla strips lightly with nonstick cooking spray. Bake 4 to 8 minutes at 400°F or until crisp.

Nutrition information per serving

Calories: 242
Fat: 9 g
  Saturated fat: 2 g
  Monounsaturated fat: 4 g
Cholesterol: 60 mg
Sodium: 239 mg
Carbohydrate: 16 g
Fiber: 4.0 g
Protein: 25 g
Niacin: 3.9 mg
Vitamin B_6: 0.5 mg
Vitamin B_{12}: 2.6 mcg
Iron: 4.2 mg
Selenium: 26.7 mcg
Zinc: 5.9 mg

This recipe is an excellent source of protein, niacin, vitamin B_6, vitamin B_{12}, iron, selenium, and zinc, and a good source of fiber.

Mixed Greens and Steak Salad with Creamy Peppercorn Dressing

Total preparation and cooking time: 40 minutes
Makes 4 servings.

BEEF SMARTS

Protein is essential to maintain muscle while you're losing weight. Protein-rich foods, such as lean beef, provide longer-lasting satisfaction that may help you consume fewer calories throughout the day. See page 234 to learn more.

Nutrition information per serving

Calories: 236
Fat: 10 g
 Saturated fat: 3 g
 Monounsaturated fat: 2 g
Cholesterol: 60 mg
Sodium: 300 mg
Carbohydrate: 9 g
Fiber: 1.1 g
Protein: 28 g
Niacin: 8.4 mg
Vitamin B_6: 0.8 mg
Vitamin B_{12}: 1.4 mcg
Iron: 2.6 mg
Selenium: 31.6 mcg
Zinc: 5.2 mg

This recipe is an excellent source of protein, niacin, vitamin B_6, vitamin B_{12}, selenium, and zinc, and a good source of iron.

Red bell peppers are a great source of vitamins A and C, which are important for a healthy immune system.

1   pound boneless beef top sirloin steak, cut ¾ inch thick
1½ teaspoons crushed mixed peppercorns (black, pink, and green)
1   medium red bell pepper, cut into 1½-inch pieces
1   medium yellow bell pepper, cut into 1½-inch pieces
    Salt, as desired

CREAMY PEPPERCORN DRESSING
¼   cup reduced-fat dairy sour cream
2   tablespoons light mayonnaise
2   tablespoons fresh lemon juice
1   large clove garlic, minced
1   teaspoon Worcestershire sauce
½   teaspoon crushed mixed peppercorns (black, pink, and green)
¼   teaspoon salt
3 to 4 tablespoons skim milk

1   package (5 ounces) mixed baby salad greens

1. Cut beef steak into 1¼-inch pieces. Toss with crushed peppercorns.

2. Alternately thread beef and bell pepper pieces evenly onto four 12-inch metal skewers.

3. Place kabobs on rack in broiler pan so surface of beef is 3 to 4 inches from heat. Broil about 8 to 10 minutes for medium-rare to medium doneness, turning once. Season with salt, as desired.

4. Meanwhile, to prepare Creamy Peppercorn Dressing, whisk all ingredients except milk in small bowl. Stir in milk 1 tablespoon at a time until creamy consistency. Set aside.

5. Place salad greens on serving platter. Remove beef and peppers from skewers and arrange over greens. Drizzle with dressing.

> **COOK'S TIP**
> If using bamboo skewers, soak them in water for at least 10 minutes before broiling.

3

HEARTY BEEF SANDWICHES

Chipotle Sloppy Joes with Crunchy Coleslaw

Total preparation and
  cooking time: 30 minutes
Makes 4 servings.

Cool, crunchy coleslaw teams with the smoky flavor of chipotle beef to create a taste sensation you'll never forget.

CRUNCHY COLESLAW
¼ cup plain nonfat yogurt
1   tablespoon light mayonnaise
2   teaspoons cider vinegar
¼ teaspoon hot pepper sauce
⅛ teaspoon salt
1½ cups packaged coleslaw mix
½ red bell pepper, cut into ⅛-inch-thick strips
    Black pepper, as desired

1   pound ground beef (95% lean)
¼ cup chopped onion
¾ cup ketchup
½ cup frozen corn
½ cup canned black beans, rinsed, drained
½ cup tomato sauce
1 to 2 teaspoons minced chipotle peppers in adobo sauce
½ teaspoon ground cumin
¼ cup chopped fresh cilantro
¼ teaspoon salt
¼ teaspoon black pepper
4   whole wheat hamburger buns, split

COOK'S TIP
This recipe works well with all varieties of lean ground beef.

COOK'S TIP
Thinly sliced green cabbage may be substituted for the packaged coleslaw mix.

Nutrition information per serving

Calories: 406
Fat: 10 g
  Saturated fat: 4 g
  Monounsaturated fat: 3 g
Cholesterol: 77 mg
Sodium: 1,344 mg
Carbohydrate: 50 g
Fiber: 6.9 g
Protein: 33 g
Niacin: 9.4 mg
Vitamin: B_6: 0.7 mg
Vitamin: B_{12}: 2.2 mcg
Iron: 5.3 mg
Selenium: 39.8 mcg
Zinc: 7.3 mg

This recipe is an excellent source of fiber, protein, niacin, vitamin B_6, vitamin B_{12}, iron, selenium, and zinc.

1. To prepare Crunchy Coleslaw, combine yogurt, mayonnaise, vinegar, pepper sauce, and salt in small bowl. Add coleslaw mix and bell pepper; toss to coat. Season with black pepper, as desired. Refrigerate, covered, until ready to serve.

2. Brown ground beef with onion in large nonstick skillet over medium heat 8 to 10 minutes or until beef is no longer pink, breaking beef up into ¾-inch crumbles. Pour off drippings. Stir in ketchup, corn, beans, tomato sauce, chipotle peppers, and cumin; bring to a boil. Reduce heat; simmer 5 minutes, stirring often. Stir in cilantro, salt, and black pepper.

3. Place beef mixture on bottom half of each bun; top with coleslaw. Close sandwiches.

Slow Good BBQ Beef Sandwiches

Love the great taste of a good BBQ beef sandwich but not all the work? Let your slow cooker do it for you while you spend your time on other fun activities.

Total preparation and cooking time on high setting: 6 hours

Total preparation and cooking time on low setting: 10 hours

Makes 8 to 10 servings.

HEALTHY LIVING TIP

Be flexible about your food choices—no need to worry about one food, one meal, or even one day. Learn to balance higher-fat food choices with lower-fat options throughout a day or a week.

1   boneless beef chuck shoulder pot roast (3 to 3½ pounds)
1   medium onion, cut into quarters
3   cloves garlic, peeled
¾   cup water
1   teaspoon salt
½   teaspoon pepper
1   bottle (18 ounces) hickory-flavored barbecue sauce
8 to 10 onion rolls, split

1. Cut beef pot roast into 4 even pieces. Place onion and garlic in 4½- to 5½-quart slow cooker; place beef on top. Add water, salt, and pepper. Cover and cook on HIGH 5 to 5½ hours, or on LOW 9 to 9½ hours, or until beef is fork-tender. (No stirring is necessary during cooking.)

2. Remove beef; cool slightly. Strain cooking liquid; skim fat. Shred beef with 2 forks.

3. Place beef in 2-quart microwave-safe dish. Stir in barbecue sauce and ½ cup cooking liquid. Cover and microwave on HIGH 6 to 8 minutes or until heated through, stirring once. Serve in rolls.

> **COOK'S TIP**
> For a Southwestern flair, serve with a side of roasted corn.

Nutrition information per serving

Calories: 405
Fat: 10 g
   Saturated fat: 3 g
   Monounsaturated fat: 4 g
Cholesterol: 64 mg
Sodium: 1,351 mg
Carbohydrate: 40 g
Fiber: 2.1 g
Protein: 36 g
Niacin: 6.5 mg
Vitamin: B_6: 0.4 mg
Vitamin: B_{12}: 2.3 mcg
Iron: 4.5 mg
Selenium: 45.8 mcg
Zinc: 8.0 mg

This recipe is an excellent source of protein, niacin, vitamin B_6, vitamin B_{12}, iron, selenium, and zinc.

Asian Express Beef Lettuce Wraps

Let these light and refreshing lettuce wraps add a new flair to your healthy eating.

1½ pounds ground beef (95% lean)
½ cup hoisin sauce
½ cup peanut sauce
1 medium cucumber, seeded, chopped
½ cup shredded carrot
¼ cup torn fresh mint
Salt and pepper, as desired
12 large Boston lettuce leaves (about 2 heads) or iceberg or romaine lettuce
Fresh mint (optional)

1. Brown ground beef in large nonstick skillet over medium heat 8 to 10 minutes or until no longer pink, breaking up into small crumbles. Pour off drippings. Stir in hoisin sauce and peanut sauce; heat through.

2. Just before serving, add cucumber, carrots, and torn mint; toss gently. Season with salt and pepper, as desired. Serve beef mixture in lettuce leaves. Garnish with mint, if desired.

Total preparation and cooking time: 30 minutes
Makes 4 servings.

COOK'S TIP
For a complete Asian meal, serve with a side of cooked brown rice.

Nutrition information per serving

Calories: 337
Fat: 11 g
 Saturated fat: 5 g
 Monounsaturated fat: 5 g
Cholesterol: 114 mg
Sodium: 641 mg
Carbohydrate: 18 g
Fiber: 2.5 g
Protein: 40 g
Niacin: 10.0 mg
Vitamin B_6: 0.7 mg
Vitamin B_{12}: 3.4 mcg
Iron: 5.8 mg
Selenium: 27.8 mcg
Zinc: 9.4 mg

This recipe is an excellent source of protein, niacin, vitamin B_6, vitamin B_{12}, iron, selenium, and zinc, and a good source of fiber.

Stir-Fry Orange Beef Lettuce Cups

Asian and citrus flavors are fused together to create a taste sensation the whole family will enjoy.

Total preparation and cooking time: 20 minutes

Makes 4 servings.

1	pound beef top round steak, cut ¾ inch thick
2	teaspoons cornstarch

ORANGE SAUCE

2	tablespoons frozen orange juice concentrate, defrosted
2	tablespoons hoisin sauce
2	tablespoons rice wine vinegar
2	tablespoons soy sauce
2	teaspoons cornstarch

1	tablespoon vegetable oil
¼	teaspoon crushed red pepper
1	cup shredded carrot
½	cup thinly sliced green onions
16	large Boston lettuce leaves (about 2 heads)

1. Cut beef steak lengthwise in half and then crosswise into ⅛-inch-thick strips. Combine beef and cornstarch in medium bowl; toss to coat. Set aside.

2. Combine Orange Sauce ingredients in small bowl; set aside.

3. Heat oil and red pepper in large nonstick skillet over medium-high heat until hot. Add half of the beef; stir-fry 1 to 2 minutes or until outside surface of beef is no longer pink. (Do not overcook.) Remove from skillet; keep warm. Repeat with remaining beef.

4. Return all beef to skillet. Add Orange Sauce, carrot, and green onions; cook and stir until sauce is thickened and bubbly.

5. Serve beef mixture in lettuce leaves.

COOK'S TIP

Serve with a side of brown rice for added fiber or try an Asian cucumber salad.

Nutrition information per serving

Calories: 261
Fat: 9 g
  Saturated fat: 2 g
  Monounsaturated fat: 4 g
Cholesterol: 62 mg
Sodium: 650 mg
Carbohydrate: 15 g
Fiber: 2.5 g
Protein: 30 g
Niacin: 5.7 mg
Vitamin B_6: 0.5 mg
Vitamin B_{12}: 1.5 mcg
Iron: 3.6 mg
Selenium: 33.6 mcg
Zinc: 5.1 mg

This recipe is an excellent source of protein, niacin, vitamin B_6, vitamin B_{12}, iron, selenium, and zinc, and a good source of fiber.

Beef and Vegetable Pizza

Feel like comfort food? Two of your favorites, pot roast and pizza, combine for a quick and healthy dinner.

Total preparation and cooking time: 30 minutes
Makes 4 servings.

1 package (16 to 17 ounces) fully cooked boneless beef pot roast with gravy
1 teaspoon olive oil
2 cups sliced baby portobello mushrooms
½ cup chopped onion
1 can (14½ ounces) Italian-style diced tomatoes, undrained
1½ cups asparagus pieces (1½ inch)
¼ cup thinly sliced fresh basil
½ cup shredded reduced-fat mozzarella cheese
1 package (14 ounces) thick prebaked pizza crust (12-inch diameter)

1. Heat oven to 450°F. Remove beef pot roast from gravy; discard gravy. Cut beef into ½-inch pieces; set aside. Heat oil in large non-stick skillet over medium heat until hot. Add mushrooms and onion; cook and stir about 5 minutes or until onion is tender.

2. Add tomatoes; bring to a boil. Reduce heat and simmer 7 minutes. Stir in asparagus and basil; simmer 5 minutes. Remove from heat.

3. Stir in beef and ¼ cup cheese. Place pizza crust on pizza pan or large baking sheet. Spread beef mixture evenly on crust. Sprinkle with remaining ¼ cup cheese.

4. Bake 8 to 10 minutes or until topping is hot and cheese is melted. Cut into 8 wedges. Serve immediately.

Nutrition information per serving

Calories: 456
Fat: 12 g
  Saturated fat: 3 g
  Monounsaturated fat: 3 g
Cholesterol: 47 mg
Sodium: 943 mg
Carbohydrate: 49 g
Fiber: 2.7 g
Protein: 36 g
Niacin: 5.0 mg
Vitamin B_6: 0.3 mg
Vitamin B_{12}: 1.6 mcg
Iron: 6.0 mg
Selenium: 27.0 mcg
Zinc: 5.6 mg

This recipe is an excellent source of protein, niacin, vitamin B_6, vitamin B_{12}, iron, selenium, and zinc, and a good source of fiber.

COOK'S TIPS

- To easily cut pizza into wedges without a pizza cutter, use a pair of kitchen scissors.
- Substitute 1½ cups broccoli, bell pepper pieces, or other favorite vegetables for asparagus.

Caribbean Grilled Burgers with Chipotle Pepper Sauce

With the spicy yogurt sauce and island-spiced beef, you can almost hear the calypso drums when you taste this burger.

CHIPOTLE-PEPPER SAUCE

½	cup nonfat plain yogurt
2	tablespoons light mayonnaise
2	tablespoons chopped fresh cilantro
1	tablespoon fresh lime juice
1 to 2	teaspoons chopped chipotle peppers in adobo sauce
1	clove garlic, minced

SEASONING

2	teaspoons brown sugar
1	teaspoon ground cumin
1	teaspoon freshly grated lime peel
½	teaspoon salt
¼	teaspoon black pepper
¼	teaspoon ground cinnamon
⅛ to ¼	teaspoon ground red pepper
⅛	teaspoon ground allspice

1	pound ground beef (95% lean)
4	whole wheat hamburger buns, split, toasted
4	slices tomato

1. Combine Chipotle Pepper Sauce ingredients in medium bowl. Set aside. Combine seasoning ingredients and ground beef in large bowl. Lightly shape ground beef mixture into four ½-inch-thick patties.

2. Place patties on grid over medium, ash-covered coals. Grill, uncovered, 11 to 13 minutes to medium (160°F) doneness, until no longer pink in center and juices show no pink color, turning once.

3. Spread sauce over cut sides of buns. Line bottom of each bun with tomato slice; top with burger. Close sandwiches. Serve with additional sauce, if desired.

COOK'S TIP

For a complete Caribbean experience, serve the burgers with a cooling and exotic fruit, such as chopped papaya or mango slices.

Total preparation and cooking time: 30 minutes
Makes 4 servings.

HEALTHY LIVING TIP

Make regular physical activity part of your lean routine. The key is consistency. Get physical for at least 30 minutes a day—and feel the difference all over.

Nutrition information per serving

Calories: 322
Fat: 10 g
    Saturated fat: 3 g
    Monounsaturated fat: 3 g
Cholesterol: 68 mg
Sodium: 647 mg
Carbohydrate: 29 g
Fiber: 4 g
Protein: 28 g
Niacin: 6.8 mg
Vitamin B_6: 0.5 mg
Vitamin B_{12}: 2.3 mcg
Iron: 3.9 mg
Selenium: 40.9 mcg
Zinc: 6.7 mg

This recipe is an excellent source of protein, niacin, vitamin B_6, vitamin B_{12}, iron, selenium, and zinc, and a good source of fiber.

Mexican Chili Beef Wrap

Total preparation and cooking time: 1 hour
Makes 6 servings.

The simple flavors of the sauce and seasoning combine into a flavor powerhouse for this terrific wrap.

SAUCE
¾ cup reduced-fat dairy sour cream
1 teaspoon minced garlic
½ teaspoon freshly grated lime peel
½ teaspoon fresh lime juice
¼ teaspoon salt
⅛ teaspoon ground red pepper

SEASONING
1 tablespoon chili powder
½ teaspoon garlic powder
½ teaspoon ground cumin

1 beef tri-tip roast (1½ to 2 pounds)
6 whole wheat flour tortillas (9-inch diameter)
¾ cup fat-free black bean salsa
¾ cup chopped seeded tomatoes
4 cups thinly sliced romaine lettuce

1. Heat oven to 425°F. Combine sauce ingredients in small bowl. Refrigerate, covered, until ready to use.

2. Combine seasoning ingredients; press evenly onto all surfaces of beef roast.

3. Place roast on rack in shallow roasting pan. Do not add water or cover. Roast in 425°F oven 30 to 40 minutes for medium-rare, 40 to 45 minutes for medium doneness.

4. Remove roast when instant-read thermometer, inserted into center of thickest part, registers 135°F for medium-rare, 150°F for medium. Transfer roast to carving board; tent loosely with aluminum foil. Let stand 15 minutes. (Temperature will continue to rise about 10°F to reach 145°F for medium-rare, 160°F for medium.) Carve roast across the grain into ¼-inch-thick slices.

5. Spread each tortilla evenly with sauce and salsa, leaving ½-inch border around edge. Place roast slices on 1 side of each tortilla. Top with tomatoes and lettuce. Fold tortillas over to cover.

Nutrition information per serving

Calories: 369
Fat: 14 g
    Saturated fat: 5 g
    Monounsaturated fat: 4 g
Cholesterol: 76 mg
Sodium: 465 mg
Carbohydrate: 29 g
Fiber: 3.6 g
Protein: 29 g
Niacin: 6.9 mg
Vitamin B_6: 0.6 mg
Vitamin B_{12}: 1.3 mcg
Iron: 3.2 mg
Selenium: 26.7 mcg
Zinc: 4.4 mg

This recipe is an excellent source of protein, niacin, vitamin B_6, vitamin B_{12}, selenium, and zinc, and a good source of fiber and iron.

Mediterranean Burgers with Hummus

Total preparation and cooking time: 30 minutes
Makes 4 servings.

Almost anything is great on a burger. Here's one with a Middle Eastern flair, combining traditional toppings with a zesty hummus sauce.

SAUCE

8	ounces nonfat plain hummus (about 1 cup)
1½	tablespoons fresh lemon juice
1	tablespoon chopped fresh parsley
¼	teaspoon black pepper
⅛ to ¼	teaspoon ground red pepper

1	pound ground beef (95% lean)
1½	teaspoons Pepper-Herb Seasoning Mix (recipe follows)
	Salt, as desired
4	whole wheat hamburger buns, split
4	romaine lettuce leaves
1	medium tomato, cut into thin slices
1	small cucumber, cut into thin slices

1. Combine sauce ingredients in small saucepan. Cook and stir over medium heat about 8 minutes or until sauce is heated through. Set aside and keep warm.

2. Combine ground beef and seasoning mix in large bowl, mixing lightly but thoroughly. Lightly shape into four ½-inch-thick patties.

3. Heat large nonstick skillet over medium heat until hot. Place patties in skillet; cook 10 to 12 minutes to medium (160°F) doneness, until no longer pink in center and juices show no pink color, turning once. Season with salt, as desired.

Nutrition information per serving

Calories: 326
Fat: 7 g
 Saturated fat: 3 g
 Monounsaturated fat: 3 g
Cholesterol: 65 mg
Sodium: 528 mg
Carbohydrate: 34 g
Fiber: 8.0 g
Protein: 31 g
Niacin: 7.5 mg
Vitamin B_6: 0.6 mg
Vitamin B_{12}: 2.6 mcg
Iron: 5.6 mg
Selenium: 40.8 mcg
Zinc: 7.6 mg

This recipe is an excellent source of fiber, protein, niacin, vitamin B_6, vitamin B_{12}, iron, selenium, and zinc.

COOK'S TIPS

- To broil, place patties on rack in broiler pan so that surface of beef is 3 to 4 inches from heat. Broil 10 to 12 minutes to medium (160°F) doneness, until no longer pink in center and juices show no pink color, turning once.
- Carrots and celery sticks make an excellent complement to this protein-packed burger.

4. Line bottom of each bun with lettuce, tomato, and cucumber slices; top with burger and 2 tablespoons sauce. Close sandwiches. Serve with remaining sauce, if desired.

PEPPER-HERB SEASONING MIX

Yield: about 3 tablespoons.

Combine 1 tablespoon dried basil leaves, crushed; 1½ teaspoons dried oregano leaves, crushed; 1½ teaspoons lemon pepper; 1½ teaspoons onion powder; and ¾ teaspoon rubbed sage. Store in airtight container. Shake well before using to blend.

Ranch Steak Panini

Total preparation and
   cooking time: 30 minutes
Makes 4 servings.

Take grilled cheese up a notch by making panini sandwiches at home using your grill!

SAUCE
¼   cup thinly sliced fresh basil
¼   cup light mayonnaise
1   clove garlic, minced
¼   teaspoon salt
¼   teaspoon pepper

SEASONING
2   tablespoons chopped fresh parsley
2   teaspoons freshly grated lemon peel
2   cloves garlic, minced
½   teaspoon pepper

2   beef shoulder center steaks (Ranch Steaks), cut ¾ inch thick
     (about 8 ounces each)
     Salt, as desired
1   loaf (1 pound) focaccia or ciabatta bread, cut horizontally in half
8   slices tomato
¾   cup shredded reduced-fat mozzarella cheese

HEALTHY LIVING TIP

Rather than think of snacks as "extras," choose snacks that contribute to food-group servings, such as sliced peaches, red pepper strips, an oat bran bagel, string cheese, or beef jerky.

1. Combine sauce ingredients in small bowl. Set aside. Combine seasoning ingredients; press evenly onto beef steaks.

2. Place steaks on grid over medium, ash-covered coals. Grill, covered, 9 to 11 minutes for medium-rare to medium doneness, turning twice. Carve steak into thin slices. Season with salt, as desired.

3. Spread sauce over bottom half of bread. Top evenly with tomato, steak, and cheese. Close sandwich.

4. Place sandwich on grid over medium, ash-covered coals. Grill, uncovered, 4 minutes or until cheese is melted, turning once and pressing down on sandwich with spatula to flatten slightly.

5. Cut sandwich crosswise in half. Cut each half diagonally to make 4 triangles.

Nutrition information per serving

Calories: 541
Fat: 14 g
   Saturated fat: 5 g
   Monounsaturated fat: 4 g
Cholesterol: 70 mg
Sodium: 1,144 mg
Carbohydrate: 62 g
Fiber: 4.0 g
Protein: 40 g
Niacin: 8.3 mg
Vitamin B_6: 0.4 mg
Vitamin B_{12}: 2.6 mcg
Iron: 6.6 mg
Selenium: 56.7 mcg
Zinc: 6.6 mg

This recipe is an excellent source of protein, niacin, vitamin B_6, vitamin B_{12}, iron, selenium, and zinc, and a good source of fiber.

COOK'S TIP
Paninis are also great made with hearty French or Italian bread. You can cook a panini in a skillet on the stove top or by using a counter-top clamshell grill.

Mushroom Merlot Burgers

The classic bistro flavors of mushrooms and wine truly enhance the flavor of these open-faced burgers.

Total preparation and
   cooking time: 55 minutes
Makes 4 servings.

SAUCE
1	teaspoon olive oil
2	tablespoons minced shallots
1	cup Merlot or other dry red wine
¼	cup ready-to-serve beef broth
2	teaspoons fresh thyme, chopped
1	tablespoon butter
2	teaspoons all-purpose flour
¼	teaspoon salt
¼	teaspoon pepper

1	pound ground beef (95% lean)
2	tablespoons chopped fresh parsley
⅛	teaspoon salt
⅛	teaspoon pepper
4	large portobello mushroom caps
4	slices French bread, cut diagonally ½ inch thick
2	ounces goat cheese (about ½ cup)
4	romaine lettuce leaves
	Chopped fresh parsley (optional)

1. To prepare sauce, heat oil in large nonstick skillet over low heat. Add shallots; cook and stir 6 to 8 minutes or until caramelized. Stir in wine, broth, and thyme. Cook over medium-high heat 8 to 10 minutes or until liquid is reduced to ½ cup. Combine butter and flour; whisk into sauce. Stir in salt and pepper. Cover; keep warm.

2. Combine ground beef, parsley, salt, and pepper in large bowl, mixing lightly but thoroughly. Lightly shape into four ½-inch-thick patties. Set aside.

3. Place mushroom caps on grid over medium, ash-covered coals; grill, uncovered, 16 to 18 minutes or until tender, turning occasionally. About 10 minutes before mushrooms are done, move mushrooms to outer edge of grid. Place patties in center of grid; grill 11 to 13 minutes to medium (160°F) doneness, until no longer pink in center and juices show no pink color, turning once. Place bread slices on grid; grill until toasted, turning once.

**Nutrition information
per serving**

Calories: 454
Fat: 15 g
   Saturated fat: 7 g
   Monounsaturated fat: 5 g
Cholesterol: 79 mg
Sodium: 557 mg
Carbohydrate: 40 g
Fiber: 3.5 g
Protein: 33 g
Niacin: 11.5 mg
Vitamin B_6: 0.5 mg
Vitamin B_{12}: 2.2 mcg
Iron: 5.2 mg
Selenium: 50.6 mcg
Zinc: 6.7 mg

This recipe is an excellent source of protein, niacin, vitamin B_6, vitamin B_{12}, iron, selenium, and zinc, and a good source of fiber.

4. Reheat sauce, if necessary. Spread half of the goat cheese on toasted bread slices. Top each with lettuce leaf, mushroom, and burger; drizzle evenly with sauce. Crumble remaining goat cheese over tops; sprinkle with parsley, as desired.

Mushroom Merlot Burgers
(continued)

COOK'S TIPS

- To broil, place patties and mushrooms on rack in broiler pan so surface of beef is 3 to 4 inches from heat. Broil mushrooms 16 to 18 minutes or until tender, turning once. Broil patties 10 to 12 minutes to medium (160°F) doneness, until no longer pink in center and juices show no pink color, turning once.
- For an elegant meal, serve with a side salad and freshly grilled vegetables.

Beef Steak Gyros

Total preparation and
cooking time: 40 minutes
Makes 4 servings.

Tender and juicy steak replaces lamb in this classic sandwich recipe.

YOGURT SAUCE

1	cup plain nonfat yogurt
¼	cup diced cucumber
1	clove garlic, minced
½	teaspoon salt
¼	teaspoon pepper

1	teaspoon dried oregano leaves, crushed
1	teaspoon minced garlic
2	beef shoulder center steaks (Ranch Steaks), cut ¾ inch thick (about 8 ounces each)
	Salt and pepper, as desired
4	whole wheat pita breads, cut crosswise in half
4	tomato slices
4	onion slices

1. Combine Yogurt Sauce ingredients in small bowl; cover and refrigerate until ready to use.

2. Combine oregano and garlic; press evenly onto beef steaks. Heat large nonstick skillet over medium heat until hot. Place steaks in skillet; cook 9 to 12 minutes for medium-rare to medium doneness, turning twice.

3. Carve steaks into thin slices; season with salt and pepper, as desired. Fill pita pockets with equal amounts of steak, tomatoes, and onions. Drizzle with sauce.

Nutrition information per serving

Calories: 251
Fat: 6 g
  Saturated fat: 2 g
  Monounsaturated fat: 3 g
Cholesterol: 58 mg
Sodium: 537 mg
Carbohydrate: 21 g
Fiber: 2.4 g
Protein: 28 g
Niacin: 3.8 mg
Vitamin B_6: 0.3 mg
Vitamin B_{12}: 2.6 mcg
Iron: 3.9 mg
Selenium: 38.1 mcg
Zinc: 5.9 mg

This recipe is an excellent source of protein, vitamin B_{12}, iron, selenium, and zinc, and a good source of niacin and vitamin B_6.

COOK'S TIPS
- To easily slice fresh tomatoes, use a serrated bread knife.
- For a colorful side dish, serve with a side of steamed summer squash seasoned with oregano.

Tenderloin Sandwich with Balsamic Caramelized Onions

Impress friends and family at your next summer picnic with this easy-to-make yet elegant sandwich.

Total preparation and cooking time: 1¼ to 1½ hours
Makes 8 servings.

1	center-cut beef tenderloin roast (about 2 pounds)
1	tablespoon fresh thyme, chopped
2	cloves garlic, minced
1	teaspoon pepper

SOUR CREAM SAUCE

5	sun-dried tomatoes, not packed in oil
¼	cup reduced-fat dairy sour cream
¼	teaspoon salt
⅛	teaspoon pepper

1	teaspoon olive oil
5	cups fresh baby spinach
2	loaves French bread (each 24 inches long)
	Balsamic Caramelized Onions (recipe follows)

1. Heat oven to 425°F. Press thyme, garlic, and pepper evenly onto all surfaces of beef roast. Place roast on rack in shallow roasting pan. Insert ovenproof thermometer so that tip is centered in thickest part of beef, not resting in fat. Do not add water or cover. Roast in 425°F oven 35 to 45 minutes for medium-rare, 45 to 50 minutes for medium doneness.

2. Remove roast when meat thermometer registers 135°F for medium-rare, 150°F for medium. Transfer roast to carving board; tent loosely with aluminum foil. Let stand 15 minutes. (Temperature will continue to rise about 10°F to reach 145°F for medium-rare, 160°F for medium.) Carve roast into ¼-inch-thick slices.

3. To prepare Sour Cream Sauce, soak sun-dried tomatoes 10 minutes in boiling water to cover; drain. Squeeze dry in paper towels. Chop tomatoes. Combine tomatoes, sour cream, salt, and pepper in small bowl. Set aside.

4. Heat oil in large nonstick skillet over medium heat until hot. Add spinach; cook and stir 2 minutes or until just wilted. Season with salt and pepper, as desired.

Nutrition information per serving

Calories: 278
Fat: 10 g
  Saturated fat: 4 g
  Monounsaturated fat: 4 g
Cholesterol: 71 mg
Sodium: 490 mg
Carbohydrate: 18 g
Fiber: 2.5 g
Protein: 28 g
Niacin: 8.1 mg
Vitamin B_6: 0.6 mg
Vitamin B_{12}: 1.4 mcg
Iron: 3.2 mg
Selenium: 30.3 mcg
Zinc: 4.9 mg

This recipe is an excellent source of protein, niacin, vitamin B_6, vitamin B_{12}, selenium, and zinc, and a good source of fiber and iron.

5. Cut each bread loaf horizontally in half, then crosswise into quarters. Evenly layer spinach, steak slices, and Balsamic Caramelized Onions on each bottom bread piece. Spread sour cream sauce evenly on cut side of each top bread piece. Close sandwiches.

BALSAMIC CARAMELIZED ONIONS

1	teaspoon olive oil
3	cups sliced onions (¼ inch thick)
¼	cup balsamic vinegar
1	teaspoon brown sugar
¼	teaspoon salt
⅛	teaspoon pepper

1. Heat oil in large nonstick skillet over medium heat until hot. Add onions; cook and stir 15 minutes. Add vinegar and brown sugar. Cook and stir about 10 minutes or until caramelized. Season with salt and pepper. Remove from skillet. Set aside.

COOK'S TIPS
- To make slicing onions easier, cut them in half first.
- Balance out this tasty sandwich with fresh-roasted asparagus or broccoli.

Tenderloin Sandwich with Balsamic Caramelized Onions (continued)

Total preparation and cooking time: 25 minutes
Makes about 1 cup.

Balsamic Marinated Steak Sandwich

Total preparation and cooking time: 55 minutes

Marinating time: 6 hours or overnight

Makes 6 servings.

Try this marinated flank steak topped with peppery arugula and tomato chutney for a flavorful dinner or pack it to go for an impromptu picnic.

MARINADE

⅓ cup balsamic vinegar
1 tablespoon Dijon-style mustard
1½ teaspoons minced garlic

1 beef flank steak (about 1½ pounds)
1 loaf whole wheat French bread (about 22 inches long)
 Salt and pepper, as desired
1 cup arugula or baby salad greens
 Tomato Chutney for Beef (page 85)

1. Combine marinade ingredients in small bowl. Place beef steak and marinade in food-safe plastic bag; turn steak to coat. Close bag securely and marinate in refrigerator 6 hours or as long as overnight.

2. Cut bread crosswise into 6 equal pieces. Split each piece lengthwise to form sandwich rolls.

3. Remove steak from marinade; discard marinade. Place steak on grid over medium, ash-covered coals. Grill, uncovered, 17 to 21 minutes for medium-rare to medium doneness, turning occasionally. About 2 minutes before steak is done, place rolls, cut sides down, on grid. Grill until lightly toasted.

4. Carve steak across the grain into thin slices. Season with salt and pepper, as desired. Divide steak slices evenly over bottom of each roll. Top beef evenly with arugula and Tomato Chutney for Beef. Close sandwiches.

COOK'S TIP

Six whole wheat sandwich rolls (2 ounces each) may be substituted for the French bread.

Nutrition information per serving

Calories: 435
Fat: 12 g
  Saturated fat: 4 g
  Monounsaturated fat: 5 g
Cholesterol: 42 mg
Sodium: 599 mg
Carbohydrate: 53 g
Fiber: 6.6 g
Protein: 31 g
Niacin: 9.7 mg
Vitamin B$_6$: 0.8 mg
Vitamin B$_{12}$: 1.4 mcg
Iron: 3.9 mg
Selenium: 60.0 mcg
Zinc: 5.8 mg

This recipe is an excellent source of fiber, protein, niacin, vitamin B$_6$, vitamin B$_{12}$, iron, selenium, and zinc.

Tomato Chutney for Beef

Serve this delicious chutney as a side with your favorite beef dishes.

Total preparation and cooking time: 20 minutes
Makes 2 cups.

1	tablespoon olive oil
1¾	cups chopped onions
1	teaspoon minced garlic
¼	cup packed brown sugar
3	tablespoons balsamic vinegar
1	tablespoon minced fresh ginger
¼	teaspoon crushed red pepper
2¼	cups chopped seeded tomatoes
2	tablespoons chopped fresh basil
½	teaspoon salt

1. Heat oil in large nonstick skillet over medium heat until hot. Add onions and garlic; cook 5 minutes or until onion is tender, stirring occasionally. Stir in sugar, vinegar, ginger, and red pepper; cook 2 minutes or until sugar dissolves and mixture thickens. Add tomatoes; cook 6 to 7 minutes or until thickened, stirring occasionally.

2. Remove from heat; stir in basil and salt. Set aside to cool.

3. Serve with Basic Lean Beef Burgers (page 88) or Balsamic Marinated Steak Sandwich (page 84).

> **COOK'S TIP**
> Tomato Chutney can be made up to 1 day ahead. Refrigerate, covered, until ready to serve.

Nutrition information per serving (¼ cup)

Calories: 72
Fat: 2 g
  Saturated fat: 0 g
  Monounsaturated fat: 1 g
Cholesterol: 0 mg
Sodium: 155 mg
Carbohydrate: 14 g
Fiber: 1.2 g
Protein: 0.9 g
Niacin: 0.4 mg
Vitamin B_6: 0.1 mg
Vitamin B_{12}: 0 mcg
Iron: 0.6 mg
Selenium: 0.6 mcg
Zinc: 0.1 mg

Sirloin Sandwich with Red Onion and Dried Fruit Marmalade

Total preparation and
    cooking time: 40 minutes
Makes 4 servings.

Don't just keep marmalade on your breakfast table. This homemade dried fruit marmalade combined with caramelized red onion and goat cheese creates a whole new flavor in this steak sandwich.

MARMALADE

1	tablespoon butter
1	tablespoon olive oil
3	cups thinly sliced red onions
½	cup Cabernet or Merlot or other dry red wine
¼	cup chopped pitted dried plums
¼	cup fig preserves
2	tablespoons red wine vinegar
2	teaspoons fresh thyme, chopped
¼	teaspoon salt

1	boneless beef top sirloin steak, cut ¾ inch thick (about 1 pound)
1	clove garlic, cut in half
¼	teaspoon pepper
2	mini baguette rolls (each 8 inches long), split
¼	cup crumbled goat cheese

COOK'S TIPS

- Four 4-inch-long French rolls, split, may be substituted for mini baguettes.
- Serve with a bulgur side salad for a complete meal and added fiber boost.

1. To prepare marmalade, heat butter and olive oil in large nonstick skillet over medium heat until hot. Add onions; cook 8 to 10 minutes or until tender and beginning to brown, stirring occasionally. Stir in wine, dried plums, preserves, and vinegar. Cook 5 minutes or until liquid evaporates and marmalade thickens and turns dark, stirring occasionally. Remove from heat; stir in thyme and salt. Set aside to cool.

2. Rub both sides of beef steak with garlic; sprinkle evenly with pepper. Place steak on grid over medium, ash-covered coals. Grill, uncovered, 13 to 16 minutes for medium-rare to medium doneness, turning occasionally. About 2 minutes before steaks are done, place rolls, cut sides down, on grid. Grill until lightly toasted.

3. Carve steak into thin slices. Evenly layer steak slices, marmalade, and cheese on bottom of each roll. Close sandwiches; cut each crosswise in half.

**Nutrition information
per serving**

Calories: 509
Fat: 13 g
    Saturated fat: 5 g
    Monounsaturated fat: 6 g
Cholesterol: 60 mg
Sodium: 555 mg
Carbohydrate: 59 g
Fiber: 3.4 g
Protein: 33 g
Niacin: 10.3 mg
Vitamin B_6: 0.7 mg
Vitamin B_{12}: 1.4 mcg
Iron: 4.5 mg
Selenium: 32.7 mcg
Zinc: 5.2 mg

This recipe is an excellent source of protein, niacin, vitamin B_6, vitamin B_{12}, iron, selenium, and zinc, and a good source of fiber.

Basic Lean Beef Burgers

Total preparation and
  cooking time: 20 minutes
Makes 4 servings.

HEALTHY
LIVING TIP
• • • • •

Plan ahead and thaw
frozen meat in the
refrigerator. In a pinch,
you can also use a
"fast-thaw" method,
such as defrosting in
the microwave, and
cook immediately. Or
you can immerse
wrapped meat in cold
water and change it
every 30 minutes. To
reduce risk for food-
borne illness, never
thaw frozen meat on
the counter.

Keep this basic lean beef burger recipe to use as is or add a sauce or topping!

1	pound ground beef (95% lean)
¼	cup soft bread crumbs
1	egg white
¼	teaspoon salt
⅛	teaspoon pepper
4	whole wheat hamburger buns, split

TOPPINGS
Lettuce leaves, tomato slices (optional)

1. Combine ground beef, bread crumbs, egg white, salt, and pepper in large bowl, mixing lightly but thoroughly. Lightly shape into four ½-inch-thick patties.

2. Place patties on grid over medium, ash-covered coals. Grill, uncovered, 11 to 13 minutes to medium (160°F) doneness, until no longer pink in center and juices show no pink color, turning occasionally.

3. Line bottom of each bun with lettuce and tomato, if desired; top with burger. Close sandwiches.

COOK'S TIP
To broil, place patties on rack in broiler pan so surface of beef is 3 to 4 inches from heat. Broil 10 to 12 minutes to medium (160°F) doneness, until no longer pink in center and juices show no pink color, turning once.

Nutrition information per serving

Calories: 272
Fat: 8 g
  Saturated fat: 3 g
  Monounsaturated fat: 3 g
Cholesterol: 65 mg
Sodium: 439 mg
Carbohydrate: 24 g
Fiber: 3.6 g
Protein: 27 g
Niacin: 6.8 mg
Vitamin B_6: 0.4 mg
Vitamin B_{12}: 2.1 mcg
Iron: 3.6 mg
Selenium: 41.9 mcg
Zinc: 6.4 mg

This recipe is an excellent source of protein, niacin, vitamin B_6, vitamin B_{12}, iron, selenium, and zinc, and a good source of fiber.

Spinach and Portobello Topping for Burgers

There's something irresistible about mushrooms and burgers. Add colorful green spinach and you've achieved not only greatness in nutrition but also heaven for the taste buds.

Total preparation and cooking time: 15 minutes
Makes 4 servings.

2	teaspoons olive oil
1	teaspoon minced garlic
3	cups packed fresh spinach, stemmed, coarsely chopped
2	cups chopped portobello mushrooms
1	teaspoon freshly grated lemon peel
¼	teaspoon crushed red pepper
½	cup crumbled feta cheese
⅛	teaspoon salt

1. Heat oil in large nonstick skillet over medium-high heat until hot. Add garlic; cook and stir 30 seconds to 1 minute. Add spinach; toss to coat. Add mushrooms, lemon peel, and red pepper; cook and stir 2 minutes or until spinach wilts and mushrooms are tender. Remove from heat. Add cheese and salt; mix well.

2. Serve as a topping for Basic Lean Beef Burgers (page 88).

> **COOK'S TIP**
> Serve on toasted whole-grain buns or rolls, if desired.

Nutrition information per serving

Calories: 84
Fat: 6 g
  Saturated fat: 3 g
  Monounsaturated fat: 3 g
Cholesterol: 17 mg
Sodium: 301 mg
Carbohydrate: 3 g
Fiber: 1 g
Protein: 4 g
Niacin: 1.4 mg
Vitamin B_6: 0.2 mg
Vitamin B_{12}: 0.3 mcg
Iron: 1.0 mg
Selenium: 5.6 mcg
Zinc: 0.8 mg

This recipe is a good source of vitamin B_6.

Creamy Cucumber-Yogurt Sauce for Burgers

This refreshing Cucumber-Yogurt Sauce found inspiration in the tzatziki sauce used on traditional Greek gyros.

½ cup finely chopped seeded cucumber
½ cup plain nonfat yogurt
1 teaspoon minced garlic
1 teaspoon finely chopped fresh mint
1 teaspoon finely chopped fresh parsley
¼ teaspoon salt
¼ teaspoon pepper

1. Combine Creamy Cucumber-Yogurt Sauce ingredients in small bowl; cover and refrigerate until ready to use.
2. Serve as a topping for Basic Lean Beef Burgers (page 88).

Total preparation and cooking time: 15 minutes
Makes 4 servings.

COOK'S TIP
Serve with burgers in whole wheat pita bread halves with sliced cucumbers and tomatoes, shredded lettuce, and chopped red onion, if desired.

Nutrition information per serving

Calories: 16
Fat: 0 g
  Saturated fat: 0 g
  Monounsaturated fat: 0 g
Cholesterol: 1 mg
Sodium: 163 mg
Carbohydrate: 3 g
Fiber: 0.0 g
Protein: 1 g
Niacin: 0.0 mg
Vitamin B_6: 0.0 mg
Vitamin B_{12}: 0.0 mcg
Iron: 0.2 mg
Selenium: 0.1 mcg
Zinc: 0.0 mg

Mango-Pineapple Salsa for Burgers

Let this tropical salsa liven up your burgers.

2 medium mangoes, finely diced (about 2 cups)
¼ cup canned crushed pineapple, drained
¼ cup finely chopped red bell pepper
2 tablespoons finely chopped fresh cilantro
2 tablespoons fresh lime juice
1 tablespoon finely chopped jalapeño pepper
¼ teaspoon salt

1. Combine Mango-Pineapple Salsa ingredients in small bowl; cover and refrigerate until ready to use.
2. Serve as a topping for Basic Lean Beef Burgers (page 88).

Total preparation and cooking time: 15 minutes
Makes 4 servings.

COOK'S TIPS
- For a more authentic meal, serve burger open-faced on lettuce-lined toasted Hawaiian bread slices and top with Mango-Pineapple Salsa.
- For best flavor, refrigerate salsa a few hours before serving.

Nutrition information per serving

Calories: 24
Fat: 0 g
  Saturated fat: 0 g
  Monounsaturated fat: 0 g
Cholesterol: 0 mg
Sodium: 147 mg
Carbohydrate: 6 g
Fiber: 1.3 g
Protein: 1 g
Niacin: 0.5 mg
Vitamin B_6: 0.1 mg
Vitamin B_{12}: 0.0 mcg
Iron: 0.3 mg
Selenium: 0.2 mcg
Zinc: 0.5 mg

Asian Burgers with Ginger-Lemon Mayonnaise

Total preparation and
cooking time: 35 minutes
Makes 4 servings.

America's favorite food gets an Asian spin.

GINGER-LEMON MAYONNAISE
¼   cup light mayonnaise
1½   tablespoons finely chopped fresh chives or green onion tops
1½   teaspoons fresh lemon juice
1½   teaspoons soy sauce
1   teaspoon grated fresh ginger
¼   teaspoon dark sesame oil
⅛   teaspoon ground red pepper (optional)

Basic Lean Beef Burgers (page 88)
2   tablespoons soy sauce
4   whole wheat hamburger buns, split

TOPPINGS
Shredded Napa cabbage or lettuce, bell pepper strips, bean sprouts

BEEF SMARTS

Lean beef is a *smart* food for growing children. A 3-ounce serving provides more than 30 percent of the average daily requirement of iron needed by girls and boys ages 9 to 13.

1. Combine Ginger-Lemon Mayonnaise ingredients in small bowl; refrigerate until ready to use.

2. Prepare Basic Lean Beef Burger recipe. Place patties on grid over medium, ash-covered coals. Grill, uncovered, 11 to 13 minutes to medium (160°F) doneness, until no longer pink in center and juices show no pink color, turning occasionally and basting with soy sauce during last 5 minutes of grilling. About 2 minutes before burgers are done, place buns, cut sides down, on grid. Grill until lightly toasted.

3. Place burger on bottom of each bun; top with equal amount of mayonnaise and toppings, if desired. Close sandwiches.

**Nutrition information
per serving**

Calories: 340
Fat: 14 g
  Saturated fat: 4 g
  Monounsaturated fat: 3 g
Cholesterol: 70 mg
Sodium: 937 mg
Carbohydrate: 26 g
Fiber: 3.4 g
Protein: 28 g
Niacin: 6.8 mg
Vitamin B_6: 0.4 mg
Vitamin B_{12}: 2.1 mcg
Iron: 3.6 mg
Selenium: 41.9 mcg
Zinc: 6.4 mg

This recipe is an excellent source of protein, niacin, vitamin B_6, vitamin B_{12}, iron, selenium, and zinc, and a good source of fiber.

COOK'S TIP
Serve with Jasmine rice to complement this Asian-influenced burger.

Blue Cheese and Caramelized Onion Burgers

Onions, blue cheese, and beef have had a long-standing partnership, and this simple but fantastic burger shows why.

Total preparation and cooking time: 35 minutes
Makes 4 servings.

CARAMELIZED ONIONS

1	tablespoon butter
1	large Vidalia or other sweet onion, cut crosswise into ⅛-inch-thick slices (4 cups)
2	teaspoons brown sugar
	Salt and pepper, as desired

	Basic Lean Beef Burgers (page 88)
1	teaspoon minced fresh sage
4	whole wheat hamburger buns, split
¼	cup crumbled blue cheese

1. To prepare Caramelized Onions, heat butter in large nonstick skillet over medium heat until hot. Add onion and brown sugar; cook and stir 16 to 18 minutes or until onion is caramelized. Season with salt and pepper, as desired. Set aside.

2. Prepare Basic Lean Beef Burgers, adding sage with other ingredients.

3. Place patties on grid over medium, ash-covered coals. Grill, uncovered, 11 to 13 minutes to medium (160°F) doneness, until no longer pink in center and juices show no pink color, turning occasionally.

4. Place burger on bottom of each bun; top with equal amounts of blue cheese and Caramelized Onions. Close sandwiches.

Nutrition information per serving

Calories: 403
Fat: 13 g
   Saturated fat: 6 g
   Monounsaturated fat: 4 g
Cholesterol: 78 mg
Sodium: 563 mg
Carbohydrate: 42 g
Fiber: 5.6 g
Protein: 30 g
Niacin: 7.0 mg
Vitamin B_6: 0.7 mg
Vitamin B_{12}: 2.2 mcg
Iron: 4.0 mg
Selenium: 43.9 mcg
Zinc: 6.8 mg

This recipe is an excellent source of fiber, protein, niacin, vitamin B_6, vitamin B_{12}, iron, selenium, and zinc.

COOK'S TIP
Serve this elegant burger at your next dinner party, paired with steamed broccoli and a garden salad.

Taco Burgers

Total preparation and cooking time: 35 minutes
Makes 4 servings.

Put a burger on your dinner table and they'll love it. Flavor it with taco seasonings and toppings and they'll say, "Ole!"

TANGY SOUR CREAM SAUCE
½   cup reduced-fat dairy sour cream
½   cup chopped seeded tomato
2   tablespoons finely chopped fresh cilantro
1   package (about 1.25 ounces) taco seasoning mix, divided
2   teaspoons fresh lime juice
¼   teaspoon pepper

     Basic Lean Beef Burgers (page 88)
8   corn tortillas (6-inch diameter), warmed
2   cups shredded lettuce
¼   cup reduced-fat shredded Mexican cheese blend
     Lime wedges (optional)

1. To prepare Tangy Sour Cream Sauce, combine sour cream, tomato, cilantro, 1 tablespoon of taco seasoning mix, lime juice, and pepper in small bowl; refrigerate sauce until ready to use.

2. Prepare Basic Lean Beef Burgers, adding remaining taco seasoning mix with other ingredients.

3. Place patties on grid over medium, ash-covered coals. Grill, uncovered, 11 to 13 minutes to medium (160°F) doneness, until no longer pink in center and juices show no pink color, turning occasionally.

4. Overlap slightly 2 corn tortillas on each of 4 plates. Layer lettuce, burgers, sour cream sauce, and cheese on 1 side of overlapped tortillas. Fold other tortilla over to cover. Serve with lime wedges, if desired.

COOK'S TIP

To warm corn tortillas, wrap 2 or 3 tortillas at a time in paper towel. Microwave on HIGH 15 to 20 seconds or until warm. Wrap warm tortillas in aluminum foil until ready to use.

Nutrition information per serving

Calories: 377
Fat: 12 g
    Saturated fat: 6 g
    Monounsaturated fat: 3 g
Cholesterol: 85 mg
Sodium: 929 mg
Carbohydrate: 36 g
Fiber: 3.8 g
Protein: 30 g
Niacin: 6.1 mg
Vitamin B_6: 0.5 mg
Vitamin B_{12}: 2.1 mcg
Iron: 3.4 mg
Selenium: 23.5 mcg
Zinc: 6.0 mg

This recipe is an excellent source of protein, niacin, vitamin B_6, vitamin B_{12}, selenium, and zinc, and a good source of fiber and iron.

COOK'S TIPS
- For spicier flavor, add desired amount of chopped jalapeño pepper or canned chopped chilies to Tangy Sour Cream Sauce.
- For best results, prepare Tangy Sour Cream Sauce within an hour of serving.
- Serve tacos with a side of Mexican rice, found in the rice section at your local grocer.

4

BUSY FAMILY BEEF FAVORITES

Easy Beef Tenderloin Steaks with Blue Cheese Sauce

Add the elegance of blue cheese and indulge in this simply prepared tenderloin steak.

Total preparation and cooking time: 25 minutes
Makes 4 servings.

BLUE CHEESE SAUCE
- 2 tablespoons cream cheese
- 4 teaspoons crumbled blue cheese
- 4 teaspoons plain nonfat yogurt
- 2 teaspoons minced onion
- Dash ground white pepper

- 4 beef tenderloin steaks, cut 1 inch thick (about 4 ounces each)
- 1 clove garlic, halved
- ½ teaspoon salt
- 2 teaspoons chopped fresh parsley

1. Combine Blue Cheese Sauce ingredients in small bowl. Set aside. Rub beef steaks with garlic.

2. Place steaks on rack in broiler pan so surface of beef is 2 to 3 inches from heat. Broil 13 to 16 minutes for medium-rare to medium doneness, turning once. One to 2 minutes before steaks are done, top evenly with sauce.

3. Season with salt; sprinkle with parsley.

COOK'S TIPS

- To grill, place steaks on grid over medium, ash-covered coals. Grill uncovered, 13 to 15 minutes for medium-rare to medium doneness, turning occasionally. One minute before steaks are done, top evenly with sauce.
- Pair sautéed wild mushrooms with this classic steak and prepare yourself for an umami flavor explosion. Umami, known as the fifth taste, is often described as meaty and savory and is derived from the Japanese word *umai*, which means "delicious."

Nutrition information per serving

Calories: 210
Fat: 11 g
  Saturated fat: 5 g
  Monounsaturated fat: 4 g
Cholesterol: 78 mg
Sodium: 411 mg
Carbohydrate: 1 g
Fiber: 0.1 g
Protein: 26 g
Niacin: 7.3 mg
Vitamin B_6: 0.6 mg
Vitamin B_{12}: 1.4 mcg
Iron: 1.8 mg
Selenium: 30.5 mcg
Zinc: 4.8 mg

This recipe is an excellent source of protein, niacin, vitamin B_6, vitamin B_{12}, selenium, and zinc, and a good source of iron.

Beef and Tomato Sauce with Pasta

Total preparation and
cooking time: 30 minutes
Makes 4 servings.

Fresh spinach adds a nutritious and colorful twist to this fun Italian rotini dish.

1   pound beef round tip steaks, cut ⅛ to ¼ inch thick
2   cloves garlic, minced
2   teaspoons olive oil
2   cups uncooked rotini (spiral) pasta
1   package (10 ounces) fresh spinach leaves, stems removed, coarsely chopped
1   can (14 to 14½ ounces) seasoned chunky tomatoes for pasta, undrained
¼   cup grated Parmesan cheese

COOK'S TIP
Serve this hearty pasta with a side of steamed peas.

1. Stack beef steaks; cut lengthwise in half and then crosswise into 1-inch-wide strips. Combine beef, garlic, and oil in medium bowl; toss to coat. Set aside.

2. Cook pasta according to package directions, adding spinach to water during last minute of cooking. Drain well; do not rinse.

3. Meanwhile, heat large nonstick skillet over medium-high heat until hot. Add half of the beef; stir-fry 1 to 2 minutes or until outside surface is no longer pink. (Do not overcook.) Remove from skillet; keep warm. Repeat with remaining beef.

4. In same skillet, add tomatoes and cook over medium-high heat until sauce is thickened. Return beef to skillet and add pasta mixture; heat through, mixing lightly. Stir in 3 tablespoons cheese; garnish with remaining cheese.

Nutrition information per serving

Calories: 414
Fat: 9 g
   Saturated fat: 3 g
   Monounsaturated fat: 4 g
Cholesterol: 73 mg
Sodium: 697 mg
Carbohydrate: 48 g
Fiber: 6.0 g
Protein: 34 g
Niacin: 6.4 mg
Vitamin B_6: 0.4 mg
Vitamin B_{12}: 2.6 mcg
Iron: 6.8 mg
Selenium: 50.7 mcg
Zinc: 6.7 mg

This recipe is an excellent source of fiber, protein, niacin, vitamin B_6, vitamin B_{12}, iron, selenium, and zinc.

Seasoned Steaks with Brown Rice and Vegetables

These lightly seasoned steaks pair nicely with the nutty flavor of brown rice.

1	boneless beef top sirloin steak, cut ¾ inch thick (about 1 pound)
⅓	cup prepared noncreamy Caesar dressing
2	teaspoons lemon-pepper seasoning
1	cup uncooked instant brown rice
2	cups frozen vegetable mixture, such as baby green and yellow beans and carrots
2	tablespoons prepared noncreamy Caesar dressing
2	tablespoons shredded Parmesan cheese (optional)

1. Cut beef steak crosswise into four equal pieces. Place steaks and ⅓ cup dressing in food-safe plastic bag; turn steaks to coat. Close bag securely and marinate in refrigerator 15 minutes to 2 hours. Remove steaks from marinade; discard marinade. Season steaks with lemon-pepper seasoning.

2. Heat large nonstick skillet over medium heat until hot. Place steaks in skillet; cook 10 to 13 minutes for medium-rare to medium doneness, turning once.

3. Meanwhile, cook rice according to package directions, including salt but omitting butter. When adding rice to saucepan, stir in vegetables. Just before serving, stir in 2 tablespoons dressing. Serve with steaks. Sprinkle with cheese, if desired.

Total preparation and cooking time: 25 minutes
Marinating time: 15 minutes
Makes 4 servings.

HEALTHY LIVING TIP
• • • • •

For your 3 daily servings of whole grains, try whole-grain breads and cereals and stir-fries, soups, and salads made with barley, brown rice, cracked wheat, buckwheat, bulgur, or quinoa.

Nutrition information per serving

Calories: 343
Fat: 12 g
  Saturated fat: 3 g
  Monounsaturated fat: 2 g
Cholesterol: 56 mg
Sodium: 554 mg
Carbohydrate: 25 g
Fiber: 3.3 g
Protein: 30 g
Niacin: 8.4 mg
Vitamin B_6: 0.6 mg
Vitamin B_{12}: 1.4 mcg
Iron: 2.5 mg
Selenium: 31.5 mcg
Zinc: 4.9 mg

This recipe is an excellent source of protein, niacin, vitamin B_6, vitamin B_{12}, selenium, and zinc, and a good source of fiber and iron.

Szechuan Beef Stir-Fry

Total preparation and
  cooking time: 15 minutes
Makes 4 servings.

This fast and easy stir-fry gets a spicy kick from crushed red pepper.

1   package (10 ounces) fresh vegetable stir-fry blend
3   tablespoons water
2   beef shoulder center steaks (Ranch Steaks), cut ¾ inch thick (about 8
    ounces each)
1   clove garlic, minced
½   cup prepared sesame-ginger stir-fry sauce
¼   teaspoon crushed red pepper
2   cups hot cooked white or brown rice, prepared without butter or salt
¼   cup dry-roasted peanuts

1. Combine vegetables and water in large nonstick skillet; cover and
   cook over medium-high heat 4 minutes or until crisp-tender.
   Remove and drain vegetables. Set aside.

2. Meanwhile, cut beef steaks into ¼-inch-thick strips.

3. Heat same skillet over medium-high heat until hot. Add half of the
   beef and half of the garlic; stir-fry 1 to 2 minutes or until outside
   surface of beef is no longer pink. Remove from skillet; keep warm.
   Repeat with remaining beef and garlic.

4. Return beef and vegetables to skillet. Add stir-fry sauce and red
   pepper; cook and stir 1 to 2 minutes or until heated through. Serve
   over rice. Sprinkle with peanuts.

**Nutrition information
per serving**

Calories: 351
Fat: 11 g
    Saturated fat: 3 g
    Monounsaturated fat: 5 g
Cholesterol: 64 mg
Sodium: 1,147 mg
Carbohydrate: 29 g
Fiber: 3.0 g
Protein: 32 g
Niacin: 5.4 mg
Vitamin B_6: 0.3 mg
Vitamin B_{12}: 2.9 mcg
Iron: 4.1 mg
Selenium: 33.0 mcg
Zinc: 6.6 mg

**This recipe is an excellent
source of protein, niacin,
vitamin B_{12}, iron, selenium,
and zinc, and a good source
of fiber and vitamin B_6.**

COOK'S TIPS

- Four cups assorted fresh vegetables, such as sugar snap peas,
  broccoli florets, bell pepper strips, and shredded carrots, may be
  substituted for 1 package vegetable stir-fry blend.
- Your favorite stir-fry sauce flavor may be substituted for the sesame-
  ginger flavor.

Bistro Beef Kabobs with Broccoli Pilaf

Total preparation and
cooking time: 30 minutes
Makes 4 servings.

*Your family will never know you spent so little time preparing this
meal. The presentation is beautiful, and everyone loves getting their
own kabob.*

1¼	pounds boneless beef top sirloin steak, cut 1 inch thick
2	teaspoons vegetable oil
2	teaspoons coarse-grain Dijon-style mustard
2	teaspoons red wine vinegar
1	clove garlic, minced
½	teaspoon cracked black pepper
	Broccoli Pilaf (recipe follows)

1. Cut beef steak into 1¼-inch pieces. Combine oil, mustard, vinegar, garlic, and pepper in medium bowl; add beef, tossing to coat.

2. Thread equal amounts of beef onto four 12-inch metal skewers, leaving small space between pieces. Place kabobs on rack in broiler pan so surface of beef is 3 to 4 inches from heat. Broil 8 to 10 minutes for medium-rare to medium doneness, turning occasionally. Serve with Broccoli Pilaf.

BROCCOLI PILAF

2	teaspoons vegetable oil
1	small onion, chopped
1	clove garlic, minced
⅔	cup uncooked regular white rice
1¼	cups ready-to-serve beef broth
1	tablespoon coarse-grain Dijon-style mustard
4	cups small broccoli florets

1. Heat oil in large saucepan over medium heat until hot. Add onion and garlic; cook and stir until tender. Add rice and cook 1 minute more. Stir in broth and mustard. Bring to a boil; reduce heat to low. Cover and simmer 15 minutes. Place broccoli over rice; cover and continue cooking 7 minutes or until broccoli and rice are tender. Stir before serving.

**Nutrition information
per serving**

Calories: 576
Fat: 11 g
   Saturated fat: 3 g
   Monounsaturated fat: 4 g
Cholesterol: 50 mg
Sodium: 486 mg
Carbohydrate: 82 g
Fiber: 3.6 g
Protein: 37 g
Niacin: 12.0 mg
Vitamin B$_6$: 0.9 mg
Vitamin B$_{12}$: 1.4 mcg
Iron: 6.5 mg
Selenium: 47.9 mcg
Zinc: 6.2 mg

**This recipe is an excellent
source of protein, niacin,
vitamin B$_6$, vitamin B$_{12}$, iron,
selenium, and zinc, and a
good source of fiber.**

Ancho Chili–Rubbed Beef Steaks

Get a real taste of the Southwest with these ancho chili–rubbed steaks.

ANCHO CHILI RUB

1	tablespoon ground ancho chili powder
3	cloves garlic, minced
1½	teaspoons dried oregano leaves, crushed
1	teaspoon unsweetened cocoa powder
1	teaspoon freshly grated orange peel
½	teaspoon ground cinnamon
2	boneless beef top loin (strip) steaks, cut 1 inch thick (about 10 ounces each)
	Salt and pepper, as desired

1. Combine Ancho Chili Rub ingredients in small bowl; press evenly onto beef steaks.
2. Heat large nonstick skillet over medium heat until hot. Place steaks in skillet; cook 12 to 15 minutes for medium-rare to medium doneness, turning occasionally. Carve steaks into slices. Season with salt and pepper, as desired.

Total preparation and cooking time: 30 minutes

Makes 4 servings.

COOK'S TIPS

- To grill, place steaks on grid over medium, ash-covered coals. Grill, uncovered, 15 to 18 minutes for medium-rare to medium doneness, turning occasionally.
- Serve steaks with a cooling side dish, such as a salad with nonfat ranch dressing or a creamy coleslaw.

Nutrition information per serving

Calories: 215
Fat: 8 g
   Saturated fat: 3 g
   Monounsaturated fat: 3 g
Cholesterol: 71 mg
Sodium: 85 mg
Carbohydrate: 3 g
Fiber: 1.3 g
Protein: 32 g
Niacin: 9.3 mg
Vitamin B_6: 0.8 mg
Vitamin B_{12}: 1.7 mcg
Iron: 2.7 mg
Selenium: 37.8 mcg
Zinc :5.9 mg

This recipe is an excellent source of protein, niacin, vitamin B_6, vitamin B_{12}, selenium, and zinc, and a good source of iron.

Beef Paprikash

Introduce your friends to this classic Hungarian dish with a lean beef twist.

Total preparation and
cooking time: 30 minutes
Makes 4 servings.

1 pound boneless beef top sirloin steak, cut ¾ inch thick
4 teaspoons vegetable oil, divided
1 tablespoon minced garlic
Salt and pepper, as desired
4 cups uncooked yolk-free egg noodles
8 ounces sliced mushrooms
2 cups chopped onions
3 tablespoons sweet or hot paprika
2 tablespoons water (optional)
¾ cup ready-to-serve beef broth
1 cup frozen peas
½ cup reduced-fat dairy sour cream
½ cup chopped tomato
Chopped fresh parsley (optional)

1. Cut beef steak lengthwise in half, then crosswise into ¼-inch-thick strips.

2. Heat 2 teaspoons oil in large nonstick skillet over medium-high heat until hot. Add half of the beef and half of the garlic; stir-fry 1 to 2 minutes or until outside surface of beef is no longer pink. Remove from skillet. Repeat with remaining beef and garlic. Season with salt and pepper, as desired. Set aside.

3. Cook noodles according to package directions.

4. Meanwhile, heat remaining 2 teaspoons oil in same skillet over medium-low heat until hot. Add mushrooms, onions, and paprika; cook 12 to 14 minutes or until vegetables are tender, stirring occasionally. If pan becomes dry, add water a tablespoon at a time. Stir in broth; bring to a boil. Reduce heat; simmer 3 minutes. Add peas; simmer an additional 2 minutes or until peas are just tender. Return beef to skillet; stir in sour cream. Cook until heated through; do not boil.

5. Serve beef mixture over noodles. Top with tomato. Garnish with parsley, if desired.

Nutrition information per serving

Calories: 466
Fat: 15 g
    Saturated fat: 5 g
    Monounsaturated fat: 3 g
Cholesterol: 65 mg
Sodium: 291 mg
Carbohydrate: 46 g
Fiber: 4.5 g
Protein: 38 g
Niacin: 12.2 mg
Vitamin B_6: 0.8 mg
Vitamin B_{12}: 1.4 mcg
Iron: 4.1 mg
Selenium: 36.7 mcg
Zinc: 6.1 mg

This recipe is an excellent source of protein, niacin, vitamin B_6, vitamin B_{12}, iron, selenium, and zinc, and a good source of fiber.

Barbeque Beef Stir-Fry with Couscous

Total preparation and cooking time: 25 minutes

Makes 4 servings.

Savor your own fusion cooking with this recipe that combines Moroccan and French flavors with traditional American barbecue.

1¼ pounds boneless beef top sirloin steak, cut 1 inch thick
1 can (14 to 14½ ounces) ready-to-serve beef broth
1 cup uncooked couscous
1 tablespoon olive oil
1 medium red bell pepper, cut into ¼-inch-thick strips
½ cup coarsely chopped Vidalia or other sweet onion
½ cup prepared honey-Dijon barbecue sauce
1 tablespoon chopped fresh parsley
  Parsley sprigs (optional)

1. Cut beef steak lengthwise in half and then crosswise into ¼-inch-thick strips; set aside.

2. Bring beef broth to a boil in medium saucepan. Stir in couscous; cover pan, and remove from heat. Let stand 5 minutes.

3. Meanwhile, heat oil in large nonstick skillet over medium-high heat until hot. Add half of the beef; stir-fry 1 to 2 minutes or until outside surface of beef is no longer pink. Remove from skillet; keep warm. Repeat with remaining beef.

4. In same skillet, stir-fry bell pepper and onion 2 to 3 minutes or until crisp-tender. Return beef to skillet; stir in barbecue sauce. Cook and stir 1 to 2 minutes or until heated through. Serve beef mixture over couscous; sprinkle with chopped parsley. Garnish with parsley sprigs, as desired.

HEALTHY LIVING TIP

"Power" your calories by choosing naturally nutrient-rich foods, like colorful fruits and vegetables, low-fat dairy, whole grains, and lean meat. You'll get more essential nutrients from fewer calories.

Nutrition information per serving

Calories: 472
Fat: 10 g
  Saturated fat: 3 g
  Monounsaturated fat: 5 g
Cholesterol: 62 mg
Sodium: 733 mg
Carbohydrate: 51 g
Fiber: 2.5 g
Protein: 39 g
Niacin: 11.4 mg
Vitamin B$_6$: 0.9 mg
Vitamin B$_{12}$: 1.8 mcg
Iron: 3.0 mg
Selenium: 39.5 mcg
Zinc: 6.6 mg

This recipe is an excellent source of protein, niacin, vitamin B6, vitamin B12, selenium, and zinc, and a good source of fiber and iron.

Middle Eastern Beef Brochettes with Couscous

Experience the enticing aromas of Middle Eastern spices with this easily prepared brochette recipe.

Total preparation and cooking time: 30 minutes
Makes 4 servings.

1¼ pounds boneless beef top sirloin steak, cut 1 inch thick

SEASONING

2 tablespoons chopped fresh cilantro
2 tablespoons olive oil
3 cloves garlic, minced
2 teaspoons ground cumin
1 teaspoon sweet paprika
¼ teaspoon ground red pepper

1 medium onion, cut into 1-inch pieces
1 medium red bell pepper, cut into 1-inch pieces
½ teaspoon salt
2 cups hot cooked couscous, prepared without oil
Chopped fresh cilantro

1. Cut beef steak into 1¼-inch pieces. Combine seasoning ingredients in large bowl. Add beef, onion, and bell pepper; toss to coat.

2. Alternately thread beef and vegetable pieces onto four 12-inch metal skewers.

3. Place skewers on rack in broiler pan so surface of beef is 3 to 4 inches from heat. Broil about 8 to 10 minutes for medium-rare to medium doneness, turning once. Season with salt. Place brochettes on top of couscous; sprinkle with cilantro, as desired.

Nutrition information per serving

Calories: 375
Fat: 13 g
    Saturated fat: 3 g
    Monounsaturated fat: 7 g
Cholesterol: 62 mg
Sodium: 78 mg
Carbohydrate: 25 g
Fiber: 2.5 g
Protein: 37 g
Niacin: 10.6 mg
Vitamin B_6: 0.8 mg
Vitamin B_{12}: 1.8 mcg
Iron: 3.2 mg
Selenium: 61.3 mcg
Zinc: 6.4 mg

This recipe is an excellent source of protein, niacin, vitamin B_6, vitamin B_{12}, selenium, and zinc, and a good source of fiber and iron.

Bistro Beef Steak with Wild Mushroom Ragoût

Mushrooms and dry sherry are high in umami and work perfectly with these steaks. Umami, known as the fifth taste, is often described as meaty and savory and is derived from the Japanese word umai, *which means "delicious."*

Total preparation and cooking time: 30 minutes

Makes 4 servings.

RUB

1	teaspoon minced garlic
½	teaspoon herbes de Provence
½	teaspoon pepper
2	boneless beef top loin (strip) steaks, cut ¾ inch thick (about 8 ounces each)

WILD MUSHROOM RAGOÛT

1	tablespoon olive oil
⅓	cup finely chopped shallots
1	teaspoon minced garlic
8	ounces assorted wild mushrooms (oyster, cremini, and shiitake), sliced
¼	cup dry sherry
1	can (14 to 14½ ounces) ready-to-serve beef broth
1	tablespoon cornstarch
1	teaspoon herbes de Provence
1	tablespoon finely chopped fresh parsley
⅛	teaspoon salt
⅛	teaspoon pepper
	Salt and pepper, as desired

1. Combine rub ingredients; press evenly onto beef steaks. Place steaks on rack in broiler pan so surface of beef is 2 to 3 inches from heat. Broil 9 to 11 minutes for medium-rare to medium doneness, turning once.

2. Meanwhile, prepare Wild Mushroom Ragoût. Heat oil in large nonstick skillet over medium-high heat until hot. Add shallots and garlic; cook 1½ to 2 minutes or until shallots are tender. Add mushrooms; cook 6 to 7 minutes or until mushrooms are tender and liquid evaporates. Stir in sherry. Bring to a boil; cook about 1 minute or until liquid evaporates.

BEEF SMARTS

To keep your lean beef tender and moist, cook it enough, but not too much. A simple way to prevent overcooking is to always use a meat thermometer. See page 254 for temperatures that signal lean beef is cooked just right.

Nutrition information per serving

Calories: 244
Fat: 10 g
  Saturated fat: 3 g
  Monounsaturated fat: 5 g
Cholesterol: 56 mg
Sodium: 477 mg
Carbohydrate: 8 g
Fiber: 1.2 g
Protein: 28 g
Niacin: 9.6 mg
Vitamin B_6: 0.7 mg
Vitamin B_{12}: 1.4 mcg
Iron: 2.7 mg
Selenium: 35.3 mcg
Zinc: 5.0 mg

This recipe is an excellent source of protein, niacin, vitamin B_6, vitamin B_{12}, selenium, and zinc, and a good source of iron.

3. Whisk broth and cornstarch in small bowl. Add to skillet with herbes de Provence. Bring to a boil over high heat. Boil 7 to 8 minutes or until ragoût thickens, stirring frequently. Stir in parsley, salt, and pepper.

4. Carve steaks into thin slices; season with salt and pepper, as desired. Serve with ragoût.

COOK'S TIPS

- Herbes de Provence is a dried herb blend used in the cooking of southern France. Often sold in supermarkets, it's a blend of basil, fennel seed, lavender, marjoram, rosemary, sage, summer savory, and thyme.
- Baked potatoes pair nicely with the mushroom ragoût.

Spicy Beef and Spinach Stir-Fry

In China, noodles are a symbol of longevity, a contrast to the quick preparation of this flavorful beef stir-fry.

Total preparation and
  cooking time: 20 minutes
Marinating time: 10 minutes
Makes 4 servings.

1   pound beef round-tip steaks, cut ⅛ to ¼ inch thick

MARINADE
½   cup hoisin sauce
¼   cup chopped red chile peppers
¼   cup reduced-sodium soy sauce
2   tablespoons water
1   tablespoon dark sesame oil
4   cloves garlic, minced
½   teaspoon crushed red pepper

6   ounces uncooked thin spaghetti
1   package (10 ounces) fresh spinach, stems removed, thinly sliced
1   can (8 ounces) sliced water chestnuts, drained
¼   cup sliced green onions

1. Stack beef steaks; cut lengthwise in half and then crosswise into 1-inch-wide strips. Combine marinade ingredients in large bowl. Reserve half of the marinade; set aside. Place beef and remaining marinade in food-safe plastic bag; turn to coat. Close bag securely and marinate in refrigerator 10 minutes.

2. Meanwhile, cook pasta in stockpot according to package directions. Drain pasta and return to stockpot.

3. Remove beef from marinade; discard marinade. Heat large nonstick skillet over medium-high heat until hot. Add half of the beef; stir-fry 1 to 2 minutes or until outside surface of beef is no longer pink. (Do not overcook.) Remove from skillet; keep warm. Repeat with remaining beef.

4. Add spinach, water chestnuts, green onions, and reserved marinade to pasta; cook over medium heat 3 to 4 minutes or until spinach is wilted and mixture is heated through, stirring frequently. Add beef to stockpot; mix lightly.

HEALTHY LIVING TIP

Getting enough iron is especially important for infants and young children. It plays an important role in brain development and supports a healthy immune system. See page 231 to learn more.

Nutrition information per serving

Calories: 431
Fat: 10 g
    Saturated fat: 2 g
    Monounsaturated fat: 4 g
Cholesterol: 76 mg
Sodium: 939 mg
Carbohydrate: 52 g
Fiber: 7.2 g
Protein: 33 g
Niacin: 6.8 mg
Vitamin B_6: 0.6 mg
Vitamin B_{12}: 1.3 mcg
Iron: 5.8 mg
Selenium: 50.1 mcg
Zinc: 5.1 mg

This recipe is an excellent source of fiber, protein, niacin, vitamin B_6, vitamin B_{12}, iron, selenium, and zinc.

Thai Noodles with Beef and Broccoli

Total preparation and cooking time: 30 minutes
Makes 4 servings.

Frozen vegetables and prepared peanut sauce make this recipe a snap to prepare and a perfect weeknight dinner.

1	pound beef shoulder center steaks (Ranch Steaks), cut ¾ inch thick
¼	cup soy sauce
1	clove garlic, minced
2	teaspoons vegetable oil, divided
1	package (16 ounces) frozen vegetable mixture (broccoli, carrots, water chestnuts)
2	cups cooked rice noodles
½	cup peanut sauce

1. Cut beef steaks lengthwise in half, then crosswise into ¼-inch-thick strips. Combine soy sauce and garlic in medium bowl. Add beef; toss to coat.

2. Heat 1 teaspoon oil in large nonstick skillet over medium-high heat until hot. Add half of the beef; stir-fry 1 to 2 minutes or until outside surface of beef is no longer pink. Remove from skillet. Repeat with remaining beef.

3. Heat remaining 1 teaspoon oil in same skillet over medium heat until hot. Add frozen vegetables; cook and stir 4 to 7 minutes or until just tender. Add beef, noodles, and peanut sauce to skillet; cook and stir until heated through.

Nutrition information per serving

Calories: 364
Fat: 10 g
  Saturated fat: 3 g
  Monounsaturated fat: 4 g
Cholesterol: 66 mg
Sodium: 799 mg
Carbohydrate: 37 g
Fiber: 4.9 g
Protein: 31 g
Niacin: 5.6 mg
Vitamin B_6: 0.5 mg
Vitamin B_{12}: 2.9 mcg
Iron: 4.9 mg
Selenium: 29.0 mcg
Zinc: 6.8 mg

This recipe is an excellent source of protein, niacin, vitamin B_6, vitamin B_{12}, iron, selenium, and zinc, and a good source of fiber.

Ranch Steaks with Pepper Rub

Total preparation and
  cooking time: 30 minutes
Makes 4 servings.

Enjoy two of the classic flavors that pair beautifully with steak: black pepper and red wine.

1	teaspoon cracked black pepper or mixed cracked peppercorns (black, white, green, and pink)
1	teaspoon minced garlic
4	beef shoulder center steaks (Ranch Steaks), cut ¾ inch thick (about 5 ounces each)
2	teaspoons vegetable oil
½	cup ready-to-serve beef broth
¼	cup dry red wine

1. Combine pepper and garlic in small bowl; press evenly onto beef steaks. Heat oil in large nonstick skillet over medium heat until hot. Place steaks in skillet; cook 9 to 11 minutes for medium-rare to medium doneness, turning once. Remove to platter; keep warm.

2. Add broth and wine to skillet; increase heat to medium-high. Cook and stir 1 to 2 minutes or until browned bits attached to skillet are dissolved; continue cooking until sauce is reduced by half. Serve sauce over steaks.

COOK'S TIPS

- Four beef tenderloin steaks, cut 1 inch thick (about 4 ounces each), may be substituted for beef shoulder center steaks (Ranch Steaks). Cook steaks 10 to 13 minutes for medium-rare to medium doneness, turning once.

- The pepper rub and sauce in this recipe pairs well with a side of mashed potatoes.

**Nutrition information
per serving**

Calories: 214
Fat: 9 g
 Saturated fat: 2 g
 Monounsaturated fat: 4 g
Cholesterol: 71 mg
Sodium: 182 mg
Carbohydrate: 1 g
Fiber: 0.2 g
Protein: 29 g
Niacin: 3.8 mg
Vitamin B_6: 0.3 mg
Vitamin B_{12}: 3.3 mcg
Iron: 3.5 mg
Selenium: 32.0 mcg
Zinc: 6.8 mg

This recipe is an excellent source of protein, vitamin B_{12}, selenium, and zinc, and a good source of niacin, vitamin B_6, and iron.

Southwest Beef and Pasta Skillet

Can't decide if you're in the mood for Mexican or Italian? Try this skillet meal that combines both in very little time.

2 cups uncooked rotini (spiral) pasta
1 pound beef round tip steaks, cut ⅛ to ¼ inch thick

SEASONING
1 package (about 1.25 ounces) taco seasoning mix
1 tablespoon chopped fresh cilantro
3 cloves garlic, minced
1 tablespoon olive oil

1 jar (16 ounces) prepared mild or medium chunky salsa
1 can (15 ounces) black beans, rinsed, drained
½ cup water

1. Cook pasta according to package directions.
2. Meanwhile, stack beef steaks; cut lengthwise in half and then crosswise into 1-inch-wide strips. Combine seasoning ingredients in medium bowl. Add beef; toss to coat. Heat large nonstick skillet over medium-high heat until hot. Add half of the beef; stir-fry 1 to 2 minutes or until outside surface of beef is no longer pink. (Do not overcook.) Remove from skillet; keep warm. Repeat with remaining beef.
3. Combine pasta, salsa, beans, and water in same skillet; cook 4 to 5 minutes or until heated through, stirring occasionally. Return beef to skillet; stir to combine. Garnish as desired.

COOK'S TIP
Serve with freshly cooked corn on the cob sprinkled with chili powder for a complete Southwestern meal.

Total preparation and cooking time: 25 minutes
Makes 4 servings.

BEEF SMARTS
Starting a new exercise plan? Beef's nutrients help to fuel fitness and muscle-building, providing energy, protein, iron, and zinc. See page 236 to learn more.

Nutrition information per serving

Calories: 484
Fat: 10 g
  Saturated fat: 2 g
  Monounsaturated fat: 4 g
Cholesterol: 69 mg
Sodium: 1,786 mg
Carbohydrate: 57 g
Fiber: 7.1 g
Protein: 35 g
Niacin: 4.9 mg
Vitamin B_6: 0.4 mg
Vitamin B_{12}: 2.5 mcg
Iron: 6.2 mg
Selenium: 45.9 mcg
Zinc: 6.6 mg

This recipe is an excellent source of fiber, protein, niacin, vitamin B_6, vitamin B_{12}, iron, selenium, and zinc.

Tenderloin Steaks with Jalapeño Pepper Sauce

Total preparation and
  cooking time: 30 minutes
Makes 4 servings.

Spice up your weeknight dining experience with this sweet and spicy blend of flavors.

SPICE RUB
¾   teaspoon garlic salt
¾   teaspoon chili powder
½   teaspoon coarse-grind black pepper
¼   teaspoon ground cumin
¼   teaspoon dried oregano leaves

4   beef tenderloin steaks, cut 1 inch thick (about 4 ounces each)
½   cup ready-to-serve beef broth
¼   cup balsamic or red wine vinegar
2   tablespoons jalapeño pepper jelly

1. Combine spice rub ingredients in small bowl; press evenly onto both sides of each beef steak. Spray large nonstick skillet with cooking spray; heat over medium heat until hot. Place steaks in skillet; cook 10 to 13 minutes for medium-rare to medium doneness, turning once. Remove steaks; keep warm.

2. Add broth, vinegar, and jelly to skillet; increase heat to medium-high. Cook and stir until browned bits attached to skillet are dissolved and sauce thickens slightly. Serve sauce with steaks.

Nutrition information per serving

Calories: 211
Fat: 7 g
   Saturated fat: 3 g
   Monounsaturated fat: 3 g
Cholesterol: 67 mg
Sodium: 344 mg
Carbohydrate: 10 g
Fiber: 0.3 g
Protein: 25 g
Niacin: 7.3 mg
Vitamin B_6: 0.6 mg
Vitamin B_{12}:1.4 mcg
Iron: 1.9 mg
Selenium: 29.6 mcg
Zinc: 4.6 mg

This recipe is an excellent source of protein, niacin, vitamin B_6, vitamin B_{12}, selenium, and zinc, and a good source of iron.

COOK'S TIPS
- Jalapeño pepper jelly can be found in most supermarkets and gourmet specialty stores.
- The sweet and spicy flavor of this dish pairs well with steamed squash, seasoned with salt and pepper.

Cumin-Crusted Beef Steaks with Orange-Olive Relish

The nutty flavor of the cumin and the freshness of the orange make this a unique and easy weeknight dinner.

Total preparation and cooking time: 30 minutes
Makes 4 servings.

    2 to 3 medium oranges
    1½ teaspoons ground cumin
    1   teaspoon salt
    ½   teaspoon black pepper
    2   beef shoulder center steaks (Ranch Steaks), cut ¾ inch thick (about 8 ounces each)
    1   jar (7 ounces) roasted red peppers, drained, diced
    ⅓   cup diced red onion
    ⅓   cup coarsely chopped Kalamata olives

1. Grate 2 teaspoons orange peel from oranges; reserve oranges. Combine orange peel, cumin, and salt in small bowl. Reserve 2 teaspoons seasoning for relish.

2. Add pepper to remaining seasoning; press evenly onto beef steaks. Heat ridged grill pan or large nonstick skillet over medium heat until hot. Place steaks in grill pan; cook 9 to 12 minutes for medium-rare to medium doneness, turning twice.

3. Meanwhile, peel and chop enough reserved oranges to measure 1½ cups. Combine oranges, roasted peppers, onion, olives, and reserved seasoning in medium bowl; mix well. Serve steaks with relish.

> **COOK'S TIP**
> Serve on a bed of saucy black beans for added protein.

HEALTHY LIVING **TIP**
● ● ● ● ●

When preparing meat, poultry, and fish, use cooking methods that add little or no fat. Broil or grill, roast, braise, stew, steam, poach, stir-fry, or microwave foods rather than fry them.

Nutrition information per serving

Calories: 220
Fat: 7 g
    Saturated fat: 2 g
    Monounsaturated fat: 4 g
Cholesterol: 57 mg
Sodium: 924 mg
Carbohydrate: 16 g
Fiber: 4.7 g
Protein: 24 g
Niacin: 3.0 mg
Vitamin B_6: 0.3 mg
Vitamin B_{12}: 2.6 mcg
Iron: 3.9 mg
Selenium: 25.7 mcg
Zinc: 5.5 mg

This recipe is an excellent source of protein, vitamin B_{12}, iron, selenium, and zinc, and a good source of fiber, niacin, and vitamin B_6.

Flank Steak with Creamy Poblano Chile Sauce

Poblano chiles are best known for their use in chiles rellenos but add an interesting kick to this creamy Poblano Chile Sauce.

Total preparation and cooking time: 30 minutes

Marinating time: 6 hours or overnight

Makes 6 servings.

MARINADE

½   cup fresh lime juice
½   cup orange juice
1   teaspoon ground cumin
1   teaspoon minced garlic
½   teaspoon salt
½   teaspoon chili powder

1   beef flank steak (about 1½ pounds)

POBLANO CHILE SAUCE

1   large poblano chile (about 6 ounces)
1   teaspoon vegetable oil
⅓   cup chopped onion
½   teaspoon minced garlic
¼   cup plain nonfat yogurt
¼   cup reduced-fat dairy sour cream
¼   teaspoon salt
1   tablespoon finely chopped fresh cilantro

1. Combine marinade ingredients in small bowl. Place beef steak and marinade in food-safe plastic bag; turn steak to coat. Close bag securely and marinate in refrigerator 6 hours or as long as overnight, turning occasionally.

2. To prepare Poblano Chile Sauce, place chile in center of grid over medium, ash-covered coals. Grill, uncovered, 10 to 11 minutes or until skin is charred and blistered on all sides, turning frequently. Place in food-safe plastic bag. Close bag; let stand 10 to 12 minutes or until cool enough to handle. Remove and discard skin, stem, and seeds. Chop chile. Set aside.

3. Heat oil in small nonstick skillet over medium-high heat until hot. Add onion and garlic; cook and stir 3 to 4 minutes or until tender.

4. Place onion mixture, chile, yogurt, sour cream, and salt in food processor or blender container. Cover; process until smooth. Pour into serving bowl; stir in cilantro. Set aside.

Nutrition information per serving

Calories: 202
Fat: 8 g
   Saturated fat: 4 g
   Monounsaturated fat: 3 g
Cholesterol: 47 mg
Sodium: 256 mg
Carbohydrate: 5 g
Fiber: 0.7 g
Protein: 25 g
Niacin: 7.0 mg
Vitamin B_6: 0.6 mg
Vitamin B_{12}: 1.4 mcg
Iron: 1.7 mg
Selenium: 27.3 mcg
Zinc: 4.4 mg

This recipe is an excellent source of protein, niacin, vitamin B_6, vitamin B_{12}, selenium, and zinc, and a good source of iron.

Flank Steak with
Creamy Poblano
Chile Sauce
(continued)

5. Remove steak from marinade; discard marinade. Place steak on grid over medium, ash-covered coals. Grill, uncovered, 17 to 21 minutes for medium-rare to medium doneness, turning occasionally.

6. Carve steak across the grain into thin slices. Serve with sauce.

COOK'S TIPS
- When handling chiles, wear clean latex or rubber gloves to protect your hands from the burning oils. Avoid touching your eyes, nose, or mouth.
- To broil a chile, place on rack in broiler pan so surface is 2 inches from heat. Broil 10 to 12 minutes or until skin is charred and blistered on all sides, turning frequently.
- Serve steak and Poblano Chile Sauce with grilled tricolor peppers.

5

BEEFY ONE-DISH MEALS

121

Beef Enchiladas with Red and Green Sauces

Total preparation and
   cooking time: 1½ hours
Makes 4 servings.

Ancho chiles and tomatillos add color and authentic south-of-the-border flavor to the two sauces in these superb enchiladas.

ANCHO CHILE SAUCE

3   dried ancho chiles
2   cups boiling water
¼   cup reduced-fat dairy sour cream
3   tablespoons packed brown sugar
2   cloves garlic, minced
½   teaspoon salt

VERDE SAUCE

12   ounces tomatillos, peeled
¼   cup fresh chopped cilantro
¼   cup minced onion
¼   cup fresh lime juice
1   medium jalapeño pepper, seeded, minced
1   teaspoon minced garlic
1   teaspoon olive oil
½   teaspoon sugar
½   teaspoon salt

1   pound ground beef (95% lean)
1   cup chopped onion
¾   cup frozen corn
1   teaspoon salt
1   teaspoon ground cumin
½   teaspoon ground black pepper
¾   cup reduced-fat shredded Mexican cheese blend, divided
8   corn tortillas

Nutrition information per serving

Calories: 498
Fat: 15 g
   Saturated fat: 6 g
   Monounsaturated fat: 4 g
Cholesterol: 82 mg
Sodium: 1,426 mg
Carbohydrate: 62 g
Fiber: 9.0 g
Protein: 34 g
Niacin: 8.9 mg
Vitamin B$_6$: 1.2 mg
Vitamin B$_{12}$: 2.1 mcg
Iron: 5.8 mg
Selenium: 23.1 mcg
Zinc: 6.6 mg

This recipe is an excellent source of fiber, protein, niacin, vitamin B$_6$, vitamin B$_{12}$, iron, selenium, and zinc.

1. To prepare Ancho Chile Sauce, remove and discard stems from chiles. Pour boiling water over chiles in medium bowl; let stand 30 minutes or until chiles are softened. Drain chiles, reserving liquid. Place chiles with seeds, ½ cup reserved liquid, sour cream, brown sugar, garlic, and salt in food processor bowl. Cover; process until smooth. Set aside.

2. To prepare Verde Sauce, place tomatillos in medium saucepan. Add enough water to cover. Bring to a boil; cook 8 to 10 minutes or until tender. Drain; coarsely chop tomatillos. Combine tomatillos, cilantro, onion, lime juice, jalapeño, garlic, oil, sugar, and salt in medium bowl. Set aside.

3. Heat oven to 350°F. Brown ground beef with onion in large non-stick skillet over medium heat 8 to 10 minutes or until beef is no longer pink, breaking beef up into ¾-inch crumbles. Pour off drippings. Stir in ¾ cup of the Verde Sauce, corn, salt, cumin, and black pepper; cook 2 to 3 minutes or until heated through. Stir in ½ cup cheese; remove from heat.

4. Reserve ⅓ cup Ancho Chile Sauce; pour remaining sauce into shallow dish. Spray 11¾ × 7½-inch baking dish with nonstick cooking spray. For each enchilada, dip 1 tortilla into sauce to coat. Spoon about ½ cup beef mixture down center of tortilla. Fold 1 side of tortilla over filling and roll up. Place seam-side down in baking dish. Pour any remaining sauce from shallow dish over enchiladas.

5. Cover with aluminum foil. Bake in 350°F oven 20 minutes. Remove foil; top with reserved Ancho Chile Sauce and remaining ¼ cup cheese. Cover and bake about 5 minutes or until cheese is melted. Serve with remaining Verde Sauce.

COOK'S TIPS
- For best results, use only fresh corn tortillas, as they are less likely to break while forming enchiladas.
- Serve with a side of Mexican rice for a complete Mexican experience.
- When handling chiles, wear clean latex or rubber gloves to protect your hands from the burning oils. Avoid touching your eyes, nose, or mouth.

Beef and Broccoli with Noodles

This quick version of beef and broccoli adds colorful carrots and ramen noodles for a complete one-dish meal.

1¼ pounds boneless top round steak, cut 1 inch thick
2 packages (3 ounces each) beef-flavored instant ramen noodles, broken up
1½ teaspoons cornstarch dissolved in ½ cup water
2 tablespoons vegetable oil, divided
8 ounces broccoli florets
2 medium carrots, thinly sliced
1½ cups water
1 teaspoon freshly grated orange peel (optional)

1. Cut beef steak lengthwise in half, then crosswise into ⅛-inch-thick strips. Combine seasoning from ramen noodles with cornstarch mixture in large bowl. Add beef; toss.

2. Heat 1 tablespoon oil in large nonstick skillet over medium-high heat until hot. Stir-fry broccoli and carrots 1 minute. Add noodles and water; bring to a boil. Reduce heat; cover and simmer 3 to 5 minutes or until vegetables are tender and most of liquid is absorbed, stirring occasionally. Remove; keep warm.

3. In same skillet, heat remaining 1 tablespoon oil over medium-high heat until hot. Add half of the beef; stir-fry 1 to 2 minutes or until outside surface of beef is no longer pink. (Do not overcook.) Remove from skillet; keep warm. Repeat with remaining beef. Serve over noodles. Sprinkle with orange peel, if desired.

Total preparation and cooking time: 30 minutes
Makes 4 servings.

• • • • • • • • • • • •
BEEF SMARTS
Beef helps deliver extra amounts of nutrients, including protein, iron, zinc, and B vitamins, pregnant women need for a healthy baby.

Nutrition information per serving

Calories: 435
Fat: 14 g
    Saturated fat: 3 g
    Monounsaturated fat: 5 g
Cholesterol: 76 mg
Sodium: 541 mg
Carbohydrate: 35 g
Fiber: 3.8 g
Protein: 42 g
Niacin: 6.8 mg
Vitamin B_6: 0.6 mg
Vitamin B_{12}: 1.9 mcg
Iron: 5.1 mg
Selenium: 42.7 mcg
Zinc: 6.3 mg

This recipe is an excellent source of protein, niacin, vitamin B_6, vitamin B_{12}, iron, selenium, and zinc, and a good source of fiber.

Beef Spanish Rice

Total preparation and cooking time: 50 minutes
Makes 4 servings.

This powerhouse meal of beef, beans, rice, tomatoes, and peppers comes together easily in just one skillet.

1	pound boneless beef top round steak, cut ¾ inch thick
2	tablespoons fresh lime juice
1	teaspoon chili powder
2	teaspoons minced garlic, divided
2	teaspoons vegetable oil, divided
¼	teaspoon salt
¼	teaspoon black pepper
1	cup chopped onion
1	cup coarsely chopped green bell pepper
2	cups water
1	cup uncooked white rice
1	teaspoon ground cumin
1	can (14½ ounces) diced tomatoes with green chiles, undrained
1	can (15 ounces) black beans, rinsed, drained
	Salt and black pepper, as desired
	Finely chopped fresh cilantro (optional)
	Lime wedges (optional)

COOK'S TIP
To keep cooked beef warm, cover with aluminum foil.

1. Cut beef steak lengthwise in half, then crosswise into ⅛-inch-thick strips. Combine lime juice, chili powder, and 1 teaspoon garlic in medium bowl. Add beef, tossing to coat.

2. Heat 1 teaspoon oil in large nonstick skillet over medium-high heat until hot. Add half of the beef; stir-fry 1 to 2 minutes or until outside surface of beef is no longer pink. (Do not overcook.) Remove beef from skillet. Repeat with remaining beef. Season beef with salt and pepper; keep warm.

3. Heat remaining 1 teaspoon oil in same skillet until hot. Add onion, bell pepper, and remaining 1 teaspoon garlic; stir-fry 2 to 3 minutes or until crisp-tender. Stir in water, rice, and cumin; bring to a boil. Reduce heat; cover and cook according to rice package directions. Add tomatoes to cooked rice; cook, covered, 3 to 5 minutes or until most of liquid is absorbed, stirring occasionally.

4. Add beef and beans; cook and stir 1 to 2 minutes or until heated through. Season with salt and pepper, as desired. Serve garnished with cilantro and lime wedges, if desired.

Nutrition information per serving

Calories: 487
Fat: 8 g
  Saturated fat: 2 g
  Monounsaturated fat: 3 g
Cholesterol: 61 mg
Sodium: 914 mg
Carbohydrate: 62 g
Fiber: 9.5 g
Protein: 38 g
Niacin: 7.0 mg
Vitamin B_6: 0.7 mg
Vitamin B_{12}: 1.5 mcg
Iron: 6.8 mg
Selenium: 42.1 mcg
Zinc: 5.5 mg

This recipe is an excellent source of fiber, protein, niacin, vitamin B_6, vitamin B_{12}, iron, selenium, and zinc.

Beef Sirloin with Oven-Roasted Vegetables

Unlike steaming or stir-frying, roasting develops the natural sweetness in vegetables, creating intense, full flavors.

Total preparation and cooking time: 1¼ hours
Makes 12 servings.

1½ tablespoons chopped fresh rosemary
1 tablespoon minced garlic
1½ teaspoons salt
1 teaspoon pepper
1 boneless beef top sirloin steak, cut 2 inches thick (about 3 pounds)
¼ cup extra-virgin olive oil
2 pounds new red potatoes
4 large carrots, each cut crosswise into quarters
1 large zucchini, cut crosswise into quarters
2 medium onions, cut into 1-inch-thick wedges

1. Heat oven to 425°F. Combine rosemary, garlic, salt, and pepper; press 1½ teaspoons evenly onto beef steak. Stir oil into remaining seasoning mixture. Set aside.

2. Cut small potatoes in half and large potatoes into quarters. Cut each carrot and zucchini quarter lengthwise in half. Set aside zucchini. Combine potatoes, carrots, onions, and remaining seasoning mixture in large bowl; toss to coat. Arrange, cut sides down, in single layer on metal baking sheet. Set aside.

3. Place steak on rack in shallow roasting pan. Insert ovenproof meat thermometer so tip is centered in thickest part of beef, not resting in fat. Do not add water or cover. Roast steak and vegetables in 425°F oven for 25 minutes. Stir vegetables and add zucchini to baking pan; continue roasting 20 to 25 minutes or until vegetables are tender and meat thermometer registers 140°F for medium-rare doneness.

4. Transfer steak to carving board. Let stand 5 to 10 minutes. (Temperature will continue to rise about 5°F to reach 145°F for medium-rare.)

5. Carve steak into slices. Serve with vegetables.

HEALTHY LIVING TIP

Cook your vegetables just until tender-crisp for more color, better texture, and more nutrition.

Nutrition information per serving

Calories: 290
Fat: 10 g
  Saturated fat: 2 g
  Monounsaturated fat: 6 g
Cholesterol: 50 mg
Sodium: 372 mg
Carbohydrate: 21 g
Fiber: 3.0 g
Protein: 29 g
Niacin: 9.2 mg
Vitamin B_6: 0.8 mg
Vitamin B_{12}: 1.4 mcg
Iron: 2.5 mg
Selenium: 32.0 mcg
Zinc: 5.3 mg

This recipe is an excellent source of protein, niacin, vitamin B_6, vitamin B_{12}, selenium, and zinc, and a good source of fiber and iron.

Beef, Arugula, and Spinach Lasagna

Oven-ready noodles and prepared pasta sauce make this taste-tempting lasagna a breeze to prepare.

Total preparation and
    cooking time: 1¼ hours
Makes 6 to 8 servings

1½	pounds ground beef (95% lean)
2	teaspoons minced garlic
1¼	teaspoons salt, divided
¾	teaspoon pepper, divided
4	cups prepared pasta or spaghetti sauce
2	cups loosely packed fresh baby arugula (about 1¾ ounces)
2	cups loosely packed fresh baby spinach (about 1¾ ounces)
1	container (15 ounces) fat-free ricotta cheese
2	egg whites
2	tablespoons chopped fresh basil
2	tablespoons chopped fresh oregano
9	uncooked oven-ready (no boil) lasagna noodles (each about 6¾ × 3½ inches)
1½	cups reduced-fat shredded mozzarella cheese

COOK'S TIP
Equal amounts of chopped fresh mature spinach and arugula may be substituted for fresh baby spinach and arugula.

1. Heat oven to 375°F. Brown ground beef with garlic in large non-stick skillet over medium heat 8 to 10 minutes or until beef is no longer pink, breaking up into ¾-inch crumbles. Pour off drippings; season with ¾ teaspoon salt and ½ teaspoon pepper. Stir in pasta sauce. Set aside.

2. Combine arugula and spinach. Set aside. Combine ricotta cheese, egg whites, basil, oregano, remaining ½ teaspoon salt, and remaining ¼ teaspoon pepper in small bowl.

3. Spread 1 cup meat sauce over bottom of 11¾ × 7½-inch glass baking dish. Top with 3 noodles, half of the ricotta mixture, half of the spinach mixture, ½ cup mozzarella, and 1½ cups meat sauce. Repeat layers. Top with remaining 3 noodles and meat sauce.

4. Cover with aluminum foil. Bake in 375°F oven 45 to 50 minutes or until noodles are tender and sauce is bubbly. Remove foil; sprinkle with remaining ½ cup mozzarella. Bake, uncovered, 5 minutes or until cheese is melted. Let stand, loosely covered, 10 minutes before serving.

Nutrition information per serving

Calories: 520
Fat: 12 g
    Saturated fat: 5 g
    Monounsaturated fat: 3 g
Cholesterol: 127 mg
Sodium: 1,260 mg
Carbohydrate: 49 g
Fiber: 5.1 g
Protein: 47 g
Niacin: 8.1 mg
Vitamin B_6: 0.4 mg
Vitamin B_{12}: 2.3 mcg
Iron: 6.0 mg
Selenium: 20.3 mcg
Zinc: 6.1 mg

This recipe is an excellent source of fiber, protein, niacin, vitamin B_6, vitamin B_{12}, iron, selenium, and zinc.

Chipotle Pot Roast with Cheddar Mashed Potatoes

Total preparation and
cooking time: 3½ hours
Makes 8 servings.

You'll fall in love with the smoky spiciness of chipotle peppers in this tasty dish.

3   teaspoons vegetable oil, divided
1   boneless beef chuck shoulder pot roast (3 to 3½ pounds)
1   teaspoon salt
½   teaspoon black pepper
1   cup chopped onion
2   teaspoons minced garlic
1   cup ready-to-serve beef broth
½   cup dark beer
2   tablespoons tomato paste
1   tablespoon minced chipotle peppers in adobo sauce
2   tablespoons cornstarch dissolved in 2 tablespoons water
¼   cup reduced-fat dairy sour cream
¼   teaspoon salt (optional)

CHEDDAR MASHED POTATOES
2   packages (1 pound, 4 ounces each) refrigerated mashed potatoes
½   cup reduced-fat shredded Cheddar cheese
1   teaspoon minced garlic

COOK'S TIP
Refrigerated mashed potatoes are available in the dairy section of most large supermarkets.

Nutrition information per serving

Calories: 339
Fat: 10 g
    Saturated fat: 4 g
    Monounsaturated fat: 4 g
Cholesterol: 89 mg
Sodium: 492 mg
Carbohydrate: 27 g
Fiber: 4.6 g
Protein: 30 g
Niacin: 2.7 mg
Vitamin B$_6$: 0.3 mg
Vitamin B$_{12}$: 2.6 mcg
Iron: 3.8 mg
Selenium: 25.8 mcg
Zinc: 7.0 mg

This recipe is an excellent source of protein, vitamin B$_{12}$, iron, selenium, and zinc, and a good source of fiber, niacin, and vitamin B$_6$.

1. Heat 2 teaspoons oil in stockpot over medium heat until hot. Place beef pot roast in stockpot; brown evenly. Remove pot roast; pour off drippings and set aside. Season with 1 teaspoon salt and black pepper.

2. Add remaining 1 teaspoon oil to stockpot. Cook and stir onion and garlic 1 to 2 minutes or until onion is tender. Add broth, beer, tomato paste, and chipotle peppers; increase heat to medium-high. Cook and stir 1 to 2 minutes or until browned bits attached to bottom of stockpot are dissolved. Return pot roast to stockpot; bring to a boil. Reduce heat; cover tightly and simmer 2 to 3 hours or until pot roast is fork-tender.

3. Remove pot roast; keep warm. Skim fat from cooking liquid. Measure 2½ cups cooking liquid and return to stockpot; stir in cornstarch mixture. Bring to a boil, stirring constantly; cook and stir 1 minute or until thickened. Remove from heat; whisk in sour cream

until well blended. Season with ¼ teaspoon salt, if desired. Set aside.

4. To make Cheddar Mashed Potatoes, heat mashed potatoes according to package directions. Spoon into serving dish. Add cheese and garlic; stir until cheese is melted.

5. Carve pot roast into slices; serve with mashed potatoes and sauce.

COOK'S TIPS

- Corn with some chopped red pepper added for color and flavor goes great with this dish.
- To easily skim fat from cooking liquids, use a fat or gravy separator. The spout on this special pitcher is positioned at the bottom so that as fat rises to the surface the liquid below can be poured off separately.

Asian Beef Steaks and Noodles

Total preparation and cooking time: 20 minutes

Makes 4 servings.

Hoisin sauce, vinegar, and crushed red pepper add sweet-spicy flavor to this quick stir-fry dish.

1	pound beef shoulder center steaks (Ranch Steaks), cut ¾ inch thick (about 8 ounces each)
¼	cup hoisin sauce
1	tablespoon water
1	tablespoon red wine vinegar
¼	teaspoon crushed red pepper
2	teaspoons vegetable oil, divided
1½	cups sliced seeded peeled cucumbers
1	small red bell pepper, cut into thin strips
¼	cup sliced green onions
2	cups hot cooked broken Chinese egg noodles
1	tablespoon chopped fresh cilantro, divided

1. Cut beef steaks lengthwise in half, then crosswise into ¼-inch-thick strips. Set aside.

2. Combine hoisin sauce, water, vinegar, and red pepper in small bowl. Set aside.

3. Heat 1 teaspoon oil in large nonstick skillet over medium-high heat until hot. Add cucumbers, bell pepper, and green onions; stir-fry 1 to 2 minutes or until vegetables are crisp-tender. Add noodles, 1½ teaspoons cilantro, and half of the hoisin mixture; toss. Remove from skillet; keep warm.

4. Heat remaining 1 teaspoon oil in same skillet until hot. Add half of the beef; stir-fry 1 to 2 minutes or until outside surface of beef is no longer pink. Remove from skillet. Repeat with remaining beef. Return beef to skillet. Stir in remaining hoisin mixture; cook and stir until heated through. Serve over noodle mixture. Sprinkle with remaining 1½ teaspoons cilantro.

Nutrition information per serving

Calories: 322
Fat: 10 g
  Saturated fat: 2 g
  Monounsaturated fat: 4 g
Cholesterol: 84 mg
Sodium: 330 mg
Carbohydrate: 30 g
Fiber: 2.1 g
Protein: 28 g
Niacin: 4.7 mg
Vitamin B$_6$: 0.4 mg
Vitamin B$_{12}$: 2.7 mcg
Iron: 4.5 mg
Selenium: 43.3 mcg
Zinc: 6.1 mg

This recipe is an excellent source of protein, niacin, vitamin B$_6$, vitamin B$_{12}$, iron, selenium, and zinc.

COOK'S TIP
Two cups cooked vermicelli (4 ounces uncooked) may be substituted for the Chinese egg noodles.

Bow Tie Pasta with Beef and Beans

Total preparation and cooking time: 40 minutes

Makes 4 servings.

Pasta and beans are a classic combination. The beans give an added boost of fiber to the meal.

1	pound ground beef (95% lean)
1	cup chopped onion
2	teaspoons minced garlic
1	can (15½ ounces) great northern beans, rinsed, drained
1	can (14½ ounces) Italian-style diced tomatoes, undrained
1	can (14 to 14½ ounces) ready-to-serve beef broth
2	cups uncooked bow tie pasta
2	cups broccoli florets
	Salt and pepper, as desired
½	cup shredded Parmesan cheese

1. Brown ground beef with onion and garlic in large nonstick skillet over medium heat 8 to 10 minutes or until beef is no longer pink, breaking beef up into ¾-inch crumbles. Pour off drippings.

2. Stir in beans, tomatoes, broth, and pasta; bring to a boil. Reduce heat; cover and simmer 12 minutes. Stir in broccoli; continue simmering, covered, 5 minutes or until pasta and broccoli are just tender.

3. Season with salt and pepper, as desired. Sprinkle with cheese.

Nutrition information per serving

Calories: 595
Fat: 11 g
  Saturated fat: 5 g
  Monounsaturated fat: 4 g
Cholesterol: 83 mg
Sodium: 1,013 mg
Carbohydrate: 77 g
Fiber: 9.4 g
Protein: 46 g
Niacin: 9.2 mg
Vitamin B_6: 0.7 mg
Vitamin B_{12}: 2.4 mcg
Iron: 7.6 mg
Selenium: 54.8 mcg
Zinc: 8.0 mg

This recipe is an excellent source of fiber, protein, niacin, vitamin B_6, vitamin B_{12}, iron, selenium, and zinc.

Spinach and Beef Skillet

Dark sesame oil, which is expressed from roasted sesame seeds, adds a rich flavor accent to this colorful stir-fry.

1	pound boneless beef top sirloin steak, cut ¾ inch thick
2	teaspoons dark sesame oil
2	garlic cloves, minced
1	medium red bell pepper, cut into thin strips
3	tablespoons reduced-sodium soy sauce, divided
2	tablespoons water
3	cups coarsely chopped fresh spinach
½	cup sliced green onions
3	tablespoons ketchup
2	cups hot cooked brown rice, prepared without butter or salt

1. Cut beef steak lengthwise in half, then crosswise into ¼-inch-thick strips. Toss with sesame oil and garlic.

2. Heat large nonstick skillet over medium-high heat until hot. Add half of the beef; stir-fry 1 to 2 minutes or until outside surface of beef is no longer pink. Remove from skillet; keep warm. Repeat with remaining beef.

3. In same skillet, add bell pepper, 2 tablespoons soy sauce, and water. Cook and stir 2 to 3 minutes or until pepper is crisp-tender. Add spinach and green onions; cook and stir until spinach is just wilted. Stir in ketchup, remaining 1 tablespoon soy sauce, and beef; heat through. Serve over rice.

Total preparation and cooking time: 30 minutes
Makes 4 servings.

● ● ● ● ● ● ● ● ● ● ● ●
BEEF SMARTS
Beef provides vital nutrients for vibrant aging. Zinc helps keep older adults' immune systems strong and appetites healthy. B vitamins play important roles in maintaining cognitive health, including memory and problem-solving skills.

Nutrition information per serving

Calories: 361
Fat: 9 g
   Saturated fat: 3 g
   Monounsaturated fat: 3 g
Cholesterol: 62 mg
Sodium: 691 mg
Carbohydrate: 30 g
Fiber: 2.8 g
Protein: 37 g
Niacin: 11.5 mg
Vitamin B_6: 1.0 mg
Vitamin B_{12}: 1.8 mcg
Iron: 3.3 mg
Selenium: 49.4 mcg
Zinc: 6.9 mg

This recipe is an excellent source of protein, niacin, vitamin B_6, vitamin B_{12}, selenium, and zinc, and a good source of fiber and iron.

Beef Pot Roast with Maple Sweet Potatoes and Cider Gravy

Looking for a little touch of fall, anytime? Beef pot roast, mashed sweet potatoes, and cider gravy are the ultimate comfort food.

Total preparation and cooking time: 3½ hours

Makes 8 servings.

2	teaspoons olive oil
1	boneless beef chuck shoulder pot roast (3 to 3½ pounds)
1¾	teaspoons salt, divided
¾	teaspoon pepper, divided
1	cup chopped onion
2	teaspoons chopped fresh thyme
1	cup ready-to-serve beef broth
¾	cup apple cider
3	pounds sweet potatoes, peeled, cut crosswise into 1- to 1½-inch pieces
4	cloves garlic, peeled
2	tablespoons maple syrup
1	teaspoon minced fresh ginger
2	tablespoons cornstarch dissolved in 2 tablespoons brandy or water

1. Heat oil in stockpot over medium heat until hot. Place beef pot roast in stockpot; brown evenly. Remove pot roast; pour off drippings and season with 1 teaspoon salt and ½ teaspoon pepper.

2. Add onion and thyme to stockpot; cook and stir 3 to 5 minutes or until onion is tender. Add broth and cider; increase heat to medium-high. Cook and stir 1 to 2 minutes or until browned bits attached to stockpot are dissolved. Return pot roast to stockpot; bring to a boil. Reduce heat; cover tightly, and simmer 2½ hours.

3. Add sweet potatoes and garlic to stockpot; continue simmering, covered, 30 minutes or until sweet potatoes and pot roast are fork-tender.

> ### COOK'S TIPS
> - Sweet potatoes may also be mashed using a food processor.
> - Unlike apple juice, fresh cider is perishable and must be refrigerated before opening. Always purchase pasteurized cider.
> - To easily skim fat from cooking liquids, use a fat or gravy separator. The spout on this special pitcher is positioned at the bottom so that as fat rises to the surface the liquid below can be poured off separately.

Nutrition information per serving

Calories: 342
Fat: 7 g
    Saturated fat: 2 g
    Monounsaturated fat: 4 g
Cholesterol: 60 mg
Sodium: 511 mg
Carbohydrate: 42 g
Fiber: 5.3 g
Protein: 26 g
Niacin: 5.2 mg
Vitamin B_6: 0.7 mg
Vitamin B_{12}: 2.6 mcg
Iron 3.9 mg
Selenium: 26.2 mcg
Zinc: 6.2 mg

This recipe is an excellent source of fiber, protein, niacin, vitamin B_6, vitamin B_{12}, iron, selenium, and zinc.

4. Remove pot roast; keep warm. Remove sweet potatoes and garlic with slotted spoon to large bowl, leaving cooking liquid in stockpot.

5. Add maple syrup, ginger, remaining ¾ teaspoon salt and remaining ¼ teaspoon pepper to sweet potatoes. Beat with an electric mixer until sweet potatoes and garlic are mashed and smooth; keep warm.

6. Skim fat from cooking liquid; stir in cornstarch mixture. Bring to a boil, stirring constantly; cook and stir 1 minute or until thickened.

7. Carve pot roast into slices; serve with mashed sweet potatoes and gravy.

Basic Beef Pot Roast

Rediscover the simple pleasure of tender, flavorful pot roast. Carve into slices and serve. Or cool and shred the pot roast to use in other recipes.

Total preparation and cooking time: 2½ to 3 hours

Makes 8 servings.

2	teaspoons olive oil
1	boneless beef chuck shoulder pot roast (about 3 pounds)
½	teaspoon salt
¼	teaspoon pepper
2	cups chopped onion
3	cloves garlic, minced
1	can (14 to 14½ ounces) ready-to-serve beef broth

1. Heat oil in stockpot over medium heat until hot. Place beef pot roast in stockpot; brown evenly. Remove pot roast; season with salt and pepper. Pour off all but 1 teaspoon drippings from stockpot, if necessary.

2. Add onion and garlic to stockpot; cook and stir 3 to 4 minutes or until onion is tender. Stir in broth. Return pot roast to stockpot; bring to a boil. Reduce heat; cover tightly, and simmer on top of range or in preheated 325°F oven 2½ to 3 hours or until pot roast is fork-tender.

3. Remove pot roast; cool slightly. Trim and discard excess fat from cooked pot roast. Shred pot roast with 2 forks. Skim fat from cooking liquid; reserve for recipe use, if desired. Use pot roast to prepare Beef and Portobello Bread Pudding (page 142) and Rustic Polenta with Beef Pot Roast Ragù (page 140).

COOK'S TIPS

- Shredded pot roast may be wrapped and refrigerated for 3 to 4 days or frozen for 2 to 3 months.
- Pot roast can also be served alone with mashed potatoes and a side of vegetables for a favorite family meal.

Nutrition information per serving

Calories: 183
Fat: 7 g
    Saturated fat: 2 g
    Monounsaturated fat: 4 g
Cholesterol: 80 mg
Sodium: 300 mg
Carbohydrate: 2 g
Fiber: 0.4 g
Protein: 26 g
Niacin: 2.6 mg
Vitamin B_6: 0.2 mg
Vitamin B_{12}: 2.5 mcg
Iron: 3.4 mg
Selenium: 25.7 mcg
Zinc: 6.7 mg

This recipe is an excellent source of protein, vitamin B_{12}, selenium, and zinc, and a good source of niacin, vitamin B_6, and iron.

Rustic Polenta with Beef Pot Roast Ragù

Total preparation and
cooking time: 1 hour
Makes 4 servings.

Ragù is a thick Italian meat sauce made with tomatoes, onions, and garlic. Here, shredded beef pot roast replaces the usual ground beef.

2 teaspoons olive oil, divided
8 cups loosely packed fresh baby spinach
1 cup finely chopped onion
2 teaspoons minced garlic
1 jar (7 ounces) roasted red peppers, drained, finely chopped
⅓ cup dry red wine
1 tablespoon tomato paste
1 teaspoon dried basil leaves, crushed
1 can (14½ ounces) Italian-style diced tomatoes, undrained
1 teaspoon sugar
½ teaspoon salt
½ recipe Basic Beef Pot Roast (about 3 cups shredded) (page 139)
3 cups cooked polenta, prepared without oil or salt
½ cup shredded reduced-fat mozzarella cheese

1. Heat oven to 350°F. Heat 1 teaspoon oil in large nonstick skillet over medium-high heat until hot. Add spinach; cook and stir until just wilted. Remove spinach from skillet; drain on paper towels and press to remove excess liquid. Set aside.

2. Heat remaining 1 teaspoon oil in same skillet until hot. Add onion and garlic; cook and stir 2 to 3 minutes or until tender. Stir in roasted peppers, wine, tomato paste, and basil; cook and stir 3 to 4 minutes or until almost all liquid is evaporated. Reduce heat to medium. Stir in tomatoes, sugar, and salt; cook 8 to 10 minutes or

**Nutrition information
per serving**

Calories: 502
Fat: 12 g
  Saturated fat: 3 g
  Monounsaturated fat: 5 g
Cholesterol: 85 mg
Sodium: 1,309 mg
Carbohydrate: 58 g
Fiber: 7.3 g
Protein: 37 g
Niacin: 2.7 mg
Vitamin B_6: 0.3 mg
Vitamin B_{12}: 2.5 mcg
Iron: 6.9 mg
Selenium: 26.1 mcg
Zinc: 6.8 mg

This recipe is an excellent source of fiber, protein, vitamin B_{12}, iron, selenium, and zinc, and a good source of niacin and vitamin B_6.

COOK'S TIPS

- Polenta is an Italian side dish made from cornmeal. For best results, the cooked polenta should have a smooth and spreadable consistency. Quick-cooking or regular polenta may be used.
- To accurately measure fresh greens, such as spinach, place leaves in measuring cup and lightly pat down. Don't pack leaves too tightly to avoid using an excess amount.
- One package (10 ounces) frozen chopped spinach, defrosted and drained well, may be substituted for fresh spinach.

until thickened and almost all liquid is evaporated, stirring occasionally. Stir in shredded beef pot roast; cook until heated through. Remove from heat. Set aside.

3. Spray 2-quart glass baking dish with nonstick cooking spray. Spread half of the polenta over bottom of dish. Top evenly with spinach. Layer half of the beef mixture and half of the cheese evenly over spinach. Top with remaining polenta, beef mixture, and cheese.

4. Bake in 350°F oven 20 to 25 minutes or until heated through. Let stand 5 minutes before serving.

Beef Portobello Bread Pudding

Total preparation and cooking time: 1¼ hours
Makes 4 servings.

Serve this savory bread pudding, loaded with shredded pot roast, mushrooms, sun-dried tomatoes, and cheese, as a hearty brunch entrée.

1½	teaspoons olive oil
¼	cup finely chopped shallots
2	cloves garlic, minced
¼	teaspoon dried thyme leaves, crushed
8	ounces portobello mushrooms, coarsely chopped
½	cup sun-dried tomatoes, not packed in oil, slivered
½	cup Merlot or other dry red wine
½	recipe Basic Beef Pot Roast (about 3 cups shredded) (page 139)
½	cup reserved cooking liquid from Basic Beef Pot Roast
½	cup chopped fresh basil
1	teaspoon salt, divided
½	teaspoon pepper, divided
2	cans (12 ounces each) evaporated fat-free milk
¾	cup egg substitute
1	loaf (1 pound) French bread, cut into ¾-inch cubes
1	cup reduced-fat shredded Italian cheese blend or reduced-fat shredded mozzarella cheese, divided
2	tablespoons thinly sliced fresh basil (optional)
	Salt, as desired

Nutrition information per serving

Calories: 746
Fat: 13 g
    Saturated fat: 5 g
    Monounsaturated fat: 4 g
Cholesterol: 82 mg
Sodium: 1,933 mg
Carbohydrate: 87 g
Fiber: 4.4 g
Protein: 60 g
Niacin: 11.0 mg
Vitamin B$_6$: 0.5 mg
Vitamin B$_{12}$: 3.5 mcg
Iron: 9.5 mg
Selenium: 36.8 mcg
Zinc: 8.0 mg

This recipe is an excellent source of protein, niacin, vitamin B$_6$, vitamin B$_{12}$, iron, selenium, and zinc, and a good source of fiber.

1. Heat oven to 375°F. Heat oil in large nonstick skillet over medium heat. Add shallots, garlic, and thyme; cook and stir 3 to 4 minutes or until shallots are tender. Add mushrooms; cook 3 minutes, stirring frequently. Stir in sun-dried tomatoes and wine; cook 4 to 5 minutes or until mushrooms and tomatoes are tender, stirring frequently. Stir in shredded beef pot roast, reserved cooking liquid, ½ cup basil, ½ teaspoon salt, and ¼ teaspoon pepper; cook and stir until heated through. Remove from heat. Set aside.

2. Whisk evaporated milk, egg substitute, remaining ½ teaspoon salt, and remaining ¼ teaspoon pepper in medium bowl. Set aside.

3. Spray 11¾ × 7½-inch glass baking dish with nonstick cooking spray. Layer half of the bread cubes, beef mixture, and ½ cup cheese in dish. Top with remaining bread cubes and ½ cup cheese. Pour milk mixture evenly over top. Cover with aluminum foil sprayed with nonstick cooking spray.

4. Bake in 375°F oven 25 minutes. Remove foil. Bake, uncovered, 10 minutes or until top is lightly browned. Garnish with thinly sliced basil, if desired. Season with salt, as desired.

COOK'S TIPS
- To easily cut sun-dried tomatoes, use kitchen scissors instead of a knife.
- To release the flavorful oils in dried herbs, crush them between your fingers when adding to a recipe.
- Serve with a side of oven-baked asparagus to complement the umami flavor in this dish.

Wine Country Meatloaf with Sun-Dried Tomatoes, Basil, and Parmesan

Total preparation and
cooking time: 1¾ hours
Makes 6 servings.

• • • • •
NOTE

Certain ingredients often used in meat loaf, such as onions, celery, and bell peppers, may cause ground beef to remain pink even if a 160°F internal temperature has been reached. Always verify the internal temperature with a meat thermometer or instant-read thermometer to be certain it reaches 160°F.

Nutrition information per serving

Calories: 228
Fat: 8 g
    Saturated fat: 4 g
    Monounsaturated fat: 3 g
Cholesterol: 100 mg
Sodium: 600 mg
Carbohydrate: 11 g
Fiber: 1.0 g
Protein: 27 g
Niacin: 5.5 mg
Vitamin B$_6$: 0.4 mg
Vitamin B$_{12}$: 2.3 mcg
Iron: 3.5 mg
Selenium: 24.4 mcg
Zinc: 6.3 mg

This recipe is an excellent source of protein, niacin, vitamin B$_6$, vitamin B$_{12}$, selenium, and zinc, and a good source of iron.

Sun-dried tomatoes, fresh basil, Parmesan cheese, and a wine glaze elevate this meatloaf to gourmet status.

About 1 cup boiling water
¼ cup sun-dried tomatoes, not packed in oil
1½ pounds ground beef (95% lean)
1 cup soft bread crumbs
½ cup finely chopped onion
⅓ cup ketchup
¼ cup shredded Parmesan cheese
¼ cup loosely packed chopped fresh basil
1 egg, slightly beaten
1 tablespoon minced garlic
½ teaspoon salt
¼ teaspoon pepper
2 tablespoons Cabernet or other dry red wine
2 tablespoons ketchup
2 tablespoons shredded Parmesan cheese
Salt and pepper, as desired

1. Heat oven to 350°F. Pour enough boiling water over sun-dried tomatoes in small bowl just to cover; let stand 10 minutes or until tomatoes are softened. Drain well. Finely chop tomatoes.

2. Combine ground beef, tomatoes, bread crumbs, onion, ⅓ cup ketchup, ¼ cup cheese, basil, egg, garlic, salt, and pepper in large bowl, mixing lightly but thoroughly.

3. Spray rack of broiler pan with nonstick cooking spray. Shape beef mixture into 8 × 4½-inch loaf; place on rack. Bake in 350°F oven 50 minutes.

4. Meanwhile, combine wine and 2 tablespoons ketchup. Generously brush meatloaf with wine mixture. Continue baking 15 to 20 minutes to medium (160°F) doneness, until no longer pink in center and juices show no pink color. Remove from oven. Sprinkle with 2 tablespoons cheese; tent loosely with aluminum foil.

5. Let stand 5 minutes before cutting. Cut into 1-inch-thick slices. Season with salt and pepper, as desired.

Mole Beef

Total preparation and cooking time: 3¾ hours
Makes 8 servings.

Experience the flavor of old-time Mexico. Mole sauce is a well known sauce that has unsweetened chocolate added for richness.

2	teaspoons vegetable oil
1	boneless beef brisket, flat cut (about 2½ to 3½ pounds)
1	cup chopped onion
2	teaspoons minced garlic
½	cup water

MOLE SAUCE

2	dried ancho chiles
1½	cups boiling water
⅓	cup raisins
1	cup chopped onion
1	can (14½ ounces) diced tomatoes, drained
1	corn tortilla, torn into pieces
¼	cup slivered almonds
½	teaspoon ground cinnamon
½	teaspoon ground allspice
2	tablespoons unsweetened cocoa powder
1	tablespoon packed brown sugar
½	teaspoon salt
½	teaspoon dark sesame oil

Salt and pepper, as desired

Nutrition information per serving

Calories: 277
Fat: 9 g
    Saturated fat: 2 g
    Monounsaturated fat: 4 g
Cholesterol: 49 mg
Sodium: 268 mg
Carbohydrate: 19 g
Fiber: 3.7 g
Protein: 31 g
Niacin: 4.7 mg
Vitamin B_6: 0.5 mg
Vitamin B_{12}: 2.1 mcg
Iron: 3.6 mg
Selenium: 29.9 mcg
Zinc: 7.2 mg

This recipe is an excellent source of protein, niacin, vitamin B_6, vitamin B_{12}, iron, selenium, and zinc, and a good source of fiber.

1. Heat vegetable oil in stockpot over medium heat until hot. Place beef brisket in stockpot; brown evenly. Remove brisket; set aside. Pour off all but 1 teaspoon drippings, if necessary.

2. Add onion and garlic to stockpot; cook and stir 3 to 5 minutes or until onion is tender. Stir in water. Return brisket, fat side up, to

COOK'S TIPS

- If brisket is too large to brown in stockpot, heat 1½ teaspoons oil in large nonstick skillet over medium heat until hot. Place brisket in skillet; brown evenly. Meanwhile, heat remaining ½ teaspoon oil in stockpot. Add onions and garlic; cook as directed above. Place brisket, fat side up, over onion mixture. Proceed as directed.
- When handling chiles, wear clean latex or rubber gloves to protect your hands from the burning oils. Avoid touching your eyes, nose, or mouth.

stockpot; bring to a boil. Reduce heat; cover tightly and simmer 2½ to 3 hours or until brisket is fork-tender.

3. To make Mole Sauce, remove and discard stems and seeds from chiles. Pour boiling water over chiles and raisins in small bowl; let stand 30 minutes or until chiles are softened. Drain well.

4. Place chiles, raisins, onion, tomatoes, tortilla, almonds, cinnamon, and allspice in food processor bowl or blender. Cover; process until smooth, stopping and scraping side of container as needed. Set aside.

5. Remove brisket; keep warm. Skim fat from cooking liquid; strain out and discard solids. Measure 1½ cups cooking liquid and return to stockpot; stir in chile mixture, cocoa powder, brown sugar, and salt. Bring to a boil; reduce heat and simmer 5 to 7 minutes or until heated through and slightly thickened, stirring occasionally. Remove from heat. Stir in sesame oil.

6. Carve brisket diagonally across the grain into thin slices; season with salt and pepper, as desired. Serve with Mole Sauce.

COOK'S TIP
This recipe makes a great base for beef tacos. Shred brisket and serve with Mole Sauce in corn tortillas and your favorite toppings.

Curry Beef and Aromatic Rice

Once considered exotic, coconut milk and Thai red curry paste are now sold in most supermarkets.

1   pound boneless beef top sirloin steak, cut ¾ inch thick
2   tablespoons soy sauce
2   teaspoons minced garlic
1   can (13½ to 14 ounces) light coconut milk
1 to 2 teaspoons Thai red curry paste
     Fruit and Almond Basmati Rice (page 19)
1   teaspoon vegetable oil
8   ounces fresh green beans, trimmed
¼   cup chopped fresh basil
1   tablespoon minced fresh lemon grass
¼   teaspoon salt
     Chopped fresh basil (optional)

1. Cut beef steak lengthwise in half, then crosswise into ¼-inch strips. Combine soy sauce and garlic in medium bowl. Add beef; toss. Set aside.

2. Whisk coconut milk and curry paste in small bowl until well blended; set aside.

3. Prepare Fruit and Almond Basmati Rice.

4. Meanwhile, heat oil in large nonstick skillet over medium-high heat until hot. Add half of the beef; stir-fry 1 to 2 minutes or until outside surface of beef is no longer pink. Remove from skillet. Repeat with remaining beef. Remove from skillet; keep warm.

5. In same skillet, bring coconut milk mixture to a boil. Reduce heat; simmer 5 minutes, stirring occasionally. Add green beans, basil, lemon grass, and salt; bring to a boil. Reduce heat; simmer 11 to 13 minutes or until green beans are crisp-tender, stirring occasionally.

6. Return beef to skillet; cook and stir until heated through. Serve over rice. Garnish with basil, if desired.

COOK'S TIP
Thai red curry paste is a concentrated red chile seasoning with a hot, sweet flavor. Adjust the amount added to a dish to your desired level of spicy heat.

Total preparation and cooking time: 1 hour
Makes 4 servings.

COOK'S TIP
Eight ounces haricots verts may be substituted for regular green beans. Reduce cooking time to 8 to 10 minutes. Haricots verts (the French term for green beans) are young, slender green beans with tender pods. They are available in bulk or packages in the produce department of many large supermarkets.

Nutrition information per serving

Calories: 531
Fat: 15 g
    Saturated fat: 7 g
    Monounsaturated fat: 4 g
Cholesterol: 50 mg
Sodium: 710 mg
Carbohydrate: 69 g
Fiber: 5.7 g
Protein: 34 g
Niacin: 9.8 mg
Vitamin B_6: 0.6 mg
Vitamin B_{12}: 1.4 mcg
Iron: 5.0 mg
Selenium: 31.7 mcg
Zinc: 5.2 mg

This recipe is an excellent source of fiber, protein, niacin, vitamin B_6, vitamin B_{12}, iron, selenium, and zinc.

Beef Fried Rice

Total preparation and
   cooking time: 40 minutes
Makes 4 servings.

Jump-start the preparation of this dish by using leftover cooked rice.

1	pound boneless beef top sirloin steak, cut ¾ inch thick
5	tablespoons soy sauce, divided
1	tablespoon dark sesame oil
1	tablespoon minced fresh ginger
1½	teaspoons minced garlic
½	teaspoon black pepper
1	teaspoon vegetable oil
½	cup chopped red bell pepper
½	cup chopped green onions
½	cup frozen peas, defrosted
1	egg, slightly beaten
3	cups cooked brown rice, prepared without butter or salt
2	tablespoons finely chopped peanuts (optional)

1. Cut beef steak lengthwise in half, then crosswise into ¼-inch-thick strips. Combine 2 tablespoons soy sauce, sesame oil, ginger, garlic, and black pepper in medium bowl. Add beef; toss.

2. Heat vegetable oil in large nonstick skillet over medium-high heat until hot. Add half of the beef; stir-fry 1 to 2 minutes or until outside surface of beef is no longer pink. Remove from skillet. Repeat with remaining beef. Remove from skillet; keep warm.

3. In same skillet, stir-fry bell pepper, green onions, and peas about 1 minute. Add egg; cook and stir about 30 seconds or until scrambled. Return beef to skillet. Carefully stir in rice and remaining 3 tablespoons soy sauce; cook 2 minutes or until heated through, stirring occasionally. Sprinkle with peanuts, if desired.

BEEF SMARTS

In addition to calcium, protein may help to build bone strength. Recent research has suggested that people eating an adequate amount of high-quality protein have stronger bones.

**Nutrition information
per serving**

Calories: 416
Fat: 12 g
   Saturated fat: 3 g
   Monounsaturated fat: 5 g
Cholesterol: 103 mg
Sodium: 1,017 mg
Carbohydrate: 40 g
Fiber: 4.4 g
Protein: 34 g
Niacin: 10.4 mg
Vitamin B_6: 0.9 mg
Vitamin B_{12}: 1.6 mcg
Iron: 3.0 mg
Selenium: 50.3 mcg
Zinc: 6.1 mg

This recipe is an excellent source of protein, niacin, vitamin B_6, vitamin B_{12}, selenium, and zinc, and a good source of fiber and iron.

Basic Beef Meatballs

Baked on a rack, these lean meatballs are versatile and easy to make. Add a simple sauce and serve with pasta or tuck into sandwich rolls.

Total preparation and cooking time: 35 minutes
Makes 4 servings.

1	pound ground beef (95% lean)
½	cup soft bread crumbs
2	egg whites, slightly beaten
2	tablespoons finely chopped onion
1	teaspoon minced garlic
½	teaspoon salt
⅛	teaspoon pepper

1. Heat oven to 400°F. Combine all ingredients in large bowl, mixing lightly but thoroughly. Shape into twelve 2-inch meatballs. Place on rack in broiler pan. Bake in 400°F oven about 17 to 19 minutes to medium (160°F) doneness, until no longer pink in center and juices show no pink color.

COOK'S TIPS

- To easily shape meatballs, pat ground beef mixture into 1¼-inch-thick rectangle on waxed or parchment paper and cut into twelve 3 × 4 squares; form each square into a meatball.
- For easy cleanup, line bottom of broiler pan (not rack) with aluminum foil before baking meatballs.

Nutrition information per serving

Calories: 172
Fat: 6 g
   Saturated fat: 3 g
   Monounsaturated fat: 2 g
Cholesterol: 65 mg
Sodium: 412 mg
Carbohydrate: 4 g
Fiber: 0.2 g
Protein: 25 g
Niacin: 5.3 mg
Vitamin B_6: 0.4 mg
Vitamin B_{12}: 2.1 mcg
Iron: 2.7 mg
Selenium: 22.9 mcg
Zinc: 5.5 mg

This recipe is an excellent source of protein, niacin, vitamin B_6, vitamin B_{12}, selenium, and zinc, and a good source of iron.

Ratatouille Meatball Pasta

Total preparation and
  cooking time: 1½ hours
Makes 4 servings.

*Ratatouille is a classic vegetable dish made with eggplant, tomatoes,
bell peppers, garlic, and herbs.*

1	medium eggplant, cut into ½-inch pieces
1	large yellow bell pepper, cut into ½-inch pieces
1	cup coarsely chopped onion
2	cloves garlic, minced
1	tablespoon olive oil
½	teaspoon dried thyme leaves, crushed
¼	teaspoon salt
⅛	teaspoon black pepper
2	cups coarsely chopped seeded plum tomatoes
	Basic Beef Meatballs (page 151)
3	tablespoons chopped fresh basil
3	cups hot cooked penne pasta
2	tablespoons shredded reduced-fat mozzarella cheese
	Chopped fresh basil (optional)

1. Heat oven to 400°F. Spray metal baking sheet with nonstick cooking spray. Combine eggplant, bell pepper, onion, garlic, oil, thyme, salt, and black pepper in large bowl. Arrange in single layer on baking sheet. Roast in 400°F oven 20 minutes. Add tomatoes and toss to combine; continue roasting 10 to 15 minutes or until vegetables are tender. Remove from oven; keep warm.

2. Meanwhile, prepare Basic Beef Meatballs. Place on rack in broiler pan. Bake in 400°F oven 17 to 19 minutes to medium (160°F) doneness, until no longer pink in center and juices show no pink color.

3. Stir 3 tablespoons basil into vegetable mixture; season with salt and pepper, as desired. Toss with pasta and meatballs in shallow serving bowl. Sprinkle with cheese. Garnish with basil, if desired.

**Nutrition information
per serving**

Calories: 418
Fat: 11 g
  Saturated fat: 4 g
  Monounsaturated fat: 5 g
Cholesterol: 66 mg
Sodium: 591 mg
Carbohydrate: 47 g
Fiber: 5.5 g
Protein: 33 g
Niacin: 8.3 mg
Vitamin B_6: 0.7 mg
Vitamin B_{12}: 2.1 mcg
Iron: 4.9 mg
Selenium: 44.8 mcg
Zinc: 6.5 mg

**This recipe is an excellent
source of fiber, protein,
niacin, vitamin B_6, vitamin
B_{12}, iron, selenium, and zinc.**

Beefy Mexican Lasagna

Try this Mexican version for a fun twist on an all-time favorite!

1½ pounds ground beef (95% lean)
2   cans (10 ounces each) mild enchilada sauce
1   can (15 ounces) black beans, rinsed, drained
1½ cups frozen corn
1   teaspoon ground cumin
9   corn tortillas
1½ cups shredded Mexican cheese blend, divided
    Crunchy Tortilla Strips (optional) (page 61)
½   cup chopped tomato
2   tablespoons chopped fresh cilantro

HEALTHY LIVING **TIP**

Learn to trade off fat grams and calories by balancing your food choices. This means enjoying foods with less fat and calories, then "spending" your savings on a higher-fat food, such as ice cream. If you're trying to lose weight, "bank" your savings instead.

1. Heat oven to 350°F. Brown ground beef in large nonstick skillet over medium heat 8 to 10 minutes or until beef is no longer pink, breaking up into ¾-inch crumbles. Pour off drippings. Stir in 1 can enchilada sauce, black beans, corn, and cumin; bring to a boil. Reduce heat; simmer 5 minutes, stirring occasionally.

2. Spray 11¾ × 7½-inch glass baking dish with nonstick cooking spray. Arrange 3 tortillas in dish, cutting 1 as needed to cover bottom. Spread ¼ cup remaining enchilada sauce over tortillas; cover with one-third of the beef mixture, then one-third of the cheese. Repeat layers twice, omitting final cheese layer. Pour remaining enchilada sauce over top.

3. Cover with aluminum foil. Bake in 350°F oven 30 minutes. Remove foil; sprinkle with remaining ½ cup cheese. Bake, uncovered, 5 minutes or until cheese is melted. Top with tortilla strips, if desired, tomato, and cilantro.

Nutrition information per serving

Calories: 349
Fat: 13 g
    Saturated fat: 7 g
    Monounsaturated fat: 2 g
Cholesterol: 76 mg
Sodium: 441 mg
Carbohydrate: 29 g
Fiber: 5.4 g
Protein: 29 g
Niacin: 5.7 mg
Vitamin B_6: 0.4 mg
Vitamin B_{12}: 1.7 mcg
Iron: 3.8 mg
Selenium: 15.4 mcg
Zinc: 5.0 mg

This recipe is an excellent source of fiber, protein, niacin, vitamin B_6, vitamin B_{12}, iron, selenium, and zinc.

COOK'S TIP
Lasagna may be made up to 24 hours ahead through step 2; refrigerate, covered. Increase baking time to 45 minutes.

Bistro-Style Steak and Potatoes

Bistro cooking is irresistibly simple, and this dish brings bistro fare right to your own home.

Total preparation and cooking time: 30 minutes
Makes 4 servings.

1	pound boneless beef top sirloin steak, cut ¾ inch thick
2	tablespoons chopped fresh Italian parsley
2	cloves garlic, minced
½	teaspoon pepper
1	large red onion
1	tablespoon olive oil
	Salt, as desired
¼	cup dry red wine
1½	pounds new potatoes, steamed

1. Cut steak lengthwise in half and then crosswise into ½-inch-thick strips. Combine beef, parsley, garlic, and pepper in medium bowl; toss to coat. Set aside.

2. Cut onion into ¼-inch-thick slices; separate into rings. Heat oil in large nonstick skillet over medium-high heat until hot. Add onion; cook and stir 3 to 5 minutes or until crisp-tender. Remove to serving platter; keep warm.

3. In same skillet, add half of the beef and stir-fry 1 to 2 minutes or until outside surface of beef is no longer pink. Remove from skillet; place beef on top of onion; keep warm. Repeat with remaining beef. Season with salt, as desired.

4. Add wine to skillet; cook and stir 1 to 2 minutes or until browned bits attached to skillet are dissolved and liquid thickens slightly. Pour sauce over beef and onions. Serve with potatoes.

COOK'S TIP

To steam new potatoes, place steamer basket in large saucepan with ½ cup water (water should not touch bottom of basket). Place 10 to 12 new potatoes (about 1½ pounds) in basket. Cover tightly and heat to boiling; reduce heat. Steam 18 to 22 minutes or until tender.

Nutrition information per serving

Calories: 318
Fat: 8 g
  Saturated fat: 2 g
  Monounsaturated fat: 4 g
Cholesterol: 50 mg
Sodium: 63 mg
Carbohydrate: 26 g
Fiber: 3.9 g
Protein: 31 g
Niacin: 9.2 mg
Vitamin B_6: 0.6 mg
Vitamin B_{12}: 1.4 mcg
Iron: 2.9 mg
Selenium: 31.9 mcg
Zinc: 5.7 mg

This recipe is an excellent source of protein, niacin, vitamin B_6, vitamin B_{12}, selenium, and zinc, and a good source of fiber and iron.

Beef and Couscous with Butternut Squash

Total preparation and
cooking time: 40 minutes
Makes 4 servings.

**HEALTHY
LIVING** TIP

Watching your sodium?
One strategy is to "get
fresh." Fresh and
unprocessed foods are
naturally low in sodium.

*Butternut squash, goat cheese, almonds, and couscous turn a ground
beef skillet dish into a special meal.*

1	pound ground beef (95% lean)
½	cup chopped onion
2	teaspoons minced garlic
2	cups cubed butternut squash (¾ inch)
1	can (14½ ounces) diced tomatoes, undrained
¼	cup water
1½	teaspoons dried oregano leaves, crushed
¾	teaspoon lemon pepper
½	teaspoon salt
2	cups hot cooked couscous, prepared without oil or salt
¼	cup slivered almonds, toasted
½	cup crumbled goat cheese
2	tablespoons chopped fresh basil

1. Brown ground beef with onion and garlic in large nonstick skillet over medium heat 8 to 10 minutes or until beef is no longer pink, breaking beef up into ¾-inch crumbles. Pour off drippings.

2. Stir in squash, tomatoes, water, oregano, lemon pepper, and salt; bring to a boil. Reduce heat; cover and simmer 8 to 10 minutes or until squash is tender. Stir in couscous and almonds; cook until heated through. Top with cheese and basil.

**Nutrition information
per serving**

Calories: 403
Fat: 13 g
    Saturated fat: 5 g
    Monounsaturated fat: 6 g
Cholesterol: 82 mg
Sodium: 615 mg
Carbohydrate: 38 g
Fiber: 7.0 g
Protein: 34 g
Niacin: 8.3 mg
Vitamin B_6: 0.6 mg
Vitamin B_{12}: 2.3 mcg
Iron: 4.9 mg
Selenium: 40.9 mcg
Zinc: 6.8 mg

**This recipe is an excellent
source of fiber, protein,
niacin, vitamin B_6, vitamin
B_{12}, iron, selenium, and
zinc.**

6

BEEF SOUPS, STEWS, AND CHILIS

Bistro Beef Stew

The tantalizing aroma of this simmering beef stew is sure to beckon everyone to the table on chilly evenings.

¼ cup all-purpose flour
½ teaspoon pepper
2 pounds boneless beef bottom round roast or boneless beef chuck shoulder pot roast, cut into 1-inch pieces
5 teaspoons olive oil, divided
1 teaspoon salt
2 medium onions, chopped
6 cloves garlic, minced
2 teaspoons dried thyme leaves, crushed
1 cup dry red wine
1 can (14 to 14½ ounces) ready-to-serve beef broth
12 ounces assorted small whole mushrooms (such as cremini, shiitake, and button)
2 cups packaged baby carrots
1 cup frozen peas

1. Combine flour and pepper. Lightly coat beef with flour mixture; reserve any remaining flour mixture.

2. Heat 2 teaspoons oil in stockpot over medium heat until hot. Brown half of the beef; remove from stockpot. Repeat with 1 teaspoon oil and remaining beef. Remove beef from stockpot; season with salt.

3. Heat remaining 2 teaspoons oil in stockpot. Add onions, garlic, and thyme; cook and stir 3 to 5 minutes. Add wine; increase heat to medium-high. Cook and stir 1 to 2 minutes or until browned bits attached to stockpot are dissolved. Stir in broth and reserved flour mixture. Return beef to stockpot. Stir in mushrooms; bring to a boil. Reduce heat; cover tightly and simmer 1¼ hours. Add carrots to stockpot; continue simmering, covered, 30 minutes or until beef and carrots are fork-tender. Stir in peas; simmer 5 minutes, or until tender. Serve.

Total preparation and cooking time: 2 to 2¼ hours

Makes 6 servings.

Nutrition information per serving

Calories: 281
Fat: 9 g
  Saturated fat: 2 g
  Monounsaturated fat: 5 g
Cholesterol: 64 mg
Sodium: 711 mg
Carbohydrate: 19 g
Fiber: 3.3 g
Protein: 29 g
Niacin: 7.2 mg
Vitamin B_6: 0.5 mg
Vitamin B_{12}: 1.4 mcg
Iron: 3.5 mg
Selenium: 44.5 mcg
Zinc: 5.1 mg

This recipe is an excellent source of protein, niacin, vitamin B_6, vitamin B_{12}, selenium, and zinc, and a good source of fiber and iron.

Easy Beef Chili

Total preparation and
  cooking time: 25 minutes
Makes 4 servings.

*This fast-fixing chili is great for a quick weeknight supper or for a tail-
gate party before the big game.*

1	pound ground beef (95% lean)
¼	teaspoon salt
¼	teaspoon pepper
1	can (15½ ounces) chili beans in chili sauce, undrained
1	can (14½ ounces) chili-style chunky tomatoes, undrained
1	cup frozen corn
2	tablespoons chopped fresh cilantro

HEALTHY LIVING TIP

Calories *rule* when it comes to managing your weight. So balance what you eat with the physical activity you do to help maintain your weight.

1. Brown ground beef in large nonstick skillet over medium heat 8 to 10 minutes or until beef is no longer pink, breaking up into ¾-inch crumbles. Pour off drippings; season with salt and pepper.

2. Stir in beans, tomatoes, and corn; bring to a boil. Reduce heat; cover and simmer 10 minutes. Sprinkle with cilantro before serving.

> **COOK'S TIP**
> The recipe may be doubled using a large stockpot. For extra flavor, prepare recipe ahead of time, leaving out the cilantro until ready to serve. Refrigerate overnight, allowing flavors to blend and intensify. Reheat before serving.

**Nutrition information
per serving**

Calories: 323
Fat: 8 g
　Saturated fat: 3 g
　Monounsaturated fat: 3 g
Cholesterol: 76 mg
Sodium: 1,252 mg
Carbohydrate: 36 g
Fiber: 7.9 g
Protein: 33 g
Niacin: 6.9 mg
Vitamin B_6: 0.4 mg
Vitamin B_{12}: 2.3 mcg
Iron: 4.6 mg
Selenium: 18.3 mcg
Zinc: 6.3 mg

**This recipe is an excellent
source of fiber, protein,
niacin, vitamin B_6, vitamin
B_{12}, iron, selenium, and zinc.**

Thai Curry Beef Stew

Infused with spices and other aromatic ingredients, this is no ordinary beef stew. Serve as a cold-weather alternative to stir-fries when your taste buds crave Asian flavors.

Total preparation and cooking time: 2½ hours
Makes 6 servings.

2	teaspoons vegetable oil, divided
2	pounds beef bottom round roast, cut into 1-inch pieces
1	teaspoon salt, divided
½	teaspoon ground black pepper
1	large onion, chopped
2	teaspoons minced garlic
1 to 2	teaspoons Thai red curry paste
½	teaspoon ground cinnamon
2	whole cloves
1	bay leaf
2	cans (14½ ounces each) diced tomatoes, drained
1	can (13½ to 14 ounces) lite coconut milk
3	tablespoons prepared mango chutney
3	tablespoons fresh lemon juice
2	tablespoons minced fresh ginger
1½	cups packaged baby carrots
1	medium red bell pepper, cut into 1-inch pieces
1	package (6 to 8 ounces) fresh sugar snap peas
3	cups hot cooked jasmine rice, prepared without butter or salt

1. Heat 1 teaspoon oil in stockpot over medium heat until hot. Brown half of the beef; remove from stockpot. Repeat with remaining beef; pour off drippings. Remove beef from stockpot; season with ½ teaspoon salt and black pepper.

2. Heat remaining 1 teaspoon oil in stockpot. Add onion and garlic; cook and stir 3 to 5 minutes or until onion is tender. Return beef to stockpot. Add curry paste, cinnamon, cloves, and bay leaf; cook and stir 1 minute. Stir in tomatoes, coconut milk, chutney, lemon juice, and ginger; bring to a boil. Reduce heat; cover tightly and simmer 1¼ hours.

3. Add carrots to stockpot; continue simmering, covered, 30 to 45 minutes or until beef and carrots are fork-tender. Stir in bell pepper and peas; cook, uncovered, 5 to 6 minutes or until bell pepper and peas are crisp-tender, stirring occasionally. Remove and discard bay leaf and cloves. Stir in remaining ½ teaspoon salt.

4. Serve stew in bowls with rice.

COOK'S TIPS:

- Thai red curry paste is a concentrated red chile seasoning with a hot, sweet flavor. Adjust the amount added to a dish to control the level of spicy heat.
- Thai red curry paste, lite coconut milk, and mango chutney can be found at your local grocer in the Asian market section.

Nutrition information per serving

Calories: 435
Fat: 12 g
   Saturated fat: 6 g
   Monounsaturated fat: 3 g
Cholesterol: 56 mg
Sodium: 645 mg
Carbohydrate: 44 g
Fiber: 5.0 g
Protein: 34 g
Niacin: 5.7 mg
Vitamin B_6: 0.5 mg
Vitamin B_{12}: 2.1 mcg
Iron: 4.7 mg
Selenium: 36.4 mcg
Zinc: 7.3 mg

This recipe is an excellent source of fiber, protein, niacin, vitamin B_6, vitamin B_{12}, iron, selenium, and zinc.

Pho Beef Noodle Soup

Total preparation and
cooking time: 50 minutes
Makes 4 servings.

Made with very thinly sliced beef and rice noodles, this well-seasoned soup is popular throughout Vietnam.

CHEF RICHARD'S TIP

Ask a butcher to slice boneless beef eye round steak paper-thin (no more than 1/16 inch thick). Boneless beef round tip steaks, cut 1/8 inch thick, may be substituted for beef eye round steak. Stack round tip steaks and cut crosswise into 2-inch-wide strips.

4	cups water
4	cups ready-to-serve beef broth
1	onion, very thinly sliced
3	cloves garlic
3	tablespoons fish sauce
2	tablespoons rice vinegar
1	tablespoon minced fresh ginger
1	star anise
1/2	teaspoon salt
1/4	teaspoon pepper
2	cups hot cooked rice noodles
1	pound boneless beef eye round steak, very thinly sliced
2	cups fresh bean sprouts
1/2	cup loosely packed sliced fresh basil
1/3	cup chopped fresh cilantro
1/4	cup minced green onions
4	lime wedges
1	tablespoon Asian hot chili sauce or Sriracha sauce

1. Combine water, broth, onion, garlic, fish sauce, vinegar, ginger, and star anise in stockpot; bring to a boil. Reduce heat; simmer 30 minutes.

2. Strain out and discard solids; return broth mixture to stockpot. Season with salt and pepper; bring to a boil. Add noodles; boil 1 minute. Separate beef steak slices; add to boiling soup. Stir once; immediately remove from heat. Cover; let stand 5 minutes.

3. Evenly divide noodles and beef among 4 large soup bowls; top evenly with broth mixture, bean sprouts, basil, cilantro, and green onions. Garnish with lime wedges and hot sauce.

Nutrition information per serving

Calories: 286
Fat: 5 g
    Saturated fat: 2 g
    Monounsaturated fat: 2 g
Cholesterol: 53 mg
Sodium: 2,295 mg
Carbohydrate: 29 g
Fiber: 2.1 g
Protein: 30 g
Niacin: 5.5 mg
Vitamin B$_6$: 0.5 mg
Vitamin B$_{12}$: 1.5 mcg
Iron: 3.8 mg
Selenium: 32.0 mcg
Zinc: 4.8 mg

This recipe is an excellent source of protein, niacin, vitamin B$_6$, vitamin B$_{12}$, iron, selenium, and zinc.

COOK'S TIPS

- Prepare rice noodles according to package directions using soaking or stir-fry method.
- Fish sauce is a popular condiment and flavoring used in dishes throughout Southeast Asia. This strong-flavored liquid made from salted, fermented fish is found in the Asian section of most supermarkets.

Spring Vegetable and Beaujolais Beef Stew

Total preparation and cooking time: 2½ hours
Makes 6 servings.

The dark brown crust that forms on the bottom of the pot and dissolves when liquid is added gives the stew a rich flavor.

⅓	cup all-purpose flour
¾	teaspoon salt
½	teaspoon pepper
2	pounds boneless beef chuck shoulder pot roast, cut into 1-inch pieces
4	teaspoons olive oil, divided
1	large leek, cleaned, white and light green parts only, cut in half lengthwise
1	tablespoon minced garlic
2	cups Beaujolais or other dry red wine
2	cans (14 to 14½ ounces each) ready-to-serve beef broth
1	tablespoon dried marjoram leaves, crushed
1	pound fingerling potatoes, cut into quarters
12	ounces asparagus, cut into 1½- to 2-inch pieces
1½	cups frozen lima beans, defrosted
½	cup chopped fresh chives
1	tablespoon freshly grated lemon peel (optional)

1. Combine flour, salt, and pepper. Reserve 1 tablespoon flour mixture. Lightly coat beef with remaining flour mixture.

2. Heat 2 teaspoons oil in stockpot over medium heat until hot. Brown half of the beef; remove from stockpot. Repeat with remaining 2 teaspoons oil and remaining beef. Remove beef from stockpot.

3. Meanwhile, cut leek crosswise into thin slices. Add leek and garlic to stockpot; cook and stir 2 to 3 minutes or until leek begins to soften. Add wine; increase heat to medium-high. Cook and stir 1

COOK'S TIP

Small new potatoes can be substituted for fingerling potatoes. Cut new potatoes in half, instead of quarters, prior to cooking.

Nutrition information per serving

Calories: 392
Fat: 10 g
    Saturated fat: 2 g
    Monounsaturated fat: 5 g
Cholesterol: 80 mg
Sodium: 599 mg
Carbohydrate: 36 g
Fiber: 6.3 g
Protein: 33 g
Niacin: 4.6 mg
Vitamin B_6: 0.6 mg
Vitamin B_{12}: 2.5 mcg
Iron: 6.4 mg
Selenium: 29.4 mcg
Zinc: 7.4 mg

This recipe is an excellent source of fiber, protein, niacin, vitamin B_6, vitamin B_{12}, iron, selenium, and zinc.

COOK'S TIPS

- To easily coat beef pieces, combine flour mixture in food-safe plastic bag. Add beef, in batches, and shake to coat with flour mixture.
- During browning, a crusty layer of flour, oil, and drippings builds up on the bottom of the pot. This layer—which is normal and desirable—turns a deep, dark brown, but should not burn. It dissolves when liquid is added.

to 2 minutes or until browned bits attached to stockpot are dissolved. Stir in broth, marjoram, and reserved flour mixture. Return beef to stockpot; bring to a boil. Reduce heat; cover tightly, and simmer $1\frac{1}{4}$ hours or until beef is fork-tender.

4. Add potatoes to stockpot; bring to a boil. Reduce heat; continue simmering, covered, 15 to 20 minutes or until potatoes are tender. Add asparagus and lima beans. Cook, uncovered, 8 to 10 minutes or until asparagus is crisp-tender. Remove from heat; stir in chives.

5. Garnish with lemon peel, if desired.

Fennel, Beef, and Bean Soup

Fennel is a fragrant vegetable that imparts a delicate flavor to this hearty soup.

Total preparation and cooking time: 2½ hours
Makes 6 servings.

3	pounds beef shank cross cuts, cut 1 inch thick
2	teaspoons olive oil, divided
1	large onion, chopped
1	tablespoon minced garlic
1½	teaspoons dried thyme leaves, crushed
3	cups water
1	can (14 to 14½ ounces) ready-to-serve beef broth
1½	teaspoons salt
½	teaspoon pepper
1	large fresh fennel bulb
2	cans (15 ounces each) cannellini beans, rinsed, drained
1	cup sliced carrots (¼ inch thick)
	Pepper, as desired

1. Cut beef from bones; reserve bones. Cut beef into ¾-inch pieces. Heat 1 teaspoon oil in stockpot over medium heat until hot. Brown half of the beef and bones; remove from stockpot. Repeat with remaining beef and bones; remove from stockpot. Set aside.

2. Heat remaining 1 teaspoon oil in same stockpot until hot. Add onion, garlic, and thyme to stockpot; cook and stir 3 to 5 minutes or until onion is tender. Return beef and bones to stockpot. Stir in water, broth, salt, and pepper; bring to a boil. Reduce heat; cover tightly and simmer 1½ to 1¾ hours or until beef is fork-tender.

3. Meanwhile, trim fennel bulb, removing and reserving fronds. Cut fennel bulb lengthwise in half; remove and discard core. Slice lengthwise into thin slices. Set aside.

4. Remove and discard bones from cooking liquid. Remove beef with slotted spoon; set aside. Skim fat from cooking liquid. Return beef to cooking liquid. Stir in fennel, beans, and carrots; bring to a boil. Reduce heat; cover and simmer 15 minutes or until vegetables are tender.

5. Garnish each serving with chopped fennel fronds and pepper, as desired.

COOK'S TIP

Choose clean, crisp fennel bulbs with no sign of browning. If the feathery dill-like fronds are still attached, they should look fresh and healthy with a rich, green color.

Nutrition information per serving

Calories: 334
Fat: 8 g
    Saturated fat: 2 g
    Monounsaturated fat: 4 g
Cholesterol: 66 mg
Sodium: 1,199 mg
Carbohydrate: 28 g
Fiber: 7.9 g
Protein: 36 g
Niacin: 5.5 mg
Vitamin B_6: 0.4 mg
Vitamin B_{12}: 3.2 mcg
Iron: 6.1 mg
Selenium: 26.1 mcg
Zinc: 9.1 mg

This recipe is an excellent source of fiber, protein, niacin, vitamin B_6, vitamin B_{12}, iron, selenium, and zinc.

Tomato-Basil Meatball Soup

Total preparation and
  cooking time: 40 minutes
Makes 4 servings.

*Take a break from traditional spaghetti and meatballs and serve this
satisfying Italian soup.*

Basic Beef Meatballs (page 151)
3 tablespoons finely chopped fresh parsley
2 teaspoons olive oil
½ cup finely chopped onion
2 cloves garlic, minced
2 cans (14 to 14½ ounces each) ready-to-serve beef broth
2 cans (14½ ounces each) Italian-style stewed tomatoes, undrained,
   coarsely chopped
1 cup uncooked rotini (spiral) pasta
¼ cup thinly sliced fresh basil
4 teaspoons grated or shredded Parmesan cheese (optional)

**HEALTHY
LIVING TIP**

Get your kids involved in
meal planning, shop-
ping, and cooking.
They'll learn some life
skills—and they'll be
more likely to eat what
they help to prepare.

1. Heat oven to 400°F. Prepare Basic Beef Meatballs, adding parsley
   with other ingredients. Shape into twenty-eight 1¼-inch meatballs. Place on rack in broiler pan. Bake in 400°F oven 13 to 15
   minutes to medium (160°F) doneness, until no longer pink in center and juices show no pink color. Set aside.

2. Meanwhile, heat oil in large saucepan over medium heat until hot.
   Add onion and garlic; cook and stir 3 to 5 minutes or until onion
   is tender. Add broth and tomatoes; bring to a boil. Stir in rotini.
   Reduce heat; cover and simmer 8 to 12 minutes or until pasta is
   just tender. Stir in meatballs and continue to cook until heated
   through.

3. Garnish each serving of soup with basil and cheese, if desired.

**Nutrition information
per serving**

Calories: 333
Fat: 9 g
   Saturated fat: 3 g
   Monounsaturated fat: 4 g
Cholesterol: 65 mg
Sodium: 1,423 mg
Carbohydrate: 34 g
Fiber: 4.6 g
Protein: 30 g
Niacin: 6.3 mg
Vitamin B_6: 0.4 mg
Vitamin B_{12}: 2.1 mcg
Iron: 4.4 mg
Selenium: 34.1 mcg
Zinc: 5.9 mg

**This recipe is an excellent
source of protein, niacin,
vitamin B_6, vitamin B_{12}, iron,
selenium, and zinc, and a
good source of fiber.**

COOK'S TIPS

- To coarsely chop stewed tomatoes, use kitchen scissors to snip them
  while in the can before adding to the recipe.
- To easily shape meatballs, pat ground beef mixture into 1¼-inch-thick
  rectangle on waxed or parchment paper and cut into 28 squares
  (7 × 4); form each square into a meatball.
- For easy cleanup, line bottom of broiler pan (not rack) with aluminum foil
  before baking meatballs.

Beef and Butternut Squash Soup with Chipotle Cream

Chipotle peppers are dried, smoked jalapeños. Swirled into sour cream, they add a spicy, smoky flavor accent to this delicious soup.

Total preparation and cooking time: 2½ hours

Makes 6 to 8 servings.

CHIPOTLE CREAM
⅓ cup reduced-fat dairy sour cream
1 to 1½ teaspoons minced chipotle peppers in adobo sauce

4 teaspoons olive oil, divided
2½ pounds beef bottom round roast, cut into ¾-inch pieces
1 teaspoon salt
¼ teaspoon black pepper
1 large onion, chopped
2 cloves garlic, minced
1 teaspoon dried thyme leaves, crushed
1 can (14 to 14½ ounces) ready-to-serve beef broth
1 large butternut squash (about 2¼ pounds)
Cooking spray
1 teaspoon ground cumin
Water, as desired

1. Combine Chipotle Cream ingredients in small bowl. Cover and refrigerate.

2. Heat oven to 400°F. Heat 1 teaspoon oil in stockpot over medium heat until hot. Brown one-third of the beef; remove from stockpot. Repeat twice with 2 teaspoons oil and remaining beef, removing beef from stockpot; season with salt and black pepper.

3. Heat remaining 1 teaspoon oil in stockpot. Add onion, garlic, and thyme; cook and stir 3 to 5 minutes or until onion is tender and lightly browned. Add broth; increase heat to medium-high. Cook and stir 1 to 2 minutes or until browned bits attached to stockpot are dissolved. Return beef to stockpot; bring to a boil. Reduce heat; cover tightly and simmer 1¼ hours.

4. Meanwhile, cut squash lengthwise in half. Scoop out and discard seeds from each half. Place squash, cut sides down, on metal baking sheet sprayed with nonstick cooking spray. Roast in 400°F oven 40 to 45 minutes or until very soft. Cool slightly. Scoop squash flesh into medium bowl; discard shells. Mash squash with back of spoon until almost smooth.

Nutrition information per serving

Calories: 286
Fat: 11 g
    Saturated fat: 4 g
    Monounsaturated fat: 5 g
Cholesterol: 63 mg
Sodium: 683 mg
Carbohydrate: 16 g
Fiber: 3.9 g
Protein: 31 g
Niacin: 5.3 mg
Vitamin B_6: 0.5 mg
Vitamin B_{12}: 2.1 mcg
Iron: 5.6 mg
Selenium: 31.0 mcg
Zinc: 7.0 mg

This recipe is an excellent source of protein, niacin, vitamin B_6, vitamin B_{12}, iron, selenium, and zinc, and a good source of fiber.

5. Stir squash and cumin into beef mixture; bring to a boil. Reduce heat; continue simmering, covered, 20 to 30 minutes or until beef is fork-tender. If necessary, thin soup with small amount of water for desired consistency.

6. Serve soup with Chipotle Cream.

COOK'S TIP
Two packages (12 ounces each) frozen butternut squash, defrosted, may be substituted for the roasted fresh butternut squash. However, the soup will have a more mild squash flavor.

Cajun Beef Fricassee

A fricassee is a chunky meat and vegetable stew from France. Crawfish, andouille sausage, and seasonings add Cajun flair to this spicy rendition.

Total preparation and cooking time: 2½ hours
Makes 6 servings.

2	teaspoons olive oil, divided
2	pounds beef bottom round roast, cut into 1-inch pieces
1	teaspoon salt
1	teaspoon black pepper
2	cups chopped onions
1	cup chopped red bell pepper
1½	tablespoons minced garlic
2	cans (14½ ounces each) stewed tomatoes, undrained
1	can (14 to 14½ ounces) ready-to-serve beef broth
1	tablespoon Cajun or Creole seasoning
1	tablespoon tomato paste
1	bay leaf
6	ounces andouille sausage, cut into ½-inch pieces
3	cups hot cooked basmati rice, prepared without butter or salt
4	ounces shrimp, peeled, deveined (50 to 60 count)
4	ounces crawfish tails

1. Heat 1 teaspoon oil in stockpot over medium heat until hot. Brown half of the beef; remove from stockpot. Repeat with remaining beef; pour off drippings, if necessary. Remove beef from stockpot; season with salt and black pepper.

2. Heat remaining 1 teaspoon oil in stockpot. Add onions, bell pepper, and garlic; cook and stir 4 to 5 minutes or until onions are tender. Return beef to stockpot. Stir in tomatoes, broth, Cajun seasoning, tomato paste, and bay leaf; bring to a boil. Reduce heat; cover tightly and simmer 1¾ to 2¼ hours or until beef is fork-tender. Remove and discard bay leaf.

3. Add sausage; continue simmering, uncovered, 8 to 10 minutes or until liquid is reduced to desired consistency. Stir in rice, shrimp, and crawfish; cook 3 to 4 minutes or until shrimp just turn opaque.

COOK'S TIP
Freeze leftover tomato paste in 1-tablespoon portions wrapped in plastic wrap and use as handy premeasured amounts to add to your favorite dishes.

COOK'S TIP
If using frozen shrimp or crawfish tails, defrost before adding to the stew.

CHEF RICHARD'S TIP
Fresh crabmeat may be substituted for crawfish. Add Tabasco sauce for an extra Cajun kick!

Nutrition information per serving

Calories: 400
Fat: 13 g
    Saturated fat: 5 g
    Monounsaturated fat: 4 g
Cholesterol: 127 mg
Sodium: 1,402 mg
Carbohydrate: 26 g
Fiber: 2.7 g
Protein: 43 g
Niacin: 5.4 mg
Vitamin B_6: 0.5 mg
Vitamin B_{12}: 2.7 mcg
Iron: 4.4 mg
Selenium: 43.9 mcg
Zinc: 7.4 mg

This recipe is an excellent source of protein, niacin, vitamin B_6, vitamin B_{12}, iron, selenium, and zinc, and a good source of fiber.

Indian Beef Stew

Aromatic spices of India and a creamy yogurt sauce lend an exotic flair to this enticing beef and vegetable stew.

Total preparation and cooking time: 2¾ hours
Makes 6 servings.

2   teaspoons olive oil, divided
2   pounds boneless beef bottom round roast, cut into 1-inch pieces
1   cup chopped onion
1   tablespoon minced garlic
1½ teaspoons curry powder
1   teaspoon cumin seeds
½   teaspoon ground ginger
½   teaspoon turmeric
2   cans (14 to 14½ ounces each) ready-to-serve beef broth
1   can (14½ ounces) diced tomatoes, undrained
1¼ cups uncooked yellow split peas, rinsed, picked over
¾   cup water
1   teaspoon salt
¼   teaspoon ground red pepper
1½ cups cauliflower florets, cut into bite-sized pieces
1   cup frozen peas

YOGURT SAUCE
¾   cup plain nonfat yogurt
1   tablespoon chopped fresh cilantro
½   teaspoon ground ginger
⅛   teaspoon ground red pepper

1. Heat 1 teaspoon oil in stockpot over medium heat until hot. Brown half of the beef; remove from stockpot. Repeat with remaining 1 teaspoon oil and remaining beef. Remove beef from stockpot.

2. Add onion, garlic, curry powder, cumin seeds, ginger, and turmeric to stockpot; cook and stir 3 to 5 minutes or until onion is tender. Stir in broth, tomatoes, split peas, water, salt, and red pepper. Return beef to stockpot; bring to a boil. Reduce heat; cover tightly and simmer 1¾ to 2¼ hours or until beef is fork-tender.

3. Meanwhile, combine Yogurt Sauce ingredients in small bowl. Cover and refrigerate.

4. Stir cauliflower and green peas into stew. Cook, covered, 5 to 7 minutes or until cauliflower is crisp-tender.

5. Serve stew with Yogurt Sauce.

COOK'S TIPS

- Before using dried legumes, including lentils and split peas, rinse them under cold water to remove surface dirt and pick through them to remove small stones or shriveled legumes.

- To save on prep time, look for packaged, precut cauliflower florets in the produce department of supermarkets.

Nutrition information per serving

Calories: 276
Fat: 7 g
    Saturated fat: 2 g
    Monounsaturated fat: 3 g
Cholesterol: 64 mg
Sodium: 789 mg
Carbohydrate: 23 g
Fiber: 7.1 g
Protein: 32 g
Niacin: 5.2 mg
Vitamin B$_6$: 0.5 mg
Vitamin B$_{12}$: 1.3 mcg
Iron: 3.9 mg
Selenium: 28.2 mcg
Zinc: 4.9 mg

This recipe is an excellent source of fiber, protein, niacin, vitamin B$_6$, vitamin B$_{12}$, iron, selenium, and zinc.

Southwest Beef Stew

Total preparation and
  cooking time: 3¼ hours
Makes 6 servings.

Topped with sour cream, cilantro, and crisp tortilla strips, this chunky stew is similar to a hearty "bowl of red."

3	teaspoons olive oil, divided
2	pounds boneless beef chuck shoulder steak, cut into 1-inch pieces
1	teaspoon salt
¾	teaspoon black pepper
2	medium red bell peppers, chopped
1	medium onion, chopped
1	medium leek, cleaned, white and light green parts only, chopped
2	large jalapeño peppers, seeded, finely chopped
2	tablespoons minced garlic
2	teaspoons sugar
¼	cup dried oregano leaves, crushed
2	tablespoons cornmeal
1	cup dry red wine
1	can (14½ ounces) diced tomatoes, undrained
1	can (14 to 14½ ounces) ready-to-serve beef broth
1	can (15 ounces) black beans, rinsed, drained
1	tablespoon fresh lime juice
	Salt and black pepper, as desired

TOPPINGS
Chopped green onions, chopped fresh cilantro, Crunchy Tortilla Strips (page 61), reduced-fat dairy sour cream (optional)

COOK'S TIP
When handling chiles, wear clean latex or rubber gloves to protect your hands from the burning oils. Avoid touching your eyes, nose, or mouth.

1. Heat 1 teaspoon oil in stockpot over medium heat until hot. Brown half of the beef; remove from stockpot. Repeat with remaining beef; pour off drippings, if necessary. Remove beef from stockpot; season with salt and black pepper.

2. Heat remaining 2 teaspoons oil in stockpot. Add bell peppers, onion, leek, jalapeños, garlic, and sugar; cook and stir 4 to 5 minutes or until vegetables are tender. Stir in oregano and cornmeal; cook 1 minute. Add wine; cook about 5 minutes or until reduced by half, stirring frequently. Return beef with juices to stockpot. Stir in tomatoes and broth; bring to a boil. Reduce heat; cover tightly and simmer 1¾ to 2¼ hours or until beef is fork-tender. Add beans; cook, uncovered, 8 minutes or until stew thickens. Stir in lime juice. Season with salt and black pepper, as desired.

3. Top each serving with green onions, cilantro, Crunchy Tortilla Strips, and sour cream, if desired.

Nutrition information per serving

Calories: 336
Fat: 9 g
  Saturated fat: 2 g
  Monounsaturated fat: 5 g
Cholesterol: 80 mg
Sodium: 982 mg
Carbohydrate: 27 g
Fiber: 8.1 g
Protein: 32 g
Niacin: 3.4 mg
Vitamin B_6: 0.4 mg
Vitamin B_{12}: 2.5 mcg
Iron: 7.5 mg
Selenium: 26.2 mcg
Zinc: 6.9 mg

This recipe is an excellent source of fiber, protein, vitamin B_6, vitamin B_{12}, iron, selenium, and zinc, and a good source of niacin.

Beef and Broccoli Soup

Unlike herbs, fresh and powdered ginger are not interchangeable in most recipes. For best results, use only fresh ginger in this savory soup.

Total preparation and
 cooking time: 30 minutes
Makes 4 servings.

1	pound beef round tip steaks, cut ⅛ to ¼ inch thick
2	tablespoons reduced-sodium soy sauce
1	tablespoon minced fresh ginger
2	teaspoons minced garlic
1	teaspoon vegetable oil
2	cans (14 to 14½ ounces each) ready-to-serve beef broth
1	red bell pepper, cut into thin strips, then crosswise in half
1	cup broccoli florets, cut into bite-sized pieces
½	cup thinly sliced fresh shiitake mushrooms
½	cup thinly sliced green onions
1	tablespoon rice vinegar
1	teaspoon dark sesame oil
⅛ to ¼	teaspoon crushed red pepper flakes
1	cup hot cooked rice, prepared without butter or salt

1. Stack beef steaks; cut lengthwise in half, then crosswise into 1-inch-wide strips. Combine beef, soy sauce, ginger, and garlic in medium bowl; toss to coat. Set aside.

2. Heat vegetable oil in large nonstick skillet over medium-high heat until hot. Add half of the beef; stir-fry 1 to 2 minutes or until outside surface of beef is no longer pink. (Do not overcook.) Remove from skillet. Repeat with remaining beef.

3. Meanwhile, bring broth to a boil in 4-quart saucepan. Add bell pepper and broccoli. Reduce heat; simmer, uncovered, 2 to 3 minutes or until vegetables are crisp-tender. Remove from heat. Stir in mushrooms, green onions, vinegar, sesame oil, pepper flakes, and beef. Serve immediately over rice in soup bowls.

COOK'S TIP
Asian noodles (1 cup cooked) may easily be substituted for rice, if desired.

HEALTHY LIVING TIP

Tame your taste for salt by cutting back gradually. In many recipes, salt can be reduced or even eliminated, especially if other sodium-containing ingredients are used, such as broth or soy sauce. Boost the natural flavors of food with fresh or dried herbs and spices.

Nutrition information per serving

Calories: 275
Fat: 8 g
  Saturated fat: 2 g
  Monounsaturated fat: 3 g
Cholesterol: 69 mg
Sodium: 1,084 mg
Carbohydrate: 20 g
Fiber: 2.0 g
Protein: 29 g
Niacin: 4.6 mg
Vitamin B_6: 0.6 mg
Vitamin B_{12}: 2.5 mcg
Iron: 3.9 mg
Selenium: 31.8 mcg
Zinc: 6.7 mg

This recipe is an excellent source of protein, niacin, vitamin B_6, vitamin B_{12}, iron, selenium, and zinc.

Cowboy Beef and Black Bean Chili

This easy-to-make dish simmers for over an hour, melding the seasonings into an incredibly flavorful chili.

Total preparation and
cooking time: 2 hours
Makes 8 servings.

2	pounds ground beef (95% lean)
1	tablespoon vegetable oil
1½	cups chopped onions
2	tablespoons minced garlic
2	medium yellow bell peppers, chopped
1	large jalapeño pepper, seeded, finely chopped
¼	cup chili powder
1	tablespoon ground cumin
1	teaspoon dried oregano leaves, crushed
1	teaspoon dried thyme leaves, crushed
⅛	teaspoon ground red pepper
1	can (28 ounces) crushed tomatoes, undrained
1	can (14½ ounces) chili-seasoned or zesty-style diced tomatoes, undrained
1	can (14 to 14½ ounces) ready-to-serve beef broth
12	ounces dark beer
⅓	cup tomato paste
1	tablespoon honey
2	cans (15 ounces each) black beans, rinsed, drained
	Salt and black pepper, as desired
	Chopped fresh cilantro (optional)

HEALTHY LIVING **TIP**

Be active—walk the dog, don't just watch the dog walk. Small changes in your level of activity can make a big fitness difference.

1. Brown ground beef in stockpot over medium heat 8 to 10 minutes or until beef is no longer pink, breaking up into ¾-inch crumbles. Remove from stockpot with slotted spoon. Set aside. Pour off drippings.

2. Heat oil in same stockpot over medium heat until hot. Add onions and garlic; cook and stir 3 to 5 minutes or until onions are tender. Add bell peppers and jalapeño; cook and stir 4 to 5 minutes or until peppers are tender.

3. Return beef crumbles to stockpot. Add chili powder, cumin, oregano, thyme, and red pepper; cook and stir for 2 to 3 minutes. Stir in crushed tomatoes, diced tomatoes, broth, beer, tomato paste, and honey; bring to a boil. Reduce heat; cover and simmer 45 minutes. Uncover stockpot; continue simmering 30 minutes or until thickened to desired consistency, stirring occasionally. Stir in beans; cook 5 to 10 minutes or until beans are heated through. Season with salt and black pepper, as desired. Garnish with cilantro, if desired.

**Nutrition information
per serving**

Calories: 364
Fat: 10 g
    Saturated fat: 3 g
    Monounsaturated fat: 4 g
Cholesterol: 76 mg
Sodium: 1,131 mg
Carbohydrate: 39 g
Fiber: 10.6 g
Protein: 34 g
Niacin: 8.1 mg
Vitamin B_6: 0.8 mg
Vitamin B_{12}: 2.2 mcg
Iron: 7.3 mg
Selenium: 19.3 mcg
Zinc: 6.5 mg

This recipe is an excellent source of fiber, protein, niacin, vitamin B_6, vitamin B_{12}, iron, selenium, and zinc.

Provençal Beef Stew

Total preparation and cooking time: 2 to 2¼ hours
Makes 6 servings.

Stew often tastes better the next day because the flavors have time to blend and intensify, so make it a day or two ahead of time and reheat for an easy dinner.

⅓	cup all-purpose flour
¾	teaspoon salt
½	teaspoon pepper
2	pounds boneless beef chuck shoulder pot roast, cut into 1-inch pieces
4	teaspoons olive oil, divided
1	cup chopped onion
1	tablespoon minced garlic
1	cup dry red wine
3	cups ready-to-serve beef broth
1	can (14½ ounces) diced tomatoes with garlic, undrained
1	tablespoon herbes de Provence
1	pound new potatoes, cut into quarters
2	small zucchini, cut lengthwise in half, then crosswise into ½-inch-thick slices
2	small yellow squash, cut lengthwise in half, then crosswise into ½-inch-thick slices
½	cup niçoise olives, pitted and cut in half
¼	cup chopped fresh basil
	Grated Parmesan cheese (optional)

1. Combine flour, salt, and pepper. Reserve 1 tablespoon flour mixture. Lightly coat beef with remaining flour mixture.

2. Heat 2 teaspoons oil in stockpot over medium heat until hot. Brown half of the beef; remove from stockpot. Repeat with remaining 2 teaspoons oil and remaining beef. Remove beef from stockpot.

Nutrition information per serving

Calories: 358
Fat: 11 g
    Saturated fat: 3 g
    Monounsaturated fat: 6 g
Cholesterol: 80 mg
Sodium: 1,179 mg
Carbohydrate: 31 g
Fiber: 4.1 g
Protein: 30 g
Niacin: 4.4 mg
Vitamin B_6: 0.6 mg
Vitamin B_{12}: 2.5 mcg
Iron: 6.0 mg
Selenium: 28.9 mcg
Zinc: 7.3 mg

This recipe is an excellent source of protein, niacin, vitamin B_6, vitamin B_{12}, iron, selenium, and zinc, and a good source of fiber.

COOK'S TIPS

- Niçoise olives are from the Provence region of France. Small, oval, and purplish-brown in color, they are packed in olive oil and have a nutty, mellow flavor. Greek Kalamata olives may be substituted for niçoise olives.
- Herbes de Provence is a dried herb blend used in the cooking of southern France. Often sold in supermarkets, it's commonly a blend of basil, fennel seed, lavender, marjoram, rosemary, sage, summer savory, and thyme.

3. Add onion and garlic to stockpot; cook and stir 3 to 5 minutes or until onions are tender. Add wine; increase heat to medium-high. Cook and stir 1 to 2 minutes or until browned bits attached to stockpot are dissolved. Stir in broth, tomatoes, herbes de Provence, and reserved flour mixture. Return beef to stockpot; bring to a boil. Reduce heat; cover tightly and simmer $1\frac{1}{2}$ hours or until beef is fork-tender.

4. Add potatoes, zucchini, and yellow squash to stockpot; continue simmering, covered, 15 minutes or until potatoes are tender. Add olives and basil; cook, uncovered, 2 to 3 minutes or until olives are heated through. Serve with cheese, if desired.

Bold Beef Chili with Queso Anejo

Laced with fiery peppers, this chili is for daring, not timid, taste buds.

1½ pounds ground beef (95% lean)
1   tablespoon olive oil
1   large yellow onion, chopped
8   cloves garlic, chopped
1 to 2 tablespoons chopped seeded serrano peppers
2 to 3 tablespoons ground ancho chili powder
2   tablespoons chili powder
1   tablespoon ground cumin
1   teaspoon dried oregano leaves, crushed
½   teaspoon salt
1   can (28 ounces) diced tomatoes, undrained
1   can (14 to 14½ ounces) ready-to-serve beef broth
1   can (8 ounces) tomato sauce
1 to 2 tablespoons adobo sauce from chipotle peppers
1   tablespoon minced chipotle peppers in adobo sauce
6   tablespoons crumbled queso anejo cheese
     Crunchy Tortilla Strips (page 61)

1. Brown ground beef in stockpot over medium heat 8 to 10 minutes or until beef is no longer pink, breaking up into ¾-inch crumbles. Remove from stockpot with slotted spoon. Set aside. Pour off drippings.

2. Heat oil in same stockpot over medium heat until hot. Add onion and garlic; cook and stir 5 minutes or until onion is tender. Add serrano peppers; cook and stir 2 minutes. Stir in chili powders, cumin, oregano, and salt; cook and stir 2 minutes.

3. Return beef crumbles to stockpot. Add tomatoes, broth, tomato sauce, adobo sauce, and chipotle peppers; bring to a boil. Reduce heat; cover and simmer 30 minutes. Uncover stockpot; continue simmering 15 minutes or until thickened to desired consistency. Serve topped with cheese and Crunchy Tortilla Strips.

COOK'S TIP

Queso anejo is an aged, hard Mexican cheese used for shredding or crumbling over cooked dishes. It has a mild, slightly spicy flavor and is coated in paprika or red chili paste. Queso fresco or feta cheese may be substituted for queso anejo.

Total preparation and cooking time: 1 hour and 20 minutes
Makes 8 servings.

COOK'S TIPS

- To easily seed and puree chipotle peppers in adobo sauce, place peppers in a garlic press and squeeze. The peppers will be pureed and the seeds can easily be discarded.
- Adjust the amounts of serrano pepper, chipotle pepper, and adobo sauce to control the level of spicy heat.

Nutrition information per serving

Calories: 319
Fat: 13 g
   Saturated fat: 5 g
   Monounsaturated fat: 5 g
Cholesterol: 84 mg
Sodium: 1,050 mg
Carbohydrate: 21 g
Fiber: 5.9 g
Protein: 31 g
Niacin: 7.2 mg
Vitamin B_6: 0.7 mg
Vitamin B_{12}: 2.4 mcg
Iron: 5.2 mg
Selenium: 20.7 mcg
Zinc: 6.6 mg

This recipe is an excellent source of fiber, protein, niacin, vitamin B_6, vitamin B_{12}, iron, selenium, and zinc.

Tortilla Beef Soup

A purchased fully cooked beef pot roast makes this hearty bean soup a breeze to prepare. A topping of crisp tortilla strips makes it fun to eat!

1 package (16 to 17 ounces) refrigerated fully cooked boneless beef pot roast with gravy
1 teaspoon olive oil
1 cup chopped onion
2 teaspoons minced garlic
1 tablespoon ground cumin
1 can (15 ounces) black beans, rinsed, drained
1 can (14½ ounces) diced tomatoes, undrained
1 can (14 to 14½ ounces) ready-to-serve beef broth
1 cup frozen corn
1 tablespoon jalapeño hot pepper sauce
2 tablespoons chopped fresh cilantro
   Crunchy Tortilla Strips (page 61)
¼ cup shredded reduced-fat Cheddar cheese
   Chopped fresh cilantro (optional)

1. Remove beef pot roast from package; discard gravy. Shred pot roast with 2 forks. Set aside.

2. Heat oil in 4-quart saucepan over medium heat until hot. Add onion and garlic; cook 3 to 5 minutes or until onion is tender, stirring occasionally. Add cumin; cook and stir 1 minute. Stir in beef, beans, tomatoes, broth, corn, and pepper sauce; bring to a boil. Reduce heat; simmer 10 minutes, stirring occasionally. Stir in 2 tablespoons cilantro.

3. Meanwhile, prepare Crunchy Tortilla Strips.

4. Ladle soup into bowls. Top each serving evenly with tortilla strips and cheese. Garnish with cilantro, if desired.

COOK'S TIPS

- Two small jalapeño peppers, seeded and thinly sliced, may be substituted for jalapeño pepper hot sauce. Cook jalapeño peppers with onion and garlic.
- A half recipe of the Basic Beef Pot Roast (page 139) (about 3 cups shredded) may be substituted for shredded fully cooked beef pot roast. Season Beef Basic Pot Roast with salt, as desired.

Total preparation and cooking time: 35 minutes
Makes 4 servings.

HEALTHY LIVING TIP
● ● ● ● ●

Feel a cold coming on? The zinc in beef may help to lessen the length and severity of a common cold. Help fight your cold with the comfort of a heartwarming lean beef soup or stew.

Nutrition information per serving

Calories: 405
Fat: 11 g
   Saturated fat: 3 g
   Monounsaturated fat: 4 g
Cholesterol: 85 mg
Sodium: 988 mg
Carbohydrate: 40 g
Fiber: 10.3 g
Protein: 37 g
Niacin: 3.6 mg
Vitamin B_6: 0.4 mg
Vitamin B_{12}: 2.6 mcg
Iron: 7.0 mg
Selenium: 27.0 mcg
Zinc: 7.5 mg

This recipe is an excellent source of fiber, protein, vitamin B_6, vitamin B_{12}, iron, selenium, and zinc, and a good source of niacin.

Panhandle Beef Chili

Total preparation and
  cooking time: 2 hours
Makes 6 servings.

The hint of cinnamon and coriander makes this chili an American pan-handle classic.

2	medium poblano chiles
1½	pounds ground beef (95% lean)
1	tablespoon olive oil
1½	cups chopped onions
2	medium jalapeño peppers, seeded, chopped
2	tablespoons minced garlic
3	tablespoons chili powder
1	teaspoon dried oregano leaves, crushed
½	teaspoon ground coriander
¼	teaspoon ground cinnamon
2	cans (14½ ounces each) diced tomatoes, undrained
1	can (14 to 14½ ounces) ready-to-serve beef broth
1	tablespoon tomato paste
1	teaspoon salt
1	can (15 ounces) pinto beans, rinsed, drained
1	cup frozen corn
¼ to ½	teaspoon black pepper
1	teaspoon cornstarch dissolved in 1 tablespoon water
	Sliced green onions (optional)

**Nutrition information
per serving**

Calories: 372
Fat: 11 g
   Saturated fat: 4 g
   Monounsaturated fat: 5 g
Cholesterol: 76 mg
Sodium: 1,078 mg
Carbohydrate: 36 g
Fiber: 11.2 g
Protein: 34 g
Niacin: 7.4 mg
Vitamin B_6: 0.9 mg
Vitamin B_{12}: 2.3 mcg
Iron: 5.8 mg
Selenium: 19.2 mcg
Zinc: 6.5 mg

**This recipe is an excellent
source of fiber, protein,
niacin, vitamin B_6, vitamin
B_{12}, iron, selenium, and zinc.**

1. Heat oven to 425°F. Line metal baking sheet with aluminum foil; spray with nonstick cooking spray. Place whole poblano chiles on baking sheet. Roast in 425°F oven 30 minutes, turning once. Place chiles in food-safe plastic bag; close bag. Let stand until skins are loosened. Remove and discard skins, stems, and seeds; chop chiles. Set aside.

2. Brown ground beef in stockpot over medium heat 8 to 10 minutes or until beef is no longer pink, breaking up into ¾-inch crumbles. Remove from stockpot with slotted spoon. Set aside. Pour off drippings.

3. Heat oil in same stockpot over medium heat until hot. Add onions, poblano chiles, jalapeños, and garlic; cook and stir 5 minutes or until onions are tender. Stir in chili powder, oregano, coriander, and cinnamon; cook 30 seconds to 1 minute or until fragrant.

4. Return beef crumbles to stockpot. Add tomatoes, broth, tomato paste, and salt; bring to a boil. Reduce heat; cover and simmer 30 minutes. Uncover stockpot; continue simmering 15 minutes, stirring occasionally. Stir in beans, corn, and black pepper; continue simmering 10 minutes or until heated through. Stir in cornstarch mixture; cook and stir. Boil 1 minute or until slightly thickened. Garnish with green onions, if desired.

EASY ENTERTAINING WITH BEEF

7

Three-Mustard Beef Round Tip with Roasted Baby Carrots and Brussels Sprouts

Nutrition information per serving

Calories: 265
Fat: 11 g
   Saturated fat: 3 g
   Monounsaturated fat: 5 g
Cholesterol: 74 mg
Sodium: 680 mg
Carbohydrate: 14 g
Fiber: 3.2 g
Protein: 28 g
Niacin: 4.3 mg
Vitamin B$_6$: 0.5 mg
Vitamin B$_{12}$: 2.5 mcg
Iron: 4.4 mg
Selenium: 25.1 mcg
Zinc: 6.6 mg

This recipe is an excellent source of protein, niacin, vitamin B$_6$, vitamin B$_{12}$, iron, selenium, and zinc, and a good source of fiber.

Served with a creamy, triple-mustard sauce, this savory roast beef dinner is sure to please guests.

3	tablespoons Dijon-style mustard
1	tablespoon fresh thyme, chopped
½	teaspoon coarse-grind black pepper
1	boneless beef round tip roast (3 pounds)
2	tablespoons dry bread crumbs

VEGETABLES

1	pound small Brussels sprouts, trimmed
2	pounds packaged baby carrots
2	tablespoons olive oil
2	teaspoons fresh thyme, chopped
1	teaspoon salt
½	teaspoon coarse-grind black pepper

THREE-MUSTARD SAUCE

1	tablespoon olive oil
¼	cup minced shallots
½	cup Dijon-style mustard
2	teaspoons mustard seeds
1	teaspoon dry mustard
2	tablespoons fresh lemon juice
½	cup reduced-fat dairy sour cream
2	tablespoons chopped fresh parsley
¼	teaspoon coarse-grind black pepper

1. Heat oven to 325°F. Combine mustard, thyme, and pepper in small bowl. Spread mustard mixture evenly over all surfaces of beef roast. Press bread crumbs evenly onto roast over mustard.

2. Place roast on rack in shallow roasting pan. Insert ovenproof meat thermometer so tip is centered in thickest part of beef, not resting in fat. Do not add water or cover. Roast in 325°F oven 1¾ to 2 hours for medium-rare, 2¼ to 2½ hours for medium doneness.

3. Meanwhile, prepare vegetables. Cut shallow "X" into bottom of each Brussels sprout. Toss Brussels sprouts, carrots, oil, thyme,

salt, and pepper in large bowl. Transfer to metal baking sheet. Cover tightly with aluminum foil. Roast in 325°F oven with beef roast 1 to 1¼ hours or until crisp-tender. Uncover baking sheet; continue roasting 5 minutes or until lightly browned.

4. Remove roast when meat thermometer registers 140°F for medium-rare, 155°F for medium. Transfer roast to carving board; tent loosely with aluminum foil. Let stand, covered, 20 minutes. (Temperature will continue to rise about 5°F to reach 145°F for medium-rare, 160°F for medium.)

5. Meanwhile, prepare Three-Mustard Sauce. Heat oil in small saucepan over medium heat until hot. Add shallots; cook and stir 3 to 5 minutes or until tender. Add Dijon-style mustard, mustard seeds, and dry mustard; cook and stir 30 seconds. Remove from heat; stir in lemon juice until well blended. Add sour cream, parsley, and pepper; stir until smooth. Keep warm.

6. Carve roast into thin slices. Serve with vegetables and sauce.

Honey Mustard Beef Tenderloin with Tarragon Sauce

Tenderloin and other tender beef cuts are marinated only for a brief time to add extra flavor.

Total preparation and cooking time: 1½ hours
Marinating time: 20 minutes
Makes 8 to 12 servings.

MARINADE

¼ cup coarse-grain Dijon-style mustard
2 tablespoons honey
1 tablespoon sherry vinegar
1 teaspoon olive oil

1 center-cut beef tenderloin roast (2 to 3 pounds)
½ teaspoon pepper

TARRAGON SAUCE

½ cup sherry vinegar
¼ cup minced shallots
2 tablespoons chopped fresh tarragon
1 cup dry sherry
1 cup Madeira
1 can (14 to 14½ ounces) ready-to-serve beef broth
1½ teaspoons cornstarch dissolved in 1 tablespoon dry sherry
2 tablespoons coarse-grain Dijon-style mustard
4 teaspoons honey
2 teaspoons butter

Salt and pepper, as desired

1. Heat oven to 425°F. Combine marinade ingredients in small bowl. Place beef roast and marinade in food-safe plastic bag; turn roast to coat. Close bag securely and marinate in refrigerator 20 minutes.

2. Remove roast from marinade; discard marinade. Place roast on rack in shallow roasting pan. Season with pepper. Insert ovenproof thermometer so tip is centered in thickest part of beef. Do not add water or cover. Roast in 425°F oven 35 to 40 minutes for medium-rare, 45 to 50 minutes for medium.

3. Remove roast when meat thermometer registers 135°F for medium-rare, 150°F for medium. Transfer roast to carving board; tent loosely with aluminum foil. Let stand 15 minutes. (Temperature will continue to rise about 10°F to reach 145°F for medium-rare, 160°F for medium.)

Nutrition information per serving

Calories: 254
Fat: 9 g
    Saturated fat: 3 g
    Monounsaturated fat: 3 g
Cholesterol: 70 mg
Sodium: 410 mg
Carbohydrate: 11 g
Fiber: 0.1 g
Protein: 27 g
Niacin: 7.3 mg
Vitamin B_6: 0.6 mg
Vitamin B_{12}: 1.4 mcg
Iron: 2.0 mg
Selenium: 29.8 mcg
Zinc: 4.6 mg

This recipe is an excellent source of protein, niacin, vitamin B_6, vitamin B_{12}, selenium, and zinc, and a good source of iron.

4. Meanwhile, prepare Tarragon Sauce. Combine vinegar, shallots, and tarragon in medium saucepan; bring to a boil. Reduce heat; simmer 4 to 5 minutes or until reduced to $\frac{1}{3}$ cup. Add sherry and Madeira; bring to a boil. Reduce heat; simmer 30 to 35 minutes or until reduced to $\frac{2}{3}$ cup. Add broth; bring to a boil. Reduce heat; simmer 25 to 30 minutes or until reduced to 1 cup. Stir in cornstarch mixture; cook and stir 1 minute or until slightly thickened. Whisk in mustard and honey. Remove from heat; whisk in butter.

5. Carve roast into $\frac{1}{2}$-inch-thick slices. Season with salt and pepper, as desired. Serve with sauce.

COOK'S TIPS

- If desired, $\frac{3}{4}$ teaspoon dried tarragon may be substituted for fresh tarragon.
- It's easy to add a stylish side dish to any meal by using frozen vegetable blends.

Grilled Beef Bruschetta with Feta Cheese

Guests will savor these delectable appetizers of grilled beef, vegetables, and tangy feta cheese atop toasty bread slices.

1	package (4 ounces) crumbled feta cheese
3	tablespoons reduced-fat dairy sour cream
1	medium red bell pepper, cut lengthwise in half, seeded, stemmed
1	small yellow onion, cut into ¼-inch-thick slices
1	loaf French baguette bread (about 20 inches long), cut into 32 ½-inch-thick slices
1	boneless beef top sirloin steak, cut ¾ inch thick (about 1 pound)
1	cup chopped seeded plum tomatoes
2	tablespoons finely chopped fresh basil
2	tablespoons minced Kalamata olives
1	tablespoon olive oil
1½	teaspoons balsamic vinegar
1	large clove garlic, finely chopped
¼	teaspoon salt
¼	teaspoon black pepper

1. Place cheese and sour cream in food processor bowl. Cover; process until smooth. Transfer to small bowl. Cover and refrigerate.

2. Place bell pepper and onion on grid over medium, ash-covered coals. Grill, uncovered, 10 to 12 minutes or until bell pepper is slightly blackened and onion is tender, turning once. Set onion aside. Place bell pepper in food-safe plastic bag; close bag. Let stand until skin is loosened.

3. Place bread slices on grid over medium, ash-covered coals. Grill, uncovered, about 3 minutes, turning once. Set aside.

4. Place beef steak on grid over medium, ash-covered coals. Grill, uncovered, 13 to 16 minutes for medium-rare to medium doneness, turning occasionally. Season with salt and black pepper, as desired. Keep warm.

5. Meanwhile, remove skin from bell pepper. Coarsely chop bell pepper and onion; place in medium bowl. Add tomatoes, basil, olives, oil, vinegar, garlic, salt, and black pepper; mix well.

6. Carve steak into 32 thin slices. Divide cheese mixture equally among bread slices; spread evenly. Top each bread slice with 1 steak slice and 1 tablespoon tomato mixture.

Total preparation and cooking time: 1 hour
Makes 32 appetizers.

CHEF RICHARD'S TIP

Bell peppers may also be roasted over the flame of a gas burner.

HEALTHY LIVING TIP

Always keep juices from raw meats and poultry away from cooked or ready-to-eat foods. One way to prevent this is to designate your cutting boards; use one for raw meats and poultry and the other for ready-to-eat foods such as breads and vegetables.

Nutrition information per serving (1 appetizer)

Calories: 73
Fat: 3 g
 Saturated fat: 1 g
 Monounsaturated fat: 1 g
Cholesterol: 10 mg
Sodium: 129 mg
Carbohydrate: 7 g
Fiber: 0.6 g
Protein: 5 g
Niacin: 1.2 mg
Vitamin B$_6$: 0.1 mg
Vitamin B$_{12}$: 0.3 mcg
Iron: 0.4 mg
Selenium: 4.5 mcg
Zinc: 0.8 mg

Triple-Ginger Beef Dumplings

The combination of three gingers makes these savory appetizers a favorite among guests.

Total preparation and cooking time: 1½ hours
Makes 48 appetizers.

DIPPING SAUCE

½	cup fresh orange juice
¼	cup reduced-sodium soy sauce
¼	cup mirin (sweet rice wine)
¼	cup finely chopped crystallized ginger
1	tablespoon chopped green onion
2	teaspoons sesame seeds
2	teaspoons freshly grated orange peel

1	tablespoon dark sesame oil
4	ounces shiitake mushrooms, chopped
1	cup shredded carrots
1	tablespoon minced garlic
¼	cup chopped green onions
1	tablespoon minced fresh ginger
½	teaspoon ground ginger
1	pound ground beef (95% lean)
¼	cup reduced-sodium soy sauce
48	wonton wrappers (3¼- to 3½-inch squares)
	Water, as desired
	Green onions, cut lengthwise into strips (optional)

1. Combine dipping sauce ingredients in small bowl. Set aside.

2. Heat oil in large saucepan over medium heat until hot. Add mushrooms, carrots, and garlic; cook and stir 5 minutes. Remove from heat; add green onions, fresh ginger, and ground ginger. Transfer to large bowl; cool to room temperature. Add ground beef and soy sauce; mix lightly but thoroughly.

3. Spoon 1 tablespoon beef filling in center of 1 wonton wrapper. (Keep remaining wonton wrappers covered to prevent them from drying out.) Moisten edges of wonton wrapper with fingertip dipped in water. Bring 4 corners of wrapper up and over filling, forming pyramid shape and pinching edges together to seal. Place on metal baking sheet lined with parchment or waxed paper. Repeat with remaining wonton wrappers and filling to form 48 dumplings.

Nutrition information per serving (1 appetizer)

Calories: 49
Fat: 1 g
   Saturated fat: 0 g
   Monounsaturated fat: 0 g
Cholesterol: 6 mg
Sodium: 153 mg
Carbohydrate: 6 g
Fiber: 0.3 g
Protein: 3 g
Niacin: 0.9 mg
Vitamin B_6: 0.0 mg
Vitamin B_{12}: 0.2 mcg
Iron: 0.6 mg
Selenium: 3.9 mcg
Zinc: 0.6 mg

4. Spray steamer basket with nonstick cooking spray. Place as many dumplings into steamer basket as will fit without touching each other. Place basket over 1 inch boiling water (water should not touch bottom of basket). Cover tightly; reduce heat. Steam 6 to 7 minutes or until beef is no longer pink in center. Carefully remove dumplings to serving plate; keep warm. Repeat with remaining dumplings.

5. Garnish platter with green onion strips, if desired. Serve with dipping sauce.

COOK'S TIPS

Mirin is a low-alcohol Japanese rice wine that adds sweetness and flavor to a variety of dishes, sauces, and glazes. It is available in Japanese markets and the Asian section of most supermarkets.

Cooked appetizers can be made ahead and frozen for 2 to 3 months. Reheat from frozen using steaming method; cook for 7 to 8 minutes.

Peppered Strip Steaks with French Herb Cheese

Flavored with garlic and fresh herbs, this rich, creamy cheese is easy to make at home.

FRENCH HERB CHEESE

4	ounces reduced-fat cream cheese
2	tablespoons reduced-fat dairy sour cream
1	teaspoon finely chopped fresh basil
1	teaspoon finely chopped fresh oregano
½	teaspoon minced garlic
1	tablespoon chopped fresh chives
⅛	teaspoon salt
	Dash freshly ground black pepper

1 to 2 tablespoons coarse-grind black pepper
4 boneless beef top loin (strip) steaks, cut ¾ inch thick (about 8 ounces each)
  Salt, as desired

1. To prepare French Herb Cheese, place cream cheese, sour cream, basil, oregano, and garlic in food processor bowl. Cover; process until smooth. Transfer to small bowl. Stir in chives, salt, and pepper. Cover and refrigerate.

2. Press coarse-grind black pepper evenly onto beef steaks. Place steaks on grid over medium, ash-covered coals. Grill, uncovered, 10 to 12 minutes for medium-rare to medium doneness, turning occasionally. Season with salt, as desired.

3. Cut each steak into 2 equal portions. Top each portion with 1 tablespoon French Herb Cheese.

Total preparation and cooking time: 30 minutes
Makes 8 servings.

CHEF RICHARD'S TIP

Serve with fresh grilled asparagus and new potatoes.

HEALTHY LIVING TIP

Jazz up your guests' plates with an edible, nutritious garnish, such as a citrus slice, radish roses, celery, pepper curls, or a few toasted nuts.

Nutrition information per serving

Calories: 202
Fat: 9 g
  Saturated fat: 4 g
  Monounsaturated fat: 3 g
Cholesterol: 66 mg
Sodium: 133 mg
Carbohydrate: 2 g
Fiber: 0.2 g
Protein: 27 g
Niacin: 7.4 mg
Vitamin B_6: 0.6 mg
Vitamin B_{12}: 1.5 mcg
Iron: 2.1 mg
Selenium: 30.4 mcg
Zinc: 4.7 mg

This recipe is an excellent source of protein, niacin, vitamin B_6, vitamin B_{12}, selenium, and zinc, and a good source of iron.

Beef Beggar's Purses

The ruffled tops of these delectable beef-filled phyllo packages make them resemble tiny purses.

Total preparation and
cooking time: 1¾ hours
Makes 66 appetizers.

• • • • •
NOTE
Beef Beggar's Purses may be assembled ahead and refrigerated up to 3 hours or frozen up to 2 months. For best results, store in deep, airtight containers because purse tops are fragile. Bake refrigerated or frozen purses at same oven temperature and baking time as directed in recipe.

3	cups finely chopped cremini mushrooms (about 6 ounces)
½	cup finely chopped onion
1	pound ground beef (95% lean)
4	cloves garlic, minced
1	cup shredded Gruyère cheese
1½	cups egg substitute
¾	teaspoon salt
½	teaspoon pepper
33	sheets frozen phyllo, thawed (14 × 9-inch sheets)
3	tablespoons dry bread crumbs
66	fresh chive stems, blanched

1. Cook and stir mushrooms and onion in large nonstick skillet over medium heat 8 to 10 minutes or until liquid has evaporated. Remove from skillet. Set aside.

2. In same skillet, brown ground beef with garlic over medium heat 8 to 10 minutes or until beef is no longer pink, breaking beef up into ¾-inch crumbles. Pour off drippings. Stir in mushroom mixture and cheese. Cook and stir over low heat 30 seconds or until cheese starts to melt. Remove from skillet. Set aside.

3. In same skillet, cook egg substitute over low to medium-low heat according to package directions for scrambled eggs, stirring occasionally. Combine scrambled eggs, salt, and pepper with beef mixture.

4. Heat oven to 400°F. Layer 3 phyllo sheets on cutting board, spraying top surface of each sheet generously with cooking spray and sprinkling with ¼ teaspoon bread crumbs. (Keep remaining phyllo sheets covered with a clean, damp kitchen towel to prevent them

Nutrition information
per serving (1 appetizer)

Calories: 53
Fat: 2 g
  Saturated fat: 1 g
  Monounsaturated fat: 1 g
Cholesterol: 6 mg
Sodium: 95 mg
Carbohydrate: 6 g
Fiber: 0.3 g
Protein: 4 g
Niacin: 0.9 mg
Vitamin B$_6$: 0.1 mg
Vitamin B$_{12}$: 0.2 mcg
Iron: 0.6 mg
Selenium: 5.4 mcg
Zinc: 0.6 mg

COOK'S TIP
To blanch chive stems, cook in boiling water 10 to 15 seconds. Remove from water with tongs or slotted spoon and immediately run under cold water or place in a bowl of ice water. Drain water and dry thoroughly with paper towels.

from drying out.) Cut layered sheets into $12\frac{3}{4} \times 8\frac{1}{2}$-inch rectangle, discarding phyllo scraps. Cut rectangle into six $4\frac{1}{4}$-inch squares. Spoon 1 scant tablespoon beef filling in center of each square. Bring 4 corners of phyllo up and over filling, carefully pinching together and twisting slightly to form bundle or purse shape. Tie 1 chive around pinched top of each purse to secure closed. Place on metal baking sheets sprayed with nonstick cooking spray. Repeat with remaining phyllo, beef filling, and chives to fill three baking sheets.

5. Bake in 400°F oven 11 to 13 minutes or until filling is hot and tops are lightly browned.

Jamaican Jerk Ranch Steaks with Chipotle Island Relish

Total preparation and cooking time: 30 minutes
Makes 6 servings.

Nutrition information per serving

Calories: 213
Fat: 7 g
   Saturated fat: 2 g
   Monounsaturated fat: 4 g
Cholesterol: 57 mg
Sodium: 367 mg
Carbohydrate: 13 g
Fiber: 0.8 g
Protein: 24 g
Niacin: 3.4 mg
Vitamin B_6: 0.3 mg
Vitamin B_{12}: 2.6 mcg
Iron: 3.3 mg
Selenium: 26.0 mcg
Zinc: 5.7 mg

This recipe is an excellent source of protein, vitamin B_{12}, selenium, and zinc, and a good source of niacin, vitamin B_6, and iron.

Transport family and friends to the Caribbean with this easy dish.

JERK RUB
2   teaspoons dark brown sugar
1½   teaspoons dried thyme leaves, crushed
1   teaspoon chili powder
1   teaspoon ground allspice
½   teaspoon garlic powder
½   teaspoon onion powder
½   teaspoon salt
¼   teaspoon ground nutmeg
¼   teaspoon ground cinnamon

3   beef shoulder center steaks (Ranch Steaks), cut ¾ inch thick (about 8 ounces each)

CHIPOTLE ISLAND RELISH
1   tablespoon honey
2   teaspoons olive oil
1   teaspoon chipotle peppers in adobo sauce, seeded, pureed
¼   teaspoon salt
1   can (15 ounces) mandarin orange segments, drained
⅓   cup finely chopped red onion
2   tablespoons finely chopped fresh cilantro

1. Combine Jerk Rub ingredients in small bowl; press rub evenly onto each beef steak. Place steaks on grid over medium, ash-covered coals. Grill, covered, 9 to 11 minutes for medium-rare to medium doneness, turning once.

2. Meanwhile, prepare Chipotle Island Relish. Combine honey, oil, chipotle peppers, and salt in medium bowl. Add orange segments, red onion, and cilantro; mix gently. Set aside.

3. Carve steaks into thin slices; season with salt and pepper, as desired. Serve with relish.

Braised Brisket with Fig and Onion Confit

Sliced tender beef brisket served with savory fig confit is the perfect autumn meal.

Total preparation and cooking time: 4 hours
Makes 6 to 8 servings.

- 1 tablespoon olive oil
- 1 boneless beef brisket, flat cut (2½ to 3½ pounds)
- 1½ cups chopped onions
- 1 tablespoon minced garlic
- ½ teaspoon salt
- 1 can (14 to 14½ ounces) ready-to-serve beef broth
- ¾ cup dry red wine
- 2 tablespoons whole black peppercorns

FIG AND ONION CONFIT

- 1 teaspoon olive oil
- 1½ cups chopped onions
- ¾ teaspoon dried thyme leaves, crushed
- ¼ teaspoon dried oregano leaves, crushed
- ¾ cup dry red wine
- ½ cup chopped sweetened dried cranberries
- ½ cup finely chopped dried figs
- 2 tablespoons balsamic vinegar
- 1 tablespoon packed brown sugar
- ½ teaspoon salt

1. Heat oil in stockpot over medium heat until hot. Place brisket in stockpot; brown evenly. Remove brisket; pour off all but 1 teaspoon of drippings, if necessary.

2. Add onions and garlic to stockpot; cook and stir 3 to 5 minutes or until onions are tender. Place brisket, fat side up, over onion mixture. Season with salt. Pour broth and wine around brisket. Add peppercorns; bring to a boil. Reduce heat; cover tightly and simmer 2½ to 3 hours or until brisket is fork-tender.

3. Meanwhile, prepare Fig and Onion Confit. Heat oil in medium saucepan over medium heat until hot. Add onions, thyme, and oregano; cook 4 to 5 minutes or until onion is tender, stirring occasionally. Stir in wine, cranberries, figs, vinegar, brown sugar, and salt; bring to a boil. Reduce heat; cover and simmer 15 minutes. Uncover saucepan; continue simmering 5 to 7 minutes or until

· · · · · · · · · · · · ·
BEEF SMARTS

All trans fats are not created equal. Naturally occurring trans fats, found in beef and dairy products, have been shown to have heart-healthy and cancer-protective benefits. See page 228 to learn more.

Nutrition information per serving

Calories: 341
Fat: 9 g
  Saturated fat: 2 g
  Monounsaturated fat: 4 g
Cholesterol: 49 mg
Sodium: 479 mg
Carbohydrate: 32 g
Fiber: 3.5 g
Protein: 30 g
Niacin: 4.3 mg
Vitamin B$_6$: 0.4 mg
Vitamin B$_{12}$: 2.1 mcg
Iron: 3.4 mg
Selenium: 29.6 mcg
Zinc: 7.0 mg

This recipe is an excellent source of protein, niacin, vitamin B$_6$, vitamin B$_{12}$, selenium, and zinc, and a good source of fiber and iron.

liquid is slightly thickened, stirring occasionally. Place fig mixture in food processor bowl or blender. Cover; pulse on and off until coarsely chopped. Keep warm.

4. Remove brisket from stockpot; keep warm. Skim fat from cooking liquid; strain and discard solids. Set aside. Trim fat from brisket.

5. Carve brisket diagonally across the grain into thin slices. Place slices on serving platter; pour enough cooking liquid (about 1 cup) to moisten brisket. Serve with warm confit and additional cooking liquid, if desired.

COOK'S TIPS

- If brisket is too large to brown in stockpot, heat 1½ teaspoons oil in large nonstick skillet over medium heat until hot. Place brisket in skillet; brown evenly. Meanwhile, heat remaining 1½ teaspoons oil in stockpot. Add onions and garlic; cook as directed above. Place brisket, fat side up, over onion mixture. Proceed as directed.

- Roast acorn or butternut squash halves in the oven while the brisket is cooking. The Fig and Onion Confit will complement the squash as well as the brisket.

Tandoori Beef Skewers with Pistachio Couscous

Total preparation and
cooking time: 1 hour
Makes 6 servings.

Yogurt is often used as a tenderizing marinade in Indian cooking.

MARINADE
1½ cups plain nonfat yogurt
1 tablespoon grated fresh ginger
2 teaspoons minced garlic
1½ teaspoons paprika
1½ teaspoons freshly ground black pepper
1 teaspoon kosher or table salt
½ teaspoon ground cinnamon
½ teaspoon ground coriander
½ teaspoon ground cumin

1½ pounds beef flank steak
6 cups shredded Napa cabbage
Pistachio Couscous with Curry Vinaigrette (recipe follows)
Salt, as desired
Chopped toasted pistachios (optional)

1. Combine marinade ingredients in large bowl; mix well. Cut beef steak crosswise across the grain into ¼-inch-thick strips. Add beef; toss to coat. Cover and marinate in refrigerator 10 minutes (do not overmarinate). Soak eighteen 9-inch bamboo skewers in water 10 minutes; drain.

2. Thread an equal amount of beef, weaving back and forth, onto each skewer. Place kabobs on grid over medium, ash-covered coals. Grill, uncovered, 4 to 6 minutes for medium-rare to medium doneness, turning occasionally. Season with salt, as desired.

3. Place cabbage on serving platter. Top with Pistachio Couscous and beef skewers. Garnish with pistachios, if desired.

**Nutrition information
per serving**

Calories: 481
Fat: 15 g
  Saturated fat: 4 g
  Monounsaturated fat: 7 g
Cholesterol: 42 mg
Sodium: 346 mg
Carbohydrate: 52 g
Fiber: 5.6 g
Protein: 35 g
Niacin: 9.2 mg
Vitamin B_6: 0.8 mg
Vitamin B_{12}: 1.4 mcg
Iron: 3.1 mg
Selenium: 28.4 mcg
Zinc: 5.2 mg

This recipe is an excellent source of fiber, protein, niacin, vitamin B_6, vitamin B_{12}, selenium, and zinc, and a good source of iron.

COOK'S TIP
To toast pistachios, spread in single layer on metal baking sheet. Bake in 350°F oven about 6 minutes or until lightly browned, stirring occasionally. (Watch carefully to prevent burning.) Set aside to cool.

Pistachio Couscous with Curry Vinaigrette

- 2 cups water
- 1 package (10 ounces) couscous

CURRY VINAIGRETTE
- 2 tablespoons extra-virgin olive oil
- ⅓ cup thinly sliced green onions
- 1½ teaspoons curry powder
- ¼ teaspoon ground cumin
- ¾ cup fresh orange juice
- ¼ cup fresh lime juice
- 1 tablespoon grated fresh ginger
- 1 teaspoon freshly grated lemon peel
- 1 teaspoon dark sesame oil
- ¼ teaspoon salt
- ¼ teaspoon freshly ground black pepper

- 1 red bell pepper, cut into ⅛-inch-thick strips
- 2 carrots, cut into ⅛ × ⅛ × 2-inch strips
- ½ cup unsalted pistachios, toasted, coarsely chopped

1. Bring water to a boil in medium saucepan; stir in couscous. Remove from heat; cover and let stand about 5 minutes. Fluff with a fork. Set aside to cool.

2. To prepare Curry Vinaigrette, heat olive oil in small nonstick skillet over medium heat until hot. Add green onions; cook and stir 1 minute. Add curry powder and cumin; cook and stir 1 minute. Transfer to small bowl. Whisk in orange juice, lime juice, ginger, lemon peel, sesame oil, salt, and black pepper.

3. Add bell pepper, carrots, and pistachios to couscous. Add vinaigrette; toss to coat.

Porcini Mushroom and Beef Bolognese

Total preparation and
    cooking time: 2¼ hours
Makes 8 servings.

Served over pasta, this rich, beefy tomato sauce flavored with mush-rooms, garlic, prosciutto, pancetta, and red wine is ideal for entertaining.

2	pounds ground beef (95% lean)
½	teaspoon salt
¼ to ½ teaspoon pepper
2	tablespoons olive oil
1	large onion, chopped
1	cup sliced cremini mushrooms
3	ounces pancetta, finely chopped
2	ounces prosciutto, finely chopped
3	tablespoons minced garlic
1	cup dry red wine
2	cans (14 to 14½ ounces each) ready-to-serve beef broth
¾	cup dried porcini mushrooms, broken into small pieces (about 1 ounce)
¾	cup chopped sun-dried tomatoes, not packed in oil
⅓	cup tomato paste
1	tablespoon sugar
1	tablespoon chopped fresh thyme
	Sugar, as desired
8	cups hot cooked pasta

CHEF RICHARD'S TIP

For an impressive touch, drizzle a little good-quality truffle oil over this and other Italian dishes. Be sure to refrigerate truffle oil to keep it fresh.

1. Brown ground beef in stockpot over medium heat 8 to 10 minutes or until beef is no longer pink, breaking up into ¾-inch crumbles. Remove from stockpot with slotted spoon; season with salt and pepper. Set aside. Pour off drippings.

2. In same stockpot, heat oil over medium heat until hot. Add onion, cremini mushrooms, pancetta, prosciutto, and garlic; cook 8 to 10

**Nutrition information
per serving**

Calories: 313
Fat: 13 g
    Saturated fat: 6 g
    Monounsaturated fat: 3 g
Cholesterol: 88 mg
Sodium: 1,014 mg
Carbohydrate: 14 g
Fiber: 2.4 g
Protein: 33 g
Niacin: 7.4 mg
Vitamin B$_6$: 0.5 mg
Vitamin B$_{12}$: 2.2 mcg
Iron: 5.2 mg
Selenium: 19.8 mcg
Zinc: 6.3 mg

**This recipe is an excellent
source of protein, niacin,
vitamin B$_6$, vitamin B$_{12}$, iron,
selenium, and zinc.**

COOK'S TIPS

- To easily chop sun-dried tomatoes, use kitchen scissors to snip the tomatoes into small pieces.
- Pancetta is an Italian bacon that is cured but not smoked. Flavorful and slightly salty, it's sliced into rounds of varying thickness from a sausage-shaped roll. Pancetta is available in Italian markets and some supermarkets.
- All that's needed to finish this meal is a colorful green salad!

Porcini Mushroom and
Beef Bolognese
(continued)

minutes or until onion is tender and most of the liquid has evaporated, stirring occasionally. Add wine; bring to a boil. Reduce heat; simmer 8 to 10 minutes or until liquid is reduced by half.

3. Return beef crumbles to stockpot. Stir in broth, porcini mushrooms, sun-dried tomatoes, tomato paste, sugar, and thyme; bring to a boil. Reduce heat; cover and simmer 45 minutes. Uncover stockpot; continue simmering 10 to 15 minutes or until sauce thickens. Stir in additional sugar, as desired. Serve over pasta.

Five-Spice Tenderloin Steaks with Creamy Polenta

East meets West when Italian polenta and balsamic vinegar mingle with Chinese five-spice powder and other Asian flavors in this exceptional dish.

Total preparation and cooking time: about 35 minutes

Makes 4 servings.

SAUCE

½   cup hoisin sauce
½   cup ketchup
¼   cup unseasoned rice vinegar
2   tablespoons chopped fresh chives
2   tablespoons soy sauce
1   tablespoon balsamic vinegar
1   tablespoon honey
1   teaspoon dry mustard
½   teaspoon Chinese five-spice powder

½   teaspoon Chinese five-spice powder
4   beef tenderloin steaks, cut 1 inch thick (about 4 ounces each)
1   teaspoon olive oil
1   teaspoon dark sesame oil
    Salt and pepper, as desired

CREAMY POLENTA

1   can (14 to 14½ ounces) ready-to-serve vegetable broth
¼   cup water
½   cup cornmeal
½   cup reduced-fat dairy sour cream
1   teaspoon dark sesame oil
    Salt and pepper, as desired
    Additional ready-to-serve vegetable broth or water (optional)

1. Combine sauce ingredients in small bowl. Set aside.

2. Sprinkle Chinese five-spice powder evenly onto 1 side of each beef steak. Heat olive and sesame oils in large nonstick skillet over medium heat until hot. Place steaks, seasoned sides down, in skillet; cook 10 to 13 minutes for medium-rare to medium doneness, turning occasionally. Season with salt and pepper, as desired. Remove steaks; keep warm.

3. Pour sauce into same skillet. Reduce heat; cook until heated through, stirring frequently. Keep warm.

Nutrition information per serving

Calories: 443
Fat: 15 g
   Saturated fat: 6 g
   Monounsaturated fat: 4 g
Cholesterol: 84 mg
Sodium: 1,806 mg
Carbohydrate: 46 g
Fiber: 2.4 g
Protein: 31 g
Niacin: 9.2 mg
Vitamin B_6: 0.6 mg
Vitamin B_{12}: 1.4 mcg
Iron: 3.4 mg
Selenium: 30.3 mcg
Zinc: 4.9 mg

This recipe is an excellent source of protein, niacin, vitamin B_6, vitamin B_{12}, selenium, and zinc, and a good source of iron.

4. Meanwhile, prepare Creamy Polenta. Combine broth and water in large saucepan; bring to a boil. Add cornmeal in thin stream, whisking constantly to prevent lumps. Cook 30 seconds or until thickened, stirring frequently. Reduce heat; continue cooking, covered, 5 minutes. Stir in sour cream and oil. Season with salt and pepper, as desired; keep warm. Stir in additional broth or water to maintain soft consistency, if necessary.

5. Serve steaks with polenta and sauce, as desired.

COOK'S TIPS

- Chinese five-spice powder is a pungent mixture of five ground spices: cinnamon, cloves, fennel seeds, star anise, and Szechuan peppercorns. It is available in Asian markets and most supermarkets.
- Chinese pea pods and shredded carrots can be quickly stir-fried to provide an authentic side dish.

CHEF RICHARD'S TIP

Any leftover sauce may be covered and refrigerated up to 3 to 4 days or frozen up to 2 months. Reheat only the amount needed, as sauce cannot be reheated more than once. To reheat, place in saucepan and cook over medium heat until hot, stirring occasionally. Serve sauce with beef steak or use as a basting sauce for grilled beef steak. Discard any leftover basting sauce.

Smoked Texas Beef Brisket with Cabernet Barbecue Sauce

Cook this tender, flavorful brisket in either a smoker (the authentic Texas way) or on the stovetop. For a glazed barbecue appearance, grill it briefly just before serving.

Total preparation and stovetop cooking time: 3¾ to 4 hours (time may vary if using smoker)
Makes 6 to 8 servings.

RUB

3	tablespoons paprika
1	tablespoon granulated garlic
2	teaspoons brown sugar
2	teaspoons onion powder
1½	teaspoons kosher or table salt
1	teaspoon pepper
1	teaspoon chili powder
½	teaspoon ground cumin
1	boneless beef brisket, flat cut (2½ to 3 pounds)

CABERNET BARBECUE SAUCE

1¼	cups Cabernet Sauvignon or other dry red wine
½	cup beer
½	cup ketchup
¼	cup molasses
2	tablespoons soy sauce
2	tablespoons cider vinegar
1	tablespoon Dijon-style mustard
1	teaspoon kosher or table salt
1	teaspoon chili powder
1	cup beer (for stovetop cooking method only)

1. Combine rub ingredients in small bowl; press evenly onto beef brisket. Wrap in plastic wrap and refrigerate while preparing barbecue sauce or as long as overnight.

2. Meanwhile, combine Cabernet Barbecue Sauce ingredients in medium saucepan; bring to a boil. Reduce heat; simmer 25 to 35 minutes or until reduced to 1 cup, stirring occasionally. Cover and reserve ½ cup barbecue sauce to serve with brisket; use remaining sauce for brushing on brisket during smoking or grilling.

3. Choose desired cooking method: Smoker Method or Stovetop Method.

Nutrition information per serving (⅙ of recipe)

Calories: 263
Fat: 6 g
 Saturated fat: 2 g
 Monounsaturated fat: 2 g
Cholesterol: 49 mg
Sodium: 1,329 mg
Carbohydrate: 18 g
Fiber: 2.0 g
Protein: 30 g
Niacin: 5.0 mg
Vitamin B$_6$: 0.6 mg
Vitamin B$_{12}$: 2.1 mcg
Iron: 6.1 mg
Selenium: 32.3 mcg
Zinc: 7.2 mg

This recipe is an excellent source of protein, niacin, vitamin B$_6$, vitamin B$_{12}$, iron, selenium, and zinc.

4. Smoker Method: Prepare charcoal or gas smoker according to manufacturer's directions. Unwrap brisket and smoke according to manufacturer's instructions and cooking times or until fork-tender, brushing occasionally with barbecue sauce.

5. Stovetop Method: Unwrap brisket. Place brisket, fat side up, in stockpot. Add beer; bring to a boil. Reduce heat; cover tightly and simmer 2½ to 3 hours or until brisket is fork-tender.

6. Carve brisket diagonally across the grain into thin slices. Serve with reserved barbecue sauce.

COOK'S TIP
Briefly grilling the braised brisket caramelizes the sauce and gives the beef a barbecued appearance. After cooking, remove brisket from cooking liquid. Place, fat side up, on grid over medium, ash-covered coals; brush with barbecue sauce. Grill, uncovered, 8 to 10 minutes, turning and brushing with sauce every 2 to 3 minutes.

Italian Pot Roast with Sweet Peppers, Olives, and Capers

Browning the beef before braising is the secret to this flavorful pot roast.

Total preparation and
cooking time: 3 hours
Makes 6 servings.

CHEF RICHARD'S TIP

Serve with your
favorite mashed pota-
toes, garlic mashed
potatoes, or creamy
polenta.

**Nutrition information
per serving**

Calories: 367
Fat: 14 g
   Saturated fat: 3 g
   Monounsaturated fat: 9 g
Cholesterol: 60 mg
Sodium: 1,035 mg
Carbohydrate: 28 g
Fiber: 5.8 g
Protein: 27 g
Niacin: 3.6 mg
Vitamin B_6: 0.4 mg
Vitamin B_{12}: 2.6 mcg
Iron: 4.7 mg
Selenium: 26.2 mcg
Zinc: 5.6 mg

**This recipe is an excellent
source of fiber, protein, vitamin B_6, vitamin B_{12}, iron,
selenium, and zinc, and a
good source of niacin.**

2	teaspoons olive oil
1	boneless beef chuck shoulder pot roast (2 pounds)
½	teaspoon salt
½	teaspoon black pepper
1	medium onion, chopped
4	cloves garlic, chopped
1½	cups dry red wine
1	can (28 ounces) whole tomatoes, drained, chopped
1	can (14 to 14½ ounces) ready-to-serve beef broth
12	large green Spanish olives, cut in half
2	tablespoons balsamic vinegar
1	tablespoon sugar
1	tablespoon capers, drained
2	bay leaves
1	teaspoon dried oregano leaves, crumbled, divided
1	teaspoon dried thyme leaves, crumbled, divided
½	teaspoon crushed red pepper
4	large carrots, cut diagonally into 1-inch pieces
3	medium red bell peppers, cut into 1-inch squares
2	tablespoons olive oil
3	tablespoons cornstarch dissolved in 3 tablespoons water

1. Heat 2 teaspoons oil in stockpot over medium heat until hot. Place beef pot roast in stockpot; brown evenly. Remove pot roast; season with salt and black pepper.

2. Add onion and garlic to stockpot; cook and stir 3 to 5 minutes or until onion is tender. Add wine; increase heat to medium-high. Cook and stir 5 minutes or until browned bits attached to bottom of stockpot are dissolved. Stir in tomatoes, broth, olives, vinegar, sugar, capers, bay leaves, ½ teaspoon oregano, ½ teaspoon thyme, and crushed red pepper. Return pot roast to stockpot; bring to a boil. Reduce heat; cover tightly and simmer 2 to 2½ hours or until pot roast is fork-tender.

3. Meanwhile, heat oven to 425°F. Toss carrots and bell peppers with remaining 2 tablespoons oil, remaining ½ teaspoon oregano, and remaining ½ teaspoon thyme in large bowl. Transfer to metal

baking sheet. Roast in 425°F oven for 35 to 40 minutes or until crisp-tender.

4. Remove pot roast; keep warm. Skim fat from cooking liquid; discard bay leaves. Add roasted vegetables to cooking liquid; stir in cornstarch mixture. Bring to a boil; reduce heat and simmer 4 minutes or until sauce is thickened, stirring occasionally. Season with salt and black pepper, as desired.

5. Carve pot roast into slices; serve with vegetables and sauce.

Lemon, Parsley, and Pine Nut–Crusted Flank Steak with Sherry-Wilted Spinach

While often marinated and grilled, flank steak is also delicious pounded thin, breaded, and cooked in a skillet.

⅓   cup dry bread crumbs
3   tablespoons chopped pine nuts
2   tablespoons chopped fresh Italian parsley
2   teaspoons freshly grated lemon peel
½   teaspoon coarse-grind black pepper
¼   teaspoon salt
3   tablespoons all-purpose flour
¼   cup egg substitute
1½   pounds beef flank steak
2   tablespoons olive oil, divided
     Salt, as desired

SHERRY-WILTED SPINACH
4   teaspoons olive oil
1   tablespoon minced garlic
2   packages (10 ounces each) fresh spinach, stemmed, torn into large pieces
½   teaspoon salt
½   teaspoon pepper
¾   cup dry sherry

1   lemon, cut into 6 wedges

1. Combine bread crumbs, pine nuts, parsley, lemon peel, coarse-grind pepper, and ¼ teaspoon salt in shallow dish; mix well. Place flour on plate and egg substitute in second shallow dish. Set aside.

2. Cut beef steak diagonally across the grain into 6 equal pieces. Place 1 steak piece between 2 pieces of plastic wrap or parchment paper. Using smooth side of meat mallet, pound to ¼-inch thickness. Repeat with remaining steak pieces.

3. Dredge 1 side only of each steak piece in flour, shaking off excess. Dip floured side into egg substitute, then into bread crumb mixture to coat.

Total preparation and cooking time: 45 minutes
Makes 6 servings.

● ● ● ● ● ● ● ● ● ● ● ●
BEEF SMARTS
Accentuate the meaty, savory flavor of lean beef by pairing it with foods that bring out the umami, such as tomatoes, wine, soy sauce, mushrooms, cheese, corn, spinach, and beets, to name a few. See page 243 to find out more about umami.

Nutrition information per serving

Calories: 334
Fat: 17 g
    Saturated fat: 4 g
    Monounsaturated fat: 9 g
Cholesterol: 42 mg
Sodium: 481 mg
Carbohydrate: 13 g
Fiber: 3.0 g
Protein: 29 g
Niacin: 8.3 mg
Vitamin B_6: 0.7 mg
Vitamin B_{12}: 1.5 mcg
Iron: 5.2 mg
Selenium: 31.2 mcg
Zinc: 5.4 mg

This recipe is an excellent source of protein, niacin, vitamin B_6, vitamin B_{12}, iron, selenium, and zinc, and a good source of fiber.

4. Heat 1 tablespoon oil in large nonstick skillet over medium heat until hot. Place 3 steak pieces in skillet, breaded sides down. Cook 5 to 7 minutes for medium-rare to medium doneness, turning once after breading develops a lightly browned crust. (If necessary, reposition steaks in skillet for even browning.) Wipe out skillet with paper towel. Repeat with remaining 1 tablespoon oil and 3 steak pieces. Season with salt, as desired. Keep warm.

5. To prepare Sherry-Wilted Spinach, heat oil in large nonstick skillet over medium heat until hot. Add garlic; cook and stir 1 to 2 minutes or until fragrant and lightly browned (watch carefully to prevent burning). Add spinach a handful at a time until all spinach has been added, cooking and stirring constantly 2 to 3 minutes or until leaves are evenly coated with oil and wilted. Stir in salt and pepper. Drain spinach in colander. Add sherry to same skillet; bring to a boil. Reduce heat; simmer 3 to 5 minutes or until reduced to ⅓ cup. Return spinach to skillet; toss to coat. Cook until heated through.

6. Serve steaks with spinach and lemon wedges.

COOK'S TIP
Use the bottom of a heavy pan to flatten beef pieces if a meat mallet is not available.

Garlic and Wine Tenderloin with Cremini Mushroom Risotto

Risotto, a creamy rice dish from northern Italy, is a delicious accompaniment to roasted tenderloin.

1 teaspoon olive oil
1 center-cut beef tenderloin roast (about 2 pounds)
½ teaspoon salt
¼ teaspoon pepper
1 tablespoon minced garlic
1 cup dry white wine
1 can (14 to 14½ ounces) ready-to-serve vegetable broth
1 tablespoon chopped fresh Italian parsley

CREMINI MUSHROOM RISOTTO

3 cups water
1 can (14 to 14½ ounces) ready-to-serve beef broth
2 teaspoons olive oil
1½ cups chopped leeks, white parts only
1 tablespoon minced garlic
2½ cups sliced cremini mushrooms
1 to 2 tablespoons water (optional)
2 teaspoons finely chopped fresh thyme
¼ teaspoon salt
1¾ cups arborio rice
½ cup Madeira
1 tablespoon chopped fresh Italian parsley
½ teaspoon salt
¼ teaspoon pepper

1. Heat oven to 425°F. Heat oil in large nonstick skillet over medium heat until hot. Place beef roast in skillet; brown evenly. Remove roast from skillet. Place on rack in shallow roasting pan. Season with salt and pepper.

2. In same skillet, cook and stir garlic over medium heat 30 seconds. Add wine; cook and stir 5 to 6 minutes or until browned bits attached to skillet are dissolved and wine is reduced to ½ cup. Add vegetable broth and parsley; bring to a boil. Pour into roasting pan around roast; brush surface of roast with broth mixture.

Total preparation and cooking time: 1¼ hours
Makes 8 servings.

CHEF RICHARD'S TIP

Short-grain arborio rice is essential for risotto's creamy texture. Its high starch content allows it to absorb a large amount of liquid yet remain firm. Arborio rice is available in the rice or Italian section of most supermarkets.

Nutrition information per serving

Calories: 386
Fat: 9 g
  Saturated fat: 3 g
  Monounsaturated fat: 4 g
Cholesterol: 67 mg
Sodium: 807 mg
Carbohydrate: 40 g
Fiber: 1.2 g
Protein: 30 g
Niacin: 8.2 mg
Vitamin B_6: 0.6 mg
Vitamin B_{12}: 1.4 mcg
Iron: 2.7 mg
Selenium: 32.1 mcg
Zinc: 4.8 mg

This recipe is an excellent source of protein, niacin, vitamin B_6, vitamin B_{12}, selenium, and zinc, and a good source of iron.

3. Insert ovenproof thermometer so tip is centered in thickest part of beef. Do not add water or cover. Roast in 425°F oven 35 to 40 minutes for medium-rare, 45 to 50 minutes for medium. Baste with cooking liquid halfway through roasting.

4. Meanwhile, prepare Cremini Mushroom Risotto. Combine water and broth in medium bowl or 2-quart measuring cup. Set aside. Heat oil in large saucepan over medium heat until hot. Add leeks and garlic; cook 3 to 4 minutes or until leeks are tender but not browned, stirring frequently to prevent burning. Add mushrooms; cook and stir 2 minutes or until tender. Add 1 to 2 tablespoons water if all liquid evaporates from saucepan. Stir in thyme and salt. Add rice; cook 1 minute, stirring constantly. Add 1 cup broth mixture; cook until liquid is absorbed, stirring frequently. Add Madeira; cook and stir until absorbed. Add remaining broth mixture, ½ cup at a time, stirring frequently. Wait until each addition of broth is absorbed before adding next ½ cup. Total cooking time will be about 25 minutes or until rice is tender and creamy. Stir in parsley, salt, and pepper; keep warm.

5. Remove roast when meat thermometer registers 135°F for medium-rare, 150°F for medium. Transfer roast to carving board; tent loosely with aluminum foil. Let stand 15 to 20 minutes. (Temperature will continue to rise about 10°F to reach 145°F for medium-rare, 160°F for medium.)

6. Skim fat from cooking liquid, if necessary. Set aside liquid. Carve roast into ½-inch-thick slices. Arrange roast slices over risotto. Spoon some cooking liquid over roast slices, if desired.

COOK'S TIPS

- Successful risotto requires arborio rice, liquid added in increments, and frequent stirring. When the dish is finished, the rice is firm, yet tender, and is bound in a creamy, velvety sauce.
- Dark-brown cremini mushrooms resemble white button mushrooms but have a slightly firmer texture and fuller flavor. They are available in most supermarkets and are sometimes called baby portobellos because they are immature portobello mushrooms.

Roasted Herb-Rubbed Beef Tri-Tip with Orange and Red Onion Salsa

This colorful salsa complements the tri-tip roast beautifully. You won't believe how easy it is!

Total preparation and cooking time: 1¼ hours

Makes 6 to 8 servings.

4	garlic cloves
½	cup packed fresh parsley
2	tablespoons fresh thyme
1	teaspoon coarse-grind black pepper
½	teaspoon salt
1	beef tri-tip roast (1½ to 2 pounds)

ORANGE AND RED ONION SALSA

1½	cups drained canned mandarin orange segments, chopped
½	cup finely chopped red onion
3	tablespoons chopped fresh mint
1	tablespoon olive oil
1	tablespoon fresh lime juice
1½	teaspoons minced fresh ginger
¼	teaspoon salt

1. Heat oven to 425°F. Place garlic in food processor bowl. Cover; process until chopped. Add parsley, thyme, pepper, and salt. Process until herbs are chopped. Press herb mixture evenly onto all surfaces of beef roast.

2. Place roast on rack in shallow roasting pan. Do not add water or cover. Roast in 425°F oven 30 to 40 minutes for medium-rare, 40 to 45 minutes for medium doneness.

3. Remove roast when instant-read thermometer registers 135°F for medium-rare, 150°F for medium. Transfer roast to carving board; tent loosely with aluminum foil. Let stand 15 minutes. (Temperature will continue to rise about 10°F to reach 145°F for medium-rare, 160°F for medium.)

4. Meanwhile, combine Orange and Red Onion Salsa ingredients in small bowl.

5. Carve roast across the grain into thin slices. Serve with salsa.

COOK'S TIP

While the beef is roasting, put some potatoes in the oven to bake, too. Serve with a green vegetable such as broccoli or spinach for a naturally nutrient-rich meal.

Nutrition information per serving (⅙ of recipe)

Calories: 212
Fat: 9 g
   Saturated fat: 3 g
   Monounsaturated fat: 5 g
Cholesterol: 60 mg
Sodium: 345 mg
Carbohydrate: 9 g
Fiber: 1.2 g
Protein: 24 g
Niacin: 6.9 mg
Vitamin B_6: 0.6 mg
Vitamin B_{12}: 1.3 mcg
Iron: 2.5 mg
Selenium: 26.9 mcg
Zinc: 4.7 mg

This recipe is an excellent source of protein, niacin, vitamin B_6, vitamin B_{12}, selenium, and zinc, and a good source of iron.

Holiday Brisket with Red Cabbage and Creamy Mustard Sauce

Total preparation and
cooking time: 3¼ hours
Makes 6 to 8 servings.

CHEF RICHARD'S TIP

The spice-infused cooking liquid makes a natural and light au jus to serve with the brisket.

Served with a tangy honey-mustard sauce, this enticing brisket dish may become a holiday tradition in your family.

2	teaspoons olive oil
1	boneless beef brisket, flat cut (about 2½ to 3 pounds)
⅛	teaspoon salt
⅛	teaspoon pepper
4	cups ready-to-serve beef broth
2	tablespoons pickling spice

CREAMY MUSTARD SAUCE

½	cup reduced-fat dairy sour cream
¼	cup Dijon-style mustard
2	teaspoons honey
1	teaspoon prepared horseradish

RED CABBAGE

2	teaspoons pickling spice
2½	cups thinly sliced unpeeled Granny Smith apples
2	cups slivered red onions
6	cups thinly sliced shredded red cabbage
¾	cup ready-to-serve beef broth
⅓	cup packed brown sugar
¼	cup cider vinegar
1	teaspoon salt
½	teaspoon pepper

Nutrition information per serving

Calories: 348
Fat: 11 g
   Saturated fat: 4 g
   Monounsaturated fat: 4 g
Cholesterol: 60 mg
Sodium: 1,418 mg
Carbohydrate: 31 g
Fiber: 3.4 g
Protein: 33 g
Niacin: 4.6 mg
Vitamin B_6: 0.4 mg
Vitamin B_{12}: 2.1 mcg
Iron: 3.9 mg
Selenium: 29.9 mcg
Zinc: 7.2 mg

This recipe is an excellent source of protein, niacin, vitamin B_6, vitamin B_{12}, iron, selenium, and zinc, and a good source of fiber.

1. Heat oven to 325°F. Heat oil in large nonstick skillet over medium heat until hot. Place beef brisket in skillet; brown evenly. Remove brisket from skillet; season with salt and pepper. Pour off drippings, if necessary.

2. Place broth, pickling spice, and brisket in ovenproof stockpot. Cover tightly and cook in 325°F oven 2½ to 3 hours or until brisket is fork-tender.

3. Meanwhile, prepare Creamy Mustard Sauce and Red Cabbage. Combine sauce ingredients in small bowl. Cover and refrigerate until ready to serve.

4. To prepare Red Cabbage, cut double thickness of cheesecloth into 5-inch square. Place pickling spice in center of cheesecloth; gather

edges and tie closed with piece of kitchen string, forming small bag. Set aside. In same skillet used to brown brisket, combine apples and onions. Cover and cook over medium heat 8 to 10 minutes or until onions are tender, stirring occasionally. Add cabbage, broth, brown sugar, vinegar, and pickling spice bag; stir to combine. Bring to a boil. Reduce heat; cover and simmer 25 to 28 minutes or until cabbage is tender and begins to caramelize, stirring occasionally. Remove spice bag. Season with salt and pepper; keep warm.

5. Remove brisket from stockpot; keep warm. Skim fat from cooking liquid; strain out and discard solids. Set aside cooking liquid.

6. Carve brisket diagonally across the grain into thin slices. Spoon some cooking liquid over brisket, if desired. Serve with cabbage mixture and sauce.

COOK'S TIP
A paper coffee filter cut to similar dimensions can be substituted for cheesecloth.

Marsala Roast Tenderloin with Shiitake-Leek Compote

Ideal for special occasions, succulent beef tenderloin is roasted to perfection and served with a savory vegetable compote.

Total preparation and cooking time: 2 hours
Makes 8 servings.

COOK'S TIP

Marsala is an Italian wine imported from Sicily that can be found in most places where wine and liquor are sold.

1½ teaspoons olive oil
1 center-cut beef tenderloin roast (about 2 pounds)
2 medium shallots, chopped
1 tablespoon minced garlic
1 cup Marsala
1 can (14 to 14½ ounces) ready-to-serve beef broth
3 tablespoons chopped fresh parsley
2 teaspoons cornstarch dissolved in 1 tablespoon water

SHIITAKE-LEEK COMPOTE
6 medium leeks, cleaned, white and light green parts only, cut lengthwise in half
2 tablespoons butter, divided
2 cups sliced shiitake mushrooms
¾ cup dry white wine
1 teaspoon fresh thyme leaves
¼ teaspoon salt
¼ teaspoon freshly ground black pepper

Nutrition information per serving

Calories: 295
Fat: 11 g
  Saturated fat: 5 g
  Monounsaturated fat: 4 g
Cholesterol: 75 mg
Sodium: 317 mg
Carbohydrate: 15 g
Fiber: 1.5 g
Protein: 27 g
Niacin: 7.6 mg
Vitamin B_6: 0.7 mg
Vitamin B_{12}: 1.4 mcg
Iron: 3.6 mg
Selenium: 30.1 mcg
Zinc: 4.8 mg

This recipe is an excellent source of protein, niacin, vitamin B_6, vitamin B_{12}, iron, selenium, and zinc.

1. Heat oven to 425°F. Heat oil in large nonstick skillet over medium heat until hot. Place beef roast in skillet; brown evenly. Remove roast from skillet. Place on rack in shallow roasting pan. Season with salt and pepper, as desired.

2. In same skillet, add shallots and garlic; cook and stir 1 to 2 minutes. Add Marsala; cook and stir 6 to 7 minutes or until reduced by half. Add broth and parsley; bring to a boil. Pour into roasting pan around roast; brush surface of roast with broth mixture.

3. Insert ovenproof thermometer so tip is centered in thickest part of beef. Do not add water or cover. Roast in 425°F oven 35 to 40 minutes for medium-rare, 45 to 50 minutes for medium. Baste with cooking liquid halfway through roasting.

4. Remove roast when meat thermometer registers 135°F for medium-rare, 150°F for medium. Transfer roast to carving board; tent loosely with aluminum foil. Let stand 15 to 20 minutes.

(Temperature will continue to rise about 10°F to reach 145°F for medium-rare, 160°F for medium.)

5. Pour pan drippings into small saucepan; bring to a boil. Stir in cornstarch mixture; cook and stir 1 to 2 minutes or until thickened. Remove sauce from heat. Reserve.

6. To prepare Shiitake-Leek Compote, slice leeks crosswise into ½-inch-thick slices. Melt 1½ teaspoons butter in large nonstick skillet over medium heat. Add leeks; cook, covered, 10 minutes, stirring halfway through cooking. Add mushrooms, wine, and thyme; cook, covered, 5 minutes. Uncover skillet; continue cooking 10 minutes or until leeks are tender, stirring occasionally. Stir in reserved sauce; cook until heated through. Remove from heat; stir in remaining 1½ tablespoons butter, salt, and pepper.

7. Carve roast into ½-inch-thick slices. Serve with compote.

COOK'S TIP
Take advantage of having a roast in the oven and also roast some mixed vegetables such as potato wedges, bell peppers, onions, and tomatoes.

The Skinny on Beef and Health

● ●

You know that eating smart is a daily challenge. What you may not know is that something as rich and satisfying as beef can help you meet that challenge. That's because lean beef provides many essential nutrients needed for a healthy diet.

Now that we've grabbed your attention, it's time to "beef up" your knowledge of lean beef nutrition.

The Meaning of Lean

Beginning in the 1980s, recommendations for lowering blood cholesterol levels placed beef in a category of "foods to avoid." Today's beef cattle are leaner and the fat is trimmed more precisely from cuts you purchase at your supermarket. As a result, many cuts of beef are 20 percent leaner, on average, than they were in the 1980s.

According to government guidelines, a serving of beef qualifies as "lean" if it has less than 10 grams total fat, 4.5 grams or less saturated fat, and less than 95 milligrams cholesterol per serving (and per 100 grams, or 3.5 ounces). A serving qualifies as "extra lean" if it has less than 5 grams total fat, 2 grams or less saturated fat, and less than 95 milligrams cholesterol per serving (and per 100 grams, or 3.5 ounces).

There are at least twenty-nine cuts of beef that qualify as "lean" according to labeling guidelines. These range between 4 grams of fat (1.4 grams of saturated fat) to 8.2 grams of fat (3 grams of saturated fat) per 3-ounce serving. See the chart below showing the twenty-nine cuts of lean beef.

Twenty-nine Cuts of Lean Beef

Cut	Sat. Fat	Total Fat
Skinless Chicken Breast	0.9 g sat. fat	3.0 g total fat
Eye Round Roast and Steak*	1.4 g sat. fat	4.0 g total fat
Sirloin Tip Side Steak	1.6 g sat. fat	4.1 g total fat
Top Round Roast and Steak*	1.6 g sat. fat	4.6 g total fat
Bottom Round Roast and Steak*	1.7 g sat. fat	4.9 g total fat
Top Sirloin Steak	1.9 g sat. fat	4.9 g total fat
Brisket, Flat Half	1.9 g sat. fat	5.1 g total fat
95% Lean Ground Beef	2.4 g sat. fat	5.1 g total fat
Round Tip Roast and Steak*	1.9 g sat. fat	5.3 g total fat
Round Steak	1.9 g sat. fat	5.3 g total fat
Shank Cross Cuts	1.9 g sat. fat	5.4 g total fat
Chuck Shoulder Pot Roast	1.8 g sat. fat	5.7 g total fat
Sirloin Tip Center Roast and Steak*	2.1 g sat. fat	5.8 g total fat
Chuck Shoulder Steak	1.9 g sat. fat	6.0 g total fat
Bottom Round (Western Griller) Steak	2.2 g sat. fat	6.0 g total fat
Top Loin (Strip) Steak	2.3 g sat. fat	6.0 g total fat
Shoulder Petite Tender and Medallions*	2.4 g sat. fat	6.1 g total fat
Flank Steak	2.6 g sat. fat	6.3 g total fat
Shoulder Center (Ranch) Steak	2.4 g sat. fat	6.5 g total fat
Tri-Tip Roast and Steak*	2.6 g sat. fat	7.1 g total fat
Tenderloin Roast and Steak*	2.7 g sat. fat	7.1 g total fat
T-Bone Steak	3.0 g sat. fat	8.2 g total fat
Skinless Chicken Thigh	2.6 g sat. fat	9.2 g total fat

There are twenty-nine cuts of lean beef with fat content falling between that of a skinless chicken breast and a skinless chicken thigh when comparing cooked 3-ounce servings.

*Cuts combined for illustration purposes.

Source: US Department of Agriculture, Agricultural Research Service, 2005. USDA Nutrient Database for Standard Reference, Release 18. Based on cooked servings, visible fat trimmed.

Beef's Fat Portfolio

It's a fact that fat in your diet is essential. Fat helps your body absorb fat-soluble vitamins and form necessary hormones. It also can be used as a source of energy to fuel your body. Of course, you can overdo fat, which is why there has been so much emphasis on reducing fat in the diet. From a taste standpoint, fat contributes to the flavor, aroma, and texture of foods. Fat also helps to provide a feeling of satisfaction after a meal.

A common misperception about beef is that the majority of its fat is saturated, the type that raises blood cholesterol levels. However, like other foods with fat, beef contains a "package" of different types of fat, including saturated, monounsaturated, and polyunsaturated fats. What may surprise you is that about one-half of the fat in beef is monounsaturated, the same type found in olive oil. This type is considered a healthy fat that does not raise blood cholesterol levels and may help to increase "good" HDL cholesterol levels in the blood. See the chart below comparing the fats in beef, chicken, fish, and olive oil.

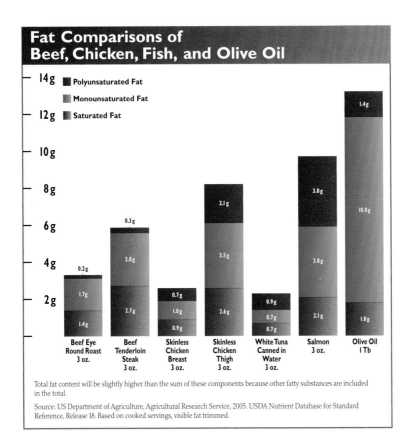

Fat Comparisons of Beef, Chicken, Fish, and Olive Oil

- Polyunsaturated Fat
- Monounsaturated Fat
- Saturated Fat

	Beef Eye Round Roast 3 oz.	Beef Tenderloin Steak 3 oz.	Skinless Chicken Breast 3 oz.	Skinless Chicken Thigh 3 oz.	White Tuna Canned in Water 3 oz.	Salmon 3 oz.	Olive Oil 1 Tb
Polyunsaturated Fat	0.2g	0.3g	0.7g	2.1g	0.9g	3.8g	1.4g
Monounsaturated Fat	1.7g	2.8g	1.0g	3.5g	0.7g	3.8g	10.0g
Saturated Fat	1.4g	2.7g	0.9g	2.6g	0.7g	2.1g	1.8g

Total fat content will be slightly higher than the sum of these components because other fatty substances are included in the total.

Source: US Department of Agriculture, Agricultural Research Service, 2005. USDA Nutrient Database for Standard Reference, Release 18. Based on cooked servings, visible fat trimmed.

Although beef also contains some polyunsaturated fat, most of the remaining fat is saturated. However, about one-third of this saturated fat is a type called stearic acid. Studies have shown that stearic acid is unique and does not raise blood cholesterol levels as do other saturated fats.

What about cholesterol? Today, there is less attention on cholesterol from food. That's because research has found dietary cholesterol has only a small effect on blood cholesterol levels in most healthy people. Even so, the cholesterol in lean beef ranges from about 40 to 80 milligrams of cholesterol per 3-ounce serving, well below the recommended 300 milligrams of cholesterol per day and comparable to skinless chicken (white and dark meat), which ranges from about 70 to 80 milligrams per 3-ounce serving. Bottom line, lean beef's fat and cholesterol profile makes it easy to fit this meat into a healthy diet. But there's even more to the fat story.

Another type of fat in food is called trans fat. The evidence is solid that this type of fat increases blood cholesterol levels. However, not all trans fats are alike. Man-made trans fat, found in many processed foods such as snack foods, cookies, vegetable shortening, and fried foods, tends to increase heart disease risk by raising blood levels of "bad" LDL cholesterol, and lowering "good" HDL cholesterol levels.

Small amounts of trans fats occur naturally in some foods, including beef, lamb, dairy products, cabbage, peas, and pomegranates. In contrast to man-made trans fat, this naturally occurring type acts very differently in the body. Research is showing that naturally occurring trans fat holds promise as a health-promoting component and may play a role in preventing disease, including cancer, heart disease, and diabetes, and it has been shown to stimulate the immune system and have positive effects on bone health.

Naturally Nutrient-Rich

The average 3-ounce serving of lean beef deliciously delivers nutrients that people of all ages need every day to stay healthy and energetic. Lean beef is considered *naturally nutrient-rich* because it packs a powerhouse of essential nutrients in a reasonable amount of calories. The next chart shows you the calorie "cost" for the nutrients supplied by lean beef.

One of the simplest strategies for improving your diet is to choose foods that are naturally nutrient-rich *first*, a cornerstone of the 2005 Dietary Guidelines for Americans. They include fruits, vegetables, whole grains, low-fat and nonfat dairy foods, lean meats, poultry, seafood, eggs, beans, and nuts. These foods have something in common—they all offer you the

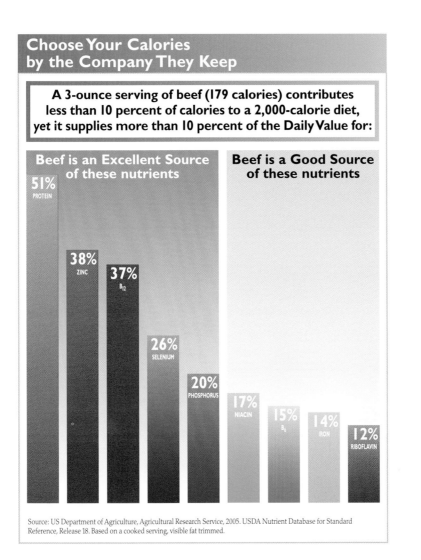

Choose Your Calories by the Company They Keep

A 3-ounce serving of beef (179 calories) contributes less than 10 percent of calories to a 2,000-calorie diet, yet it supplies more than 10 percent of the Daily Value for:

Beef is an Excellent Source of these nutrients

51% PROTEIN

38% ZINC

37% B₁₂

26% SELENIUM

20% PHOSPHORUS

Beef is a Good Source of these nutrients

17% NIACIN

15% B₆

14% IRON

12% RIBOFLAVIN

Source: US Department of Agriculture, Agricultural Research Service, 2005. USDA Nutrient Database for Standard Reference, Release 18. Based on a cooked serving, visible fat trimmed.

biggest bang (most nutrients) for your buck (calories). Of course, if your daily calorie limit allows it, you can also include other foods that supply calories but fewer nutrients, such as snack foods and desserts. See the table on page 230 for a comparison of calories and other nutrients in various meat choices.

Tales and Truths about Eating Beef

Chances are you've heard mixed messages about beef. The following statements are from people just like you. The scientific facts that follow help set the record straight.

Nutrient Bang for Your Calorie Buck

3-OUNCE COOKED SERVING	CALORIES	TOTAL FAT (g)	SAT. FAT (g)	CHOLESTEROL (mg)	PROTEIN (g)	IRON (mg)	ZINC (mg)	THIAMIN (mg)	RIBOFLAVIN (mg)	NIACIN (mg)	B_6 (mg)	PANTOTHENIC ACID (mg)	B_{12} (mcg)
BEEF													
Daily Value*	**2000**	**65**	**20**	**300**	**50**	**18**	**15**	**1.5**	**1.7**	**20**	**2**	**10**	**6**
Bottom Round Roast and Steak	139	4.9	1.7	64	23.8	2.0	4.1	0.05	0.13	4.3	0.3	0.5	1.3
95% Lean Ground Beef	139	5.1	2.4	65	21.9	2.4	5.5	0.04	0.15	5.3	0.3	0.5	2.6
Eye Round Roast and Steak	144	4.0	1.4	53	25.3	2.1	4.3	0.06	0.14	4.5	0.3	0.5	1.4
Sirloin Tip Side Steak	143	4.1	1.6	68	24.7	2.4	6.2	0.06	0.17	5.0	0.5	0.7	3.6
Chuck Shoulder Pot Roast	147	5.7	1.8	60	22.4	2.6	5.4	0.08	0.21	2.9	0.2	N/A	2.6
Round Tip Roast and Steak	148	5.3	1.9	75	23.4	2.0	4.0	0.05	0.13	4.2	0.3	0.5	1.3
Sirloin Tip Center Roast and Steak	150	5.8	2.1	65	23.1	2.1	5.8	0.05	0.18	4.4	0.4	0.6	2.7
Shoulder Petite Tender and Medallions	150	6.1	2.4	66	22.3	2.2	4.5	0.07	0.23	4.4	0.5	0.7	4.4
Round Steak	154	5.3	1.9	66	24.8	2.3	4.0	0.09	0.19	3.6	0.3	0.3	2.7
Bottom Round (Western Griller) Steak	155	6.0	2.2	65	23.4	2.5	4.3	0.06	0.18	6.4	0.6	0.7	3.4
Shoulder Center (Ranch) Steak	155	6.5	2.4	65	22.4	2.4	6.0	0.06	0.25	4.5	0.5	0.7	4.2
Top Sirloin Steak	156	4.9	1.9	49	26.0	1.7	4.9	0.07	0.13	7.4	0.6	0.5	1.5
Top Round Roast and Steak	157	4.6	1.6	61	27.1	2.3	4.7	0.06	0.15	4.9	0.4	0.5	1.5
Tri-Tip Roast and Steak	158	7.1	2.6	61	22.8	1.5	4.2	0.06	0.12	6.7	0.5	0.4	1.3
Flank Steak	158	6.3	2.6	42	23.7	1.5	4.3	0.07	0.12	6.8	0.5	0.5	1.4
Top Loin (Strip) Steak	161	6.0	2.3	56	24.9	1.6	4.6	0.07	0.13	7.1	0.5	0.5	1.4
Chuck Shoulder Steak	161	6.0	1.9	80	24.9	3.2	6.7	0.06	0.22	2.7	0.2	N/A	2.5
Brisket Flat Half	167	5.1	1.9	49	28.2	2.4	6.8	0.06	0.18	4.1	0.3	0.6	2.1
Tenderloin Roast and Steak	170	7.1	2.7	67	24.7	1.6	4.6	0.07	0.13	7.1	0.5	0.5	1.4
Shank Cross Cuts	171	5.4	1.9	66	28.6	3.3	8.9	0.12	0.18	5.0	0.3	0.3	3.2
T-Bone Steak	172	8.2	3.0	48	23.0	3.1	4.3	0.09	0.21	3.9	0.3	0.3	1.9
PORK													
Daily Value*	**2000**	**65**	**20**	**300**	**50**	**18**	**15**	**1.5**	**1.7**	**20**	**2**	**10**	**6**
Top Loin Chop	141	3.6	1.3	65	25.4	0.5	1.8	0.50	0.16	8.8	0.4	0.7	0.6
Tenderloin	159	5.4	1.9	80	25.9	1.2	2.5	0.84	0.33	4.4	0.4	0.8	0.9
Sirloin Chop	181	8.6	3.1	72	24.2	0.9	2.3	0.87	0.32	4.0	0.5	0.7	0.7
Rib Chop	186	8.3	2.9	69	26.2	0.7	2.0	0.95	0.28	5.2	0.4	0.6	0.7
POULTRY													
Daily Value*	**2000**	**65**	**20**	**300**	**50**	**18**	**15**	**1.5**	**1.7**	**20**	**2**	**10**	**6**
Skinless, Boneless Chicken Breast	140	3.0	0.9	72	26.4	0.9	0.9	0.06	0.10	11.7	0.5	0.8	0.3
Skinless, Boneless Turkey Breast	115	0.6	0.2	71	25.6	1.3	1.5	0.04	0.11	6.4	0.5	0.6	0.3
FISH													
Daily Value*	**2000**	**65**	**20**	**300**	**50**	**18**	**15**	**1.5**	**1.7**	**20**	**2**	**10**	**6**
Cod	89	0.7	0.1	47	19.4	0.4	0.5	0.08	0.07	2.1	0.2	0.2	0.9
Light Tuna Canned in Water	99	0.7	0.2	26	21.7	1.3	0.7	0.03	0.06	11.3	0.3	0.2	2.5
Halibut	119	2.5	0.4	35	22.7	0.9	0.5	0.06	0.08	6.1	0.3	0.3	1.2
Salmon	175	10.5	2.1	54	18.8	0.3	0.4	0.29	0.12	6.8	0.6	1.3	2.4

*Daily Value based on a 2000-calorie intake for adults and children 4 or more years of age. Source: USDA.

"My husband has a high cholesterol level. He heard that he shouldn't eat beef, but he's tired of eating only chicken and fish."

Avoiding beef is perhaps one of the most common misperceptions about following a heart-healthy diet. There is now clear-cut evidence that a heart-healthy diet including lean red meat (beef, veal, pork) can be just as effective at reducing blood cholesterol levels as can chicken and fish.

In the largest and longest research study of lean red meat as part of a diet designed to reduce the risk of heart disease, 145 adults with high blood cholesterol levels were followed for about eighteen months. The study participants all followed a low-fat diet, but some ate 6 ounces of lean red meat per day while others ate the same amount of lean white meat (poultry, fish). No differences in blood cholesterol levels between the two groups were observed. In fact, all of the study participants reduced their total cholesterol and "bad" LDL cholesterol levels, and they increased their "good" HDL cholesterol levels.

The practice of cutting out lean beef is not only unnecessary for most people, but it also can be potentially unhealthy. Here's why. Including lean beef in a low-fat diet offers the additional variety that may improve your ability and desire to stick with a heart-healthy diet in the long run. Studies show that when you deprive yourself of favorite foods, you can sabotage your good intentions over time. Instead of making a seemingly positive change, eliminating beef from your diet may actually make it harder to reach your diet and health goals. You *can* include sensible portions of lean beef in addition to chicken and fish. There is no rule that says being heart-healthy means sacrificing eating pleasure.

"I've heard that beef is a good source of iron, but I can also get iron from chicken or spinach."

Beef is the most readily available source of iron. To get the same amount of iron in 3 ounces of beef, you would need to eat about two and a half

HEART HELP

What if your risk for heart disease is high, or you've had a heart attack or heart surgery—do you need to swear off beef? It's true that you need to make changes in your diet. You may have been told to follow a cholesterol-lowering diet that restricts saturated fat to less than 7 percent of your total calories—a diet prescription recommended by the National Heart, Lung, and Blood Institute and the American Heart Association. How does this translate to amounts and types of meat? Even with the focus on keeping saturated fat intake low, there is room to include up to 5 ounces of meat per day, which can include lean beef. For instance, if you're following an 1,800-calorie diet, your daily limit for saturated fat is about 14 grams or less. A 3-ounce portion of lean beef supplies between 1.4 and 3 grams of saturated fat, depending on the cut. In any case, talk to your doctor or a registered dietitian for personalized advice on how much and what types of meat, including lean beef, you can eat.

When shopping for lean beef, here's a helpful tip: look for cuts of beef with "loin" or "round" on the label, such as sirloin, tenderloin, top round, or eye round. These generally have the least amount of fat. Take it a step further and choose lean cuts with the least amount of marbling and trim all visible fat around the edges before cooking.

chicken breasts or nearly 3 cups of spinach. In fact, research shows that if you eat beef regularly, you are more than twice as likely to meet 100 percent of the Daily Value for iron. Even mild, short-term iron deficiency can leave you feeling run-down and fatigued, impairing your ability to function at peak productivity.

Although iron is available in various foods, those who need it most, including children, adolescent girls, and women of child-bearing age, are the ones consuming the least. In infants and children, iron deficiency can impair growth and brain development, and lead to a weakened immune system. Low iron status is linked to lower scores on math tests among older children and adolescents. During pregnancy, without enough iron to build an increased blood supply, there is a greater risk for preterm and low-birthweight deliveries.

The iron in red meat is more completely absorbed in the body than the iron found in bread, cereal, and other plant products. In addition, eating red meat at a meal has been shown to increase your body's ability to absorb iron from plant foods at the same meal by two to four times. You'll find many recipes in this book that pair iron-enhancing beef with plant sources of iron such as spinach, legumes, and whole wheat bread. For example, try the Beef and Spinach Salad with Roasted Tomato Vinaigrette, Cowboy Beef and Black Bean Chili, and Beef Steak Gyros (made with whole wheat pita bread).

"My family loves hamburgers, tacos, and spaghetti with meatballs, but I don't serve these very often because ground beef has too much fat."

You can return these family favorites to your table because there is a new view of ground beef. The U.S. Department of Agriculture (USDA) recently updated its official nutrition data for ground beef. It now turns out that much of the ground beef available is lower in fat and calories yet remains high in many essential nutrients. In fact, the new nutrient data shows 95% lean/5% fat cooked ground beef meets government labeling guidelines for "lean" at 5 grams of fat per 3-ounce serving.

You've probably noticed that there are several varieties of ground beef available at your supermarket. You may see ground beef labeled as ground chuck, ground sirloin, or ground round. More commonly, though, you'll see ground beef labeled by the percent of lean and fat. Generally, the leanest ground beef is labeled as 95% or 96% lean (some stores may offer 97% lean), which means that most of the weight is from lean muscle with only a small amount of fat. See the following table for comparisons of several ground beef varieties.

CALORIES, FAT, AND CHOLESTEROL IN 3-OUNCE SERVINGS OF COOKED GROUND BEEF				
	Calories	Total Fat (g)	Saturated Fat (g)	Cholesterol (mg)
95% lean, pan-broiled patty	139	5.0	2.4	65
90% lean, pan-broiled patty	173	9.1	3.6	70
85% lean, pan-broiled patty	197	11.9	4.5	73
80% lean, pan-broiled patty	206	13.6	5.1	73

Source: *U.S. Department of Agriculture, Agricultural Research Service, 2005, USDA Nutrient Database for Standard Reference, Release 18*

Any type of ground beef is versatile and flavorful, which makes it a great meat for many different dishes. The easiest way to keep dishes with ground beef lower in fat is to start with at least 90% lean ground beef. But, whichever type of ground beef you use, you can take steps to reduce the fat content of the cooked beef. See page 242 for simple steps to reduce the fat in cooked ground beef.

"When I cook certain cuts of beef, they sometimes come out tough and dry."

The secret to moist and flavorful lean beef is in the cooking. There are two main reasons why beef can get tough or dry—using the wrong cooking method for the cut of meat and overcooking, either cooking too long or at a temperature that is too high.

Appendix B covers everything you need to know about selecting lean cuts of beef and matching them with appropriate cooking methods, such as roasting, broiling, grilling, stir-frying, braising, and stewing. It also covers methods for tenderizing, including marinades, natural enzyme tenderizers, and pounding. The recipes in this book take the guesswork out of cooking lean beef by suggesting the best cuts, cooking methods, and cooking times.

Fitting Beef into a Healthy Diet

About fifty different nutrients are essential to health, and no single food or food group contains all of these nutrients. When it comes to nutrients supplied by the meat group, about one-third of Americans are not meeting their daily requirements for iron, zinc, and vitamin B_6. About one in five also are not getting enough protein and other B vitamins, including niacin, thiamin, riboflavin, and vitamin B_{12}.

Considering the abundance of nutrients supplied by beef, it is not surprising that people who eat beef regularly are more likely to meet their daily needs for protein, iron, zinc, and B vitamins than people consuming less or no beef. Since no one food or food group can provide all the nutrients your body needs, your best bet is to think variety when it comes to making food choices. From the meat and bean group, this means choosing from lean beef and pork, skinless poultry, fish, and other lean protein sources. You'll get the enjoyment of eating a variety of foods and you'll be more likely to obtain the right amounts of nutrients provided by meat group foods while managing your fat and calories.

Beef's Nutrient Roster

Take a closer look at some of the key nutrients lean beef has to offer.

- *Protein.* The protein in beef (and in all animal sources of protein) is complete and high-quality. In other words, beef can supply all of the essential amino acids (building blocks of protein) the body needs to build, maintain, and repair body tissue and muscle, form hormones and enzymes, and increase resistance to infection and disease. A 3-ounce serving of lean beef supplies more than one-half of the amount of protein most people need each day.

- *Iron.* Beef is a good source of iron, which helps red blood cells carry oxygen to body tissues. It also plays an important role in cognitive health (memory, ability to learn and reason) throughout life. The iron in meat is easily utilized by the body and it helps the body absorb and use iron present in plant foods. A 3-ounce serving of lean beef supplies 14 percent of the amount of iron that most people need each day.

- *Zinc.* Beef is an excellent source of this essential mineral. Zinc helps build muscles and heal wounds, maintain the immune system, and contribute to cognitive health throughout life. A 3-ounce serving of lean beef supplies 38 percent of the amount of zinc that most people need each day.

- *B vitamins.* Beef contains significant amounts of several B vitamins. Vitamin B_{12} is needed for normal functioning of body cells and of the nervous system, and is only found naturally in animal foods. Vitamin B_6 is important for a healthy nervous system, and it helps the body fight infection and build protein needed for growth. Both vitamins B_6 and B_{12} play important roles in lowering blood levels of homocysteine, an amino acid that increases risk for heart disease. Niacin promotes healthy skin and nerves, aids digestion, and fosters normal appetite. Riboflavin helps the body use energy and promotes healthy skin and good vision. A 3-ounce serving of lean beef supplies about 37 percent of the amount of vitamin B_{12}, 17 percent of the amount of niacin, 15 percent of the amount of vitamin B_6, and 12 percent of the amount of riboflavin that most people need each day.

BEEF HELPS FUEL AN ACTIVE LIFESTYLE

Your body needs enough energy (calories), protein, vitamins, and minerals to fuel a lifestyle that includes regular physical activity. You don't need to spend hours in the gym to reap the benefits of physical activity. Simply aim to be physically active for at least thirty to sixty minutes each day. This can include walking the dog, yard work, playing with the kids—anything that gets you moving. Beef, as part of a balanced diet, helps to supply energy and several of the nutrients you need to power your body before, during, and after physical activity.

- Zinc is involved in energy metabolism during physical activity and plays a role in muscle building and recovery.

- Iron helps deliver oxygen to working muscles and is required for energy metabolism.

- Protein is essential in building and repairing muscle tissue and aids in muscle recovery after physical activity.

- B vitamins help convert foods that you eat into energy.

When it comes to certain key nutrients, beef has a nutritional edge over other foods. The figure on this page shows how beef stacks up compared to other foods.

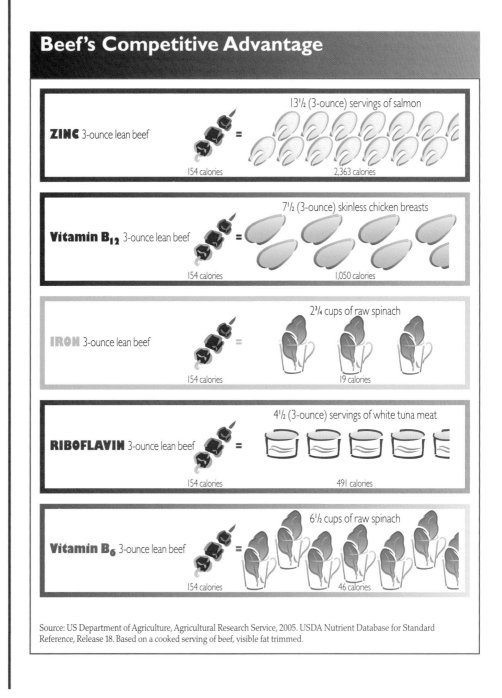

Beef's Competitive Advantage

ZINC 3-ounce lean beef = 13½ (3-ounce) servings of salmon
154 calories — 2,363 calories

Vitamin B₁₂ 3-ounce lean beef = 7½ (3-ounce) skinless chicken breasts
154 calories — 1,050 calories

IRON 3-ounce lean beef = 2¾ cups of raw spinach
154 calories — 19 calories

RIBOFLAVIN 3-ounce lean beef = 4½ (3-ounce) servings of white tuna meat
154 calories — 491 calories

Vitamin B₆ 3-ounce lean beef = 6½ cups of raw spinach
154 calories — 46 calories

Source: US Department of Agriculture, Agricultural Research Service, 2005. USDA Nutrient Database for Standard Reference, Release 18. Based on a cooked serving of beef, visible fat trimmed.

Size-wise Guidelines

Practicing portion control is the logical next step after you know how to select and cook lean beef. To keep from exceeding your daily needs for certain nutrients, such as calories and fat, one of the easiest steps you can take is to keep tabs on your portions.

The amount of food you choose to eat is considered a "portion," which may be larger or smaller than a standard "serving size" listed on a Nutrition Facts panel. Take meat, for example. The government's Dietary Guidelines recommend about 5 to 7 ounces of (cooked) meat each day, depending on your calorie needs. A "standard" serving of meat is about 3 ounces cooked, but this doesn't mean that you can only eat this amount at one time. Standard serving sizes are meant to help you plan and judge your portions so that your day's food choices will supply enough calories and nutrients without overdoing it. See the table below.

Bottom line: You can decide to eat your daily meat quota all at one meal, or you can split it between your meals. When you practice balance, you can exceed your portion on one day and cut back on another day. Occasionally, you can enjoy a larger portion of meat without feeling guilty. Simply adjust your portions on other days so that you average about 5 to 7 ounces of meat or other protein foods on most days.

HOW MUCH FROM THE MEAT AND BEANS GROUP?

Daily Calories	Daily Fat Allowance (30% of total calories)	Suggested Daily Amount from Meat and Beans Group*	Approximate Calorie and Fat Contribution of Daily Amount as Lean Beef**
1,600	53 grams	5 ounces	268 calories 10 grams of fat
2,200	69 grams	6 ounces	322 calories 12 grams of fat
2,800	86 grams	7 ounces	376 calories 14 grams of fat

*Based on recommendations from the Dietary Guidelines for Americans, 2005. One ounce from the meat and beans group is equivalent to 1 ounce of cooked lean meat, poultry, or fish, 1 egg, ¼ cup cooked dry beans or tofu, 1 tablespoon peanut butter, or ½ ounce nuts or seeds.
**Based on a broiled Top Loin (Strip) Steak in the amount indicated.

Develop an "Eye" for Portions

Without a food scale, it can be hard to judge the size of a steak or burger. But there are simple ways to visually judge a 3-ounce cooked portion of meat. For example, a 3-ounce portion of steak or hamburger is about the size of a deck of cards or a computer mouse. Use the photos below to help you judge your portions of different cuts of lean beef compared to some household items. Remember, though, your portions may be more or less than the given amounts; just be sure to keep tabs on your total meat portions over the course of the day. To show how easy and enjoyable it is to eat a moderate portion of meat, most of the recipes in this book feature about 3 ounces of beef per serving.

How a 3-ounce steak compares to a deck of cards

How a 3-ounce hamburger compares to a hockey puck

How 3 ounces of beef cubes compare to four child's blocks

How 3 ounces of beef strips compare to a 6-inch ruler

Beef Basics from the Experts

● ●

Beef is convenient, versatile, and easy to prepare. And it partners deliciously with a broad range of flavors, from Asian to Mediterranean. The information in this section takes the guesswork out of buying, storing, handling, cooking, and serving beef. You'll learn how to bring delicious lean beef dishes to your table with ease and confidence.

Smart Shopping for Beef

What to Look For

As with other perishable foods, it's a good idea to select meat last when shopping to ensure that the meat stays cold as long as possible until you get home. Follow these general guidelines for selecting beef:

- Choose beef with a bright cherry-red color, without any grayish or brown blotches. A darker purplish-red color is typical of vacuum-packaged beef. Once exposed to oxygen, beef will turn from a darker red to bright red. With extended exposure to oxygen, beef's cherry-red color will take on a brown color.
- Fresh ground beef goes through a number of color changes during its shelf life. These color changes are normal, and the ground

beef remains perfectly wholesome and safe to eat if purchased by the "sell by" date on the package label.

- A package of ground beef may appear bright red on the surface, where it is exposed to oxygen through the permeable plastic wrapping, while the interior, where oxygen is absent, remains purplish-red.

- Purchase before or on the "sell by" date printed on the package label. Generally, beef can be stored at a temperature of 35°F to 40°F for one to four days after purchase.

- Choose beef packages that are cold, tightly wrapped, and have no tears or punctures. Be sure the packages do not contain excessive liquid, an indication of temperature fluctuations, excessive storage time, or lack of full vacuum.

- Choose steaks, roasts, and pot roasts that are firm to the touch, not soft.

Which Cut?

An individual store can have more than forty different beef cuts available in the meat case. In addition, many markets provide time-saving, value-added items such as beef strips for stir-frying, kabob kits complete with beef cubes and vegetables, and stuffed, rolled, and tied flank steaks.

Thanks to industry efforts, today's beef cuts are more standardized, labeling is improved, and there is more nutrition and cooking information available at the point of sale. The illustration on the next page shows the areas where lean beef cuts come from on the animal. Also called the primal cuts, these areas include the chuck, rib, loin, round, shank, brisket, and flank.

Matching the correct beef cut to the appropriate cooking method is one of the most important steps you can take to ensure moist, juicy, flavorful beef. Tender beef cuts such as tenderloin and sirloin can be cooked relatively quickly using dry-heat methods such as grilling, roasting, and pan broiling. Less tender cuts such as shoulder steak and bottom round need the

BEEF GRADING

Beef is graded for quality by the USDA according to established standards. Grades are based on the amount of marbling (flecks of fat within the lean) and the age of the animal. Quality grades indicate palatability—tenderness, juiciness, and flavor of the cooked beef. While there are eight quality grades for beef, usually only the top three are identified and sold at retail: prime, choice and select.

Prime has the most marbling. It is produced in limited quantities and usually sold to fine restaurants and specialty meat markets. Choice falls between prime and select. Of these three, select has the least amount of marbling, making it leaner than but often not as tender, juicy, and flavorful as choice and prime grades. Most supermarkets today offer a selection of choice and select cuts.

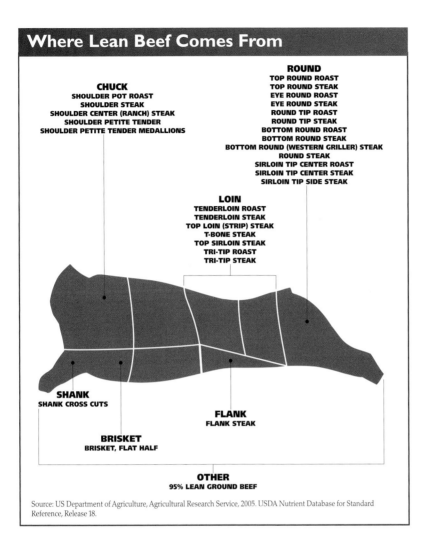

Where Lean Beef Comes From

CHUCK
SHOULDER POT ROAST
SHOULDER STEAK
SHOULDER CENTER (RANCH) STEAK
SHOULDER PETITE TENDER
SHOULDER PETITE TENDER MEDALLIONS

ROUND
TOP ROUND ROAST
TOP ROUND STEAK
EYE ROUND ROAST
EYE ROUND STEAK
ROUND TIP ROAST
ROUND TIP STEAK
BOTTOM ROUND ROAST
BOTTOM ROUND STEAK
BOTTOM ROUND (WESTERN GRILLER) STEAK
ROUND STEAK
SIRLOIN TIP CENTER ROAST
SIRLOIN TIP CENTER STEAK
SIRLOIN TIP SIDE STEAK

LOIN
TENDERLOIN ROAST
TENDERLOIN STEAK
TOP LOIN (STRIP) STEAK
T-BONE STEAK
TOP SIRLOIN STEAK
TRI-TIP ROAST
TRI-TIP STEAK

SHANK
SHANK CROSS CUTS

FLANK
FLANK STEAK

BRISKET
BRISKET, FLAT HALF

OTHER
95% LEAN GROUND BEEF

Source: US Department of Agriculture, Agricultural Research Service, 2005. USDA Nutrient Database for Standard Reference, Release 18.

longer, slower cooking methods of moist-heat cookery (such as braising or stewing). The table on page 249 shows standard retail cuts and suggested cooking methods. In "Secrets to Successful Beef Cookery," beginning on page 248, you'll learn more about dry- and moist-heat cooking methods.

Recent beef industry innovation has led to the development of new muscle cuts from the chuck and the round. Some of these cuts have unique qualities, such as a high degree of tenderness or flavor. Data from analysis of seven of these new cuts show that they also meet the government guidelines for lean. These include shoulder petite tender (roast or medallions), shoulder center (Ranch Steak), sirloin tip side steak, sirloin tip center (steak or roast), and bottom round (Western Griller) steak.

Ground Beef

Ground beef packages are labeled according to USDA standards and by supermarket preferences. Lean-to-fat ratios vary. The information on the labels will be expressed *as % lean/% fat*. Labels also may indicate the primal cut of beef that has been ground: ground chuck, ground round, or ground sirloin.

In general, ground beef that is 70% to 75% lean is suitable for dishes in which you drain the fat from the cooked beef, such as sloppy joes, chili, and spaghetti sauce. Ground beef that is 80% to 90% lean works well for meatloaf, meatballs, hamburgers, casseroles, and Salisbury steak. As you'll see in the recipes in this book, 95% lean ground beef works wonderfully in any recipe that calls for ground beef—and provides less fat and calories.

REDUCING FAT IN COOKED GROUND BEEF

Whichever leanness of ground beef you select, you can reduce the fat content using a few simple techniques.

Ground Beef Crumbles. When preparing a dish that calls for cooked ground beef crumbles, such as spaghetti sauce, chili, sloppy joes, or tacos, you can drain the drippings that accumulate as you cook the beef, or when the crumbles are fully cooked, you can rinse the beef to remove even more fat. This is an excellent way to take advantage of lower-priced ground beef, such as 70% lean/30% fat, and still have the benefits of a leaner product. Nutrition researchers have found that a simple rinsing process can reduce the fat in cooked ground beef crumbles by as much as 50 percent. Note: Because 90% and higher lean beef are lower in fat, rinsing will not produce the same results and, therefore, it is not recommended.

1. Brown ground beef in a skillet over medium heat 8 to 10 minutes or until no longer pink. Stir occasionally to break beef into large pieces (about ½ inch).
2. Meanwhile, microwave 4 cups of water in a glass measuring cup or microwavable bowl on HIGH 5 to 6 minutes or until very hot (150°F to 160°F), but not boiling.
3. Using a slotted spoon, remove beef crumbles to a large plate or other container lined with three layers of white paper towels; let sit 1 minute, blot top of beef with paper towels.
4. Next, put beef crumbles in a fine-mesh strainer or colander. Pour the hot water over beef to rinse away fat. Do not run water directly from the tap because it causes the beef to break into finer pieces, which can affect the texture of your finished dish. Drain 5 minutes.

Beef Burgers, Meatballs, and Meatloaf. For pan-broiled beef burgers, you can reduce the fat by removing excess fat as it accumulates, and by placing the cooked burgers on several layers of paper towels before serving. For meatballs or meatloaf, place the beef in a pan on a rack so that the fat drips away. After cooking, place the beef on a surface lined with several layers of paper towels. You also can blot the sides and top of the cooked beef (if not glazed) for further fat reduction.

Beef Steaks

Beef steaks can be categorized as tender or less tender. Most tender steaks are cooked by dry-heat methods. These include premium steaks and more affordable family-priced steaks, which usually come from the center section of the animal (rib and loin). Some examples of premium steaks are top loin (strip), T-bone, and tenderloin. Family-priced tender steaks include top sirloin and tri-tip.

Less tender steaks are better suited for moist-heat cooking, although some may be cooked by dry heat after being tenderized in a tenderizing marinade. Less tender steaks come from the front and rear of the animal (chuck and round) and include top round, eye round, bottom round, and flank.

Beef Roasts

A roast is a cut of beef, thicker than 2 inches, that is suitable for cooking by dry heat on a rack in a shallow open pan, either in the oven or in a covered grill (indirect heat).

Premium roasts, such as tenderloin, tend to be more costly and are wonderful for holidays, entertaining, and other special occasions. Other roasts such as tri-tip, round tip, and eye round are more suitable for family fare and casual gatherings.

For holidays or special occasions, it's a good idea to order the type and size of roast you need in advance from your meat retailer. Expect larger appetites at these times and plan on about 6 ounces cooked, trimmed beef per serving.

Choose a beef tri-tip roast or a small beef tenderloin roast for small gatherings. Boneless roasts are easiest to carve. This is a great benefit when hosting a crowd or if serving buffet style.

Pot Roasts

Pot roast cuts contain more connective tissue, which makes them less tender. They require moist-heat cooking to tenderize the meat fibers and develop the natural beef flavors.

Many pot roast cuts can be used interchangeably in pot roast recipes, requiring only slight adjustments in

BEEF FLAVOR PAIRINGS: THE POWER OF UMAMI

Did you know that your taste buds have a fifth taste, in addition to sweet, salty, bitter, and sour? Known as "umami" (oo-MOM-ee) from the Japanese word for "delicious," *umai*, this fifth taste is described as meaty and savory. Part of umami's great flavor power comes from pairing together umami-rich foods. When umami compounds from different foods are combined in a dish, they have a magnifying effect on each other. In fact, a mixture of two umami-rich foods can produce eight times as much flavor as either one of the foods alone. It's no accident that beef is often paired with certain ingredients, such as tomatoes, wine, soy sauce, mushrooms, cheese, corn, spinach, or beets, to name a few. Like beef, these ingredients also contain umami compounds. Pair them with beef and you get an explosion of savory, meaty, delicious flavors.

cooking times. Take advantage of this fact when the cut specified in a recipe is not available, when certain cuts are on special, or to accommodate family preferences.

Beef Brisket

Briskets are boneless and available in a variety of cuts. The flat half, often referred to as first cut or thin cut, is a lean beef cut. Like pot roasts, it also requires moist-heat cooking to tenderize.

How Much to Buy

The amount of edible cooked beef per pound of raw beef will vary with the cut. The table on page 245 provides general guidelines. Use it to help decide how much beef to buy when serving a given number of people, or to determine if a certain recipe is sufficient for your needs. Of course, other factors may affect the amount you need, including the occasion, side dishes, and individual appetites.

At-Home Beef Storage

Fresh beef is perishable and, like all perishable food, must be handled and stored properly to avoid spoilage and foodborne illness. Follow these food safety practices for storing raw and cooked beef:

- Refrigerate or freeze beef as soon after purchasing as possible. (If it will take longer than 30 minutes to get it home, keep it cold in a cooler in your car.)
- When refrigerating beef, place it in the meat compartment or the coldest part of the refrigerator.
- If the beef is wrapped in transparent film, it can be refrigerated (or frozen up to 2 weeks) without rewrapping. See the table on page 246 for suggested storage times to preserve wholesomeness and quality of beef. For longer freezer storage and to prevent freezer burn, repackage in heavy-duty aluminum foil, freezer paper, or plastic freezer bags, removing as much air as possible.
- Label and date frozen beef packages, including weight and/or number of servings. Practice the *FIFO* inventory system—first in, first out.
- Follow the laws of thawing: Do not defrost frozen beef at room temperature. Defrost frozen beef in the refrigerator to prevent bacterial growth. Place the package on a tray to catch any drippings and place it in the refrigerator the day before it's needed.

BEEF SERVINGS PER POUND

	Type of Beef Cut	Servings per Pound (3-ounce Cooked, Trimmed)
Steaks	Shoulder Center (Ranch Steak)	4
	Chuck Shoulder	3½
	Flank	4
	T-Bone	2½
	Tri-Tip	4
	Tenderloin	4
	Top Loin	4
	Top Round	4
	Round	4
	Bottom Round	3
	Bottom Round (Western Griller)	4
	Top Sirloin	4
	Sirloin Tip Side	4
	Sirloin Tip Center	4
	Eye Round	4
	Round Tip, thin cut	4
Roasts	Shoulder Petite Tender	4
	Sirloin Tip Center	4
	Eye Round	4
	Top Round	4
	Round Tip	4
	Tri-Tip	4
	Tenderloin	4
Pot Roasts	Chuck Shoulder	3
	Bottom Round	3
	Brisket, Flat Cut	2½ to 3
Other Cuts	95% Lean Ground Beef	4
	Shank Cross Cuts	1½ to 2½
	Shoulder Petite Tender Medallions	4

- Allow about 24 hours to defrost a 1- to 1½-inch-thick package of ground beef or beef pieces, 12 hours for ½- to ¾-inch-thick patties.
- Allow 12 to 24 hours to defrost steaks, depending on thickness.
- Allow 4 to 7 hours per pound to defrost large roasts or thick, compact pot roasts.
- Allow 3 to 5 hours per pound to defrost small roasts or thin pot roasts.

- Cook ground beef as soon as possible after defrosting. Due to the grinding process, ground beef is more perishable than roasts and steaks and has a shorter shelf life.
- Refrigerate leftovers promptly after serving, within 2 hours after cooking. To speed up the chilling, divide large quantities into smaller portions or spread food out in a shallow container.

REFRIGERATOR AND FREEZER STORAGE TIMETABLE: RECOMMENDED STORAGE TIMES FOR MAXIMUM QUALITY

	Type of Beef	Refrigerator (35°F to 40°F)	Freezer (0°F or Colder)
Fresh Beef	Steaks Roasts Pot Roasts	3 to 4 days	6 to 12 months
	Beef for stew, stir-fry, and kabobs	2 to 3 days	6 to 12 months
	Ground beef	1 to 2 days	3 to 4 months
Leftover (Cooked) Beef	All	3 to 4 days	2 to 3 months

Beef Cooking Basics

Keep It Clean

To prevent foodborne illness, follow these simple steps.

Wash your cutting board after contact with raw meat

- Wash hands thoroughly for at least 20 seconds in hot soapy water before and after handling meat and other fresh foods.
- Keep raw meat and meat juices from coming into contact with other foods, both in the refrigerator and during preparation.
- Wash all utensils, cutting surfaces, and counters with hot soapy water after contact with raw meat.
- Designate your cutting boards so you have one that is used only for raw meats and another for cooked meats.
- Do not use a platter or a plate that held raw meats or poultry for cooked foods unless it has been washed in hot soapy water.

Get It Ready

Use these smart handling tips to prepare beef for cooking.

- Leave a thin layer of fat on steaks and roasts during cooking to preserve juiciness. Trim fat after cooking.
- Pat steaks, cubes, and pot roasts dry with paper towels for better browning.
- Partially freeze beef (or partially thaw frozen beef) until it is firm to make it easier to slice beef into strips for stir-frying.
- Use a gentle touch with ground beef. Overmixing will result in burgers, meatballs, or meat loaves with a firm, compact texture.
- When roasting or broiling, place beef on a rack in the broiler or roasting pan to allow fat to drip away during cooking.
- Salt draws out moisture and inhibits browning. Therefore, salt beef after cooking or browning.

Equipment Basics

Having the right equipment and knowing how to use it can make a big difference in cooking beef.

- Choose pans that heat evenly without scorching.
- Size matters when it comes to pans. For best results, use the pan size specified in the recipe. If the pan is too small and beef is crowded, browning will be inhibited. If the pan is too large, overcooking may result.
- Nonstick pans are easier to clean and allow for cooking with less fat.
- When cooking with acidic ingredients, such as tomatoes, citrus juices, or wine, use pans with a nonreactive interior surface, such as nonstick, anodized aluminum, and stainless steel. Reactive metals such as aluminum and cast iron can affect the taste and color of dishes with acidic ingredients.
- Place beef on a rack in the broiler or roasting pan to allow fat to drip away during cooking.

Marinades and Rubs

Marinades are seasoned liquid mixtures that add flavor to beef and may tenderize depending on the ingredients. A tenderizing marinade must contain an acidic ingredient, such as lemon juice, vinegar, yogurt, wine, or a natural tenderizing enzyme found in fresh papaya, ginger, pineapple, or figs. Marinades are typically used only for beef cuts that are to be cooked by dry heat. Follow these helpful hints for mastering marinades:

- Always marinate in the refrigerator, never at room temperature.
- Tender beef cuts need only be marinated 15 minutes to 2 hours for flavor.
- Less tender cuts should be marinated at least 6 hours, but no more than 24 hours, in a tenderizing marinade. Marinating longer than 24 hours in a tenderizing marinade will result in a mushy texture. A tenderizing marinade penetrates about ¼ inch into the beef.
- Never save and reuse a marinade.
- If a marinade will be used for basting during cooking or served as a sauce, plan to reserve a portion of it before adding the beef. To ensure food safety, marinade that has been in contact with uncooked beef must be brought to a full rolling boil for at least one minute before it can be used as a sauce.
- Allow ¼ to ½ cup of marinade for each 1 to 2 pounds of beef.
- Marinate in a food-safe plastic bag or in a nonreactive container, such as a glass or plastic dish. Turn or stir the beef occasionally to allow even exposure to the marinade.

A rub is a blend of seasonings applied to the surface of beef before cooking. Dry rubs consist of herbs, spices, and perhaps garlic. Paste-type rubs often have small amounts of oil, mustard, or other moistening ingredients added. A rub adds an outer crust of flavor to beef but does not tenderize.

Secrets to Successful Beef Cookery

The secret to moist, juicy, flavorful beef is actually quite simple—just match an appropriate cooking method to the cut you've selected. Here's an easy rule of thumb: for tender cuts, dry-heat methods such as grilling, pan-broiling, broiling, roasting, and stir-frying are best. Moist-heat methods such as braising (pot roasting) or cooking in liquid (stewing) are better choices for less tender cuts of beef. For quick easy reference, see the table "How to Cook Lean Cuts of Beef" on the next page.

HOW TO COOK LEAN CUTS OF BEEF

Beef Cut		Pan-Broil	Broil	Stir-Fry	Roast	Grill	Braise	Stew
Tender Steaks	Shoulder Center Steak (Ranch Steak)	X	X	X		X		
	T-Bone Steak	X	X			X		
	Sirloin Tip Center Steak	X	X	X		X		
	Top Sirloin Steak	X	X	X		X		
	Tenderloin Steak	X	X	X		X		
	Top Loin (strip) steak	X	X	X		X		
	Tri-Tip Steak	X	X	X		X		
Less Tender Steaks	Chuck Shoulder Steak, Boneless	*	*			*	X	X
	Flank Steak		*	X		*	X	
	Top Round Steak	*	*	X		*		
	Round Steak	*	*	X		*		
	Bottom Round Steak						X	X
	Bottom Round (Western Griller) Steak	*	*			*		
	Sirloin Tip Side Steak	*	*	X		*		
	Eye Round Steak	*				*	X	
	Round Tip Steak, thin cut	X	X	X				
Roasts	Shoulder Petite Tender Roast		X		X	X		
	Eye Round Roast				X		X	
	Round Tip Roast				X			
	Top Round Roast				X			
	Sirloin Tip Center Roast				X			
	Tenderloin Roast				X	X		
	Top Loin Roast				X	X		
	Tri-Tip Roast				X	X		
Pot Roasts	Chuck Shoulder Pot Roast						X	X
	Bottom Round Roast				X		X	X
	Brisket, Flat Half						X	X
Other	95% Lean Ground Beef	X	X		X	X		
	Shank Cross Cuts						X	X
	Shoulder Petite Tender Medallions	X						

* Requires marinating

Dry-heat Cooking Methods

Dry-heat cooking methods are best for cooking tender cuts of beef, or less tender cuts that have been tenderized by marinating or pounding. The following dry-heat cooking methods are considered low-fat because they require little or no added fat. See Appendix C, "Easy Steps to Cooking

Lean Beef," for detailed instructions on dry-heat cooking, including suggested cooking times for various cuts of lean beef.

Roasting

Roasting is used when cooking large cuts of beef, such as tenderloin roasts. Although it requires more time, roasting is the simplest method because it requires little attention. The beef is placed on a rack so that fat drains off during cooking.

Broiling

When broiling, the food is cooked at a high temperature and is positioned directly underneath the heat source, only inches away. The beef is placed on a rack so that fat drains off during cooking.

Grilling

Any cut of beef that can be roasted or broiled can also be grilled by one of two grilling methods: direct or indirect. The direct method is usually used for quick-cooking cuts such as steaks, kabobs, and burgers. The beef is placed directly over the heat source. The indirect method is generally used for larger cuts of beef, such as roasts. In this method, the beef is cooked by reflective heat, similar to the way a conventional oven cooks, because the beef is shielded from direct heat. For detailed instructions, see appendix C. Cooking times for both of these methods depend on several factors, including size, shape, and type of beef; equipment used; maintaining consistent cooking temperature; and desired degree of doneness.

Pan-broiling

Pan-broiling is faster and more appropriate than oven-broiling for thinner, tender cuts of beef. It's sometimes called "frying without fat." In pan-broiling, no water or fat is added to the pan, and drippings from beef, if present, are removed as they accumulate. It's important not to overcook beef when pan-broiling, or it may become tough and dry. This method also can be used to cook ground beef crumbles. Even more fat can be removed by rinsing cooked ground beef (see page 242), which helps to reduce fat but retain nutrients.

Stir-frying

Stir-frying is a popular variation of pan-frying that typically combines meat, vegetables, and seasonings. Unlike pan-frying, however, the beef is sliced thin, cooked at a higher heat, and stirred continuously as it is being cooked. Only a small amount of fat is needed—typically 1 tablespoon or less for about four servings, or a vegetable oil cooking spray can be used to lightly coat the pan. Because overcrowding can cause beef pieces to steam, larger amounts of beef should be cooked in smaller batches (approximately ½ pound of beef strips per batch). Beef strips and vegetables should be cut into uniform sizes to help ensure even cooking.

Moist-heat Cooking Methods

Moist-heat cooking methods, including braising and stewing, are used to cook less tender cuts of lean beef. This generally involves cooking the beef in a covered pan, in a liquid of some type, such as flavored broth, wine, vegetable or fruit juice, or water. This is also called *under-cover cooking* because steam from the simmering liquid is what cooks and tenderizes the beef. It is important to keep the cooking temperature at a low setting so the liquid simmers. A high temperature that causes the liquid to boil will toughen beef.

Moist-heat cooking methods also are considered low-fat because added fat is not necessary, and drippings can be drained off after browning the beef. See Appendix C, "Easy Steps to Cooking Lean Beef," for detailed instructions on moist-heat cooking, including suggested cooking times for various cuts of lean beef.

HELPFUL HINTS FOR COOKING LEAN BEEF

- High heat can overcook or char the outside of beef cuts while the interior remains underdone. For tender beef, use medium-high heat for stir-frying, medium heat with all other dry cookery methods, and low heat for moist cookery methods.
- Turn steaks and roasts with tongs, not with a fork. A fork pierces the beef, allowing flavorful juices to be lost.
- Turn ground beef patties with a spatula; do not flatten patties. Pressing causes the loss of flavorful juices and results in a dry burger.
- Use an oven thermometer to verify that your oven is accurate.
- Cooking times are based on beef taken directly from the refrigerator.
- Cooking times for gas and electric ranges are comparable. However, since individual ranges perform differently, it's important for you to become familiar with your own range.
- Grilling times are based on charcoal grilling. Because gas grill brands vary greatly, it's best to consult your owner's manual for grilling guidelines.

Braising (Pot Roasting)

In braising, the beef is browned to develop color and flavor. Then a small amount of liquid, not enough to cover the beef, is added to the pan and the beef is covered with a tight-fitting lid. The beef is cooked slowly over low heat or in a 325°F oven until tender.

Cooking in Liquid (Stewing)

This method is very similar to braising. The beef may be browned, if desired. Then the beef is covered with liquid and gently simmered over low heat until tender.

Determining Doneness

Perfectly cooked beef is flavorful and tender. Overcooking is a common mistake that can make beef less juicy and tough. Your best bet for achieving the right balance between cooking beef enough, but not too much, is to use a meat thermometer. This inexpensive kitchen tool is essential for determining doneness of roasts, steaks, and burgers. It is simple to use and can make a big difference in the tenderness and flavor of cooked beef.

The cooking times in the tables (see Appendix C) and recipes are not absolutes but are given as guidelines. Use them along with the following tips.

Roasts and Steaks

There are two types of thermometers you can use for determining doneness of a roast. An ovenproof meat thermometer is inserted prior to roasting and left in the entire cooking time. An instant-read thermometer is not ovenproof; use it to check the temperature near the end of the recommended cooking time. Insert it just long enough to get a temperature reading, about 10 to 15 seconds, then remove it. Thermometers should be inserted into the thickest part of the roast, not resting in fat or touching bone.

Roasts should be removed from the oven when the thermometer registers 5°F to 10°F below the desired doneness and then allowed to stand for at least 15 to 20 minutes before carving. The beef actually continues to cook after you remove it from the oven; the temperature will continue to rise during standing and reach the desired temperature.

The most accurate way to determine doneness of steaks is with an instant-read thermometer. The temperature-sensing part of the thermometer should penetrate the center or thickest part of the steak. To test steaks, insert thermometer horizontally from the side into the center. Or make a small slit near the bone, or near the center for boneless steaks, and check the color.

Medium-rare beef is very pink in the center, slightly brown toward the exterior. Medium beef is light pink in center, brown toward the exterior. Well-done beef is uniformly brown throughout. For a color illustration of these stages of doneness, see the photographs below.

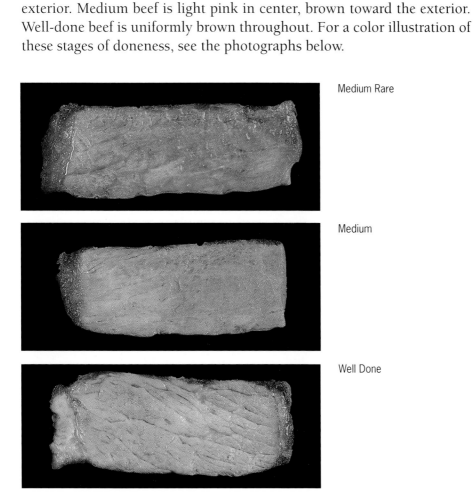

Medium Rare

Medium

Well Done

Ground Beef

Ground beef should always be cooked to a minimum internal temperature of 160°F (medium doneness), until the center is no longer pink and the juices show no pink color. The most accurate way to determine doneness is with an instant-read thermometer.

The temperature-sensing part of the thermometer should penetrate the center or thickest part of the meatloaf or patty. To test patties, insert thermometer horizontally from the side into the center, as the photograph on this page shows.

Due to the natural nitrate content of certain ingredients often used in meatloaf, such as onions, celery, and bell peppers, meatloaf may remain pink even when a 160°F internal temperature has been reached. Always check the internal temperature of meat loaf using a meat thermometer or instant-read thermometer to be certain it reaches 160°F.

Pot Roast and Beef for Stew

Due to the nature of braising, pot roasts and beef for stew will always be well done. Simmer pot roasts and beef for stew until the beef is fork-tender. To test, insert a double-pronged fork into the thickest part of the beef. When the fork can be inserted without resistance and then releases easily when pulled out, the beef is done.

Can you overcook a pot roast? Absolutely! Pot roast cooked beyond the fork-tender stage may begin to fall apart and seem very tender. Actually, when it is overcooked, it loses moisture, becoming dry, tough, and stringy.

Carving Cues

Your beef is cooked to perfection. For roasts and some steaks, the final step before serving is carving. A sharp carving knife is a must.

Roasts become firmer and easier to carve when allowed to stand 15 to 20 minutes before carving. If you slice too soon, you'll lose flavorful juices. For uniform slices, hold the knife at the same angle for each cut.

The more tender the roast, the thicker the slices may be. Beef tenderloin and shoulder petite tender roast can be sliced ½ to ¾ inch thick. Round tip, eye round, top round, shoulder tip center, and tri-tip roasts should be sliced no more than ¼ inch thick.

Tender steaks can be carved into thick or thin slices, depending on usage and personal preference. Less tender steaks, such as flank steak and round steak, should be carved into thin slices.

Brisket, tri-tip roasts, and flank steaks should be carved diagonally across the grain. Carve chuck pot roasts into medium-to-thin slices, round pot roasts into thin slices.

Easy Steps to Cooking Lean Beef

● ●

Follow the three easy steps for the various cooking methods that follow to create moist, juicy, and flavorful lean beef every time. The cooking timetables will help you determine the best cooking time for the cut you have selected. For more information on cooking times and other available beef cuts, visit www.beefitswhatsfordinner.com.

Three Easy Steps to Grilling

1. Prepare charcoal grill for direct cooking. When coals are medium ash-covered (in approximately 25 to 30 minutes), spread them out in a single layer. Check cooking temperature by cautiously holding the palm of your hand above the coals at cooking height. Count the number of seconds you can hold your hand in that position before the heat forces you to pull it away; approximately 4 seconds equals medium heat.

2. Position cooking grid. Season steak(s) with herbs or spices, as desired. Place steak(s) on cooking grid directly over coals. Charring meat, poultry, or fish is not recommended. Grill over medium to medium-low coals. Never grill while the coals are still flaming; wait until the flames subside and the coals are covered with gray ash.

3. Grill according to chart below, turning occasionally. After cooking, season with salt, if desired.

(Because gas grill brands vary greatly, consult your owner's manual for grilling guidelines.)

BEEF STEAK CHARCOAL GRILLING

Beef Steak	Thickness/ Weight	Approximate Total Cooking Time (medium-rare to medium doneness)
T-Bone Steak	¾ inch	10 to 12 minutes
	1 inch	14 to 16 minutes
	1½ inches	20 to 24 minutes (grill covered)
Shoulder Center Steak (Ranch Steak)	¾ inch	9 to 11 minutes (grill covered)
	1 inch	11 to 14 minutes (grill covered)
Shoulder Petite Tender	Varies	14 to 18 minutes (grill covered)
Top Loin Steak, boneless	¾ inch	10 to 12 minutes
	1 inch	15 to 18 minutes
Tenderloin Steak	1 inch	13 to 15 minutes
	1½ inches	14 to 16 minutes (grill covered)
Top Sirloin Steak, boneless	¾ inch	13 to 16 minutes
	1 inch	17 to 21 minutes
	1½ inches	22 to 26 minutes (grill covered)
	2 inches	28 to 33 minutes (grill covered)
Tri-Tip Roast	1¾ to 2½ pounds	25 to 35 minutes (remove roast when internal temperature reaches 140°F to 155°F)
Flank Steak (marinate)	1½ to 2 pounds	17 to 21 minutes
Sirloin Tip Center Steak	¾ inch	8 to 9 minutes (grill covered)
	1 inch	11 to 13 minutes (grill covered)
Sirloin Tip Side Steak (marinate)	¾ inch	9 to 11 minutes (grill covered)
	1 inch	12 to 14 minutes (grill covered)
Eye Round Steak (marinate) *Recommend cooking to medium-rare (145°F) doneness only.*	¾ inch	15 to 20 minutes
	1 inch	19 to 23 minutes
Top Round Steak (marinate) *Recommend cooking to medium-rare (145°F) doneness only.*	¾ inch	8 to 9 minutes
	¾ inch	9 to 11 minutes (grill covered)
	1 inch	16 to 18 minutes
	1½ inches	25 to 28 minutes (grill covered)

(continued)

Beef Steak	Thickness/ Weight	Approximate Total Cooking Time (medium-rare to medium doneness)
Bottom Round (Western Griller) Steak (marinate)	¾ inch 1 inch 1¼ inches	8 to 10 minutes 12 to 15 minutes 18 to 20 minutes
Chuck Shoulder Steak, boneless (marinate)	¾ inch 1 inch	14 to 17 minutes 16 to 20 minutes
Ground Beef Patties *USDA/FSIS recommends cooking ground beef to medium (160°F) doneness, until no longer pink in center.*	½ × 4 inches (4 oz) ¾ × 4 inches (6 oz)	11 to 13 minutes 13 to 15 minutes

All cook times are based on beef removed directly from refrigerator.
All cook times are based on medium, ash-covered coals.

Three Easy Steps to Grilling Beef Roasts (Indirect Heat)

1. Prepare charcoal grill for indirect cooking by igniting an equal number of charcoal briquettes on each side of fire grate, leaving open space in the center. When coals are medium ash-covered (about 25 to 30 minutes), add 3 to 4 new briquettes to each side. Place aluminum foil drip pan in center between coals. Position cooking grid with handles over coals so additional briquettes may be added when necessary. Check cooking temperature by cautiously holding the palm of your hand above the coals at cooking height. Count the number of seconds you can hold your hand in that position before the heat forces you to pull it away; approximately 4 seconds equals medium heat.

2. Season beef as desired. Place beef on cooking grid directly over drip pan.

3. Cover with grill lid and grill over medium heat for time indicated in chart on the next page or until thickest part of roast reaches internal temperature as specified. Turning is usually not necessary. Add 3 to 4 additional briquettes to each side every 30 minutes or as necessary to maintain proper heat during grilling. Transfer roast to carving board; tent loosely with aluminum foil. Let roast stand 10 to 15 minutes. (Temperature will continue to rise about 5° to 10°F to reach desired doneness and roast will be easier to carve.)

Beef Roast	Weight (pounds)	Approximate Total Cooking Time (over medium heat)		Remove Roast When Internal Temperature Reaches
Tenderloin Roast, well trimmed and silver skin removed	2 to 3 (center-cut)	medium-rare:	35 to 45 minutes	135°F
		medium:	45 to 60 minutes	150°F
	4 to 5 (whole)	medium-rare:	55 to 65 minutes	135°F
		medium:	65 to 75 minutes	150°F
	Place tenderloin roast on one side of cooking grid directly over coals. Sear, uncovered, 5 to 10 minutes or until bottom of roast is browned (do not turn). Turn roast over and place in center of cooking grid over drip pan. Cover and grill indirectly for time and temperature indicated in chart.			
Round Tip Roast	3 to 4	medium-rare:	70 to 90 minutes	135°F
		medium:	1½ to 1¾ hours	150°F
	4 to 6	medium-rare:	1½ to 1¾ hours	135°F
		medium:	1¾ to 2 hours	150°F
Eye Round Roast	2 to 3	medium-rare:	50 to 70 minutes	130°F

Medium-rare doneness: 145°F final meat temperature after 15 to 20 minutes standing time.
Medium doneness: 160°F final meat temperature after 15 to 20 minutes standing time.
All cook times are based on beef removed directly from refrigerator.
All cook times are based on medium, ash-covered coals.

Three Easy Steps to Pan-Broiling

1. Heat heavy nonstick skillet 5 minutes over medium heat.
2. Season steak(s) with herbs or spices, as desired. Place steak(s) in preheated skillet. Do not overcrowd. Do not add oil or water; do not cover.
3. Pan-broil according to chart on the next page, turning once. (For steaks 1 inch thick or thicker, turn occasionally.) Remove excess drippings as they accumulate. After cooking, season with salt, if desired.

Three Easy Steps to Broiling

1. Set oven regulator to broil; preheat for 10 minutes. During broiling the door of electric ovens should be left ajar; the door of gas ovens should remain closed. (However, consult your owner's manual for specific broiling guidelines.)

BEEF STEAK PAN-BROILING

Beef Steak	Thickness	Approximate Total Cooking Time over Medium Heat (medium-rare to medium doneness)
T-Bone Steak	¾ inch	11 to 13 minutes
	1 inch	14 to 17 minutes
Shoulder Center Steak (Ranch Steak)	¾ inch	9 to 12 minutes
	1 inch	13 to 16 minutes
Shoulder Petite Tender Medallions	½ to ¾ inch	5 to 6 minutes
Top Loin Steak, boneless	¾ inch	10 to 12 minutes
	1 inch	12 to 15 minutes
Tenderloin Steak	½ inch	3½ to 5½ minutes*
Use medium-high heat for ½-inch- thick steak.	¾ inch	7 to 9 minutes
	1 inch	10 to 13 minutes
Top Sirloin Steak, boneless	¾ inch	10 to 13 minutes
	1 inch	15 to 20 minutes
Sirloin Tip Center Steak	¾ inch	11 to 13 minutes
	1 inch	14 to 15 minutes
Sirloin Tip Side Steak (marinate)	¾ inch	10 to 12 minutes
	1 inch	13 to 15 minutes
Top Round Steak (marinate) *Recommend cooking to medium-rare (145°F) doneness only.*	¾ inch	11 to 12 minutes
	1 inch	15 to 16 minutes
Bottom Round (Western Griller) Steak (marinate)	¾ inch	11 to 14 minutes
	1 inch	16 to 22 minutes
Ground Beef Patties *USDA/FSIS recommends cooking ground beef to medium (160°F) doneness, until no longer pink in center.*	½ × 4 inches (4 oz)	10 to 12 minutes
	¾ × 4 inches (6 oz)	12 to 15 minutes

All cook times are based on beef removed directly from refrigerator.

2. Place beef on rack in broiler pan. Season beef with herbs or spices, as desired. Position broiler pan so that surface of beef is within specified distance from heat as indicated in chart on the next page.

3. Broil according to chart, turning once. After cooking, season with salt, if desired.

BEEF STEAK BROILING

Beef Steak	Thickness/Weight	Distance from Heat	Approximate Total Cooking Time (medium-rare to medium doneness)
T-Bone Steak	¾ inch	2 to 3 inches	10 to 13 minutes
	1 inch	3 to 4 inches	15 to 20 minutes
	1½ inches	3 to 4 inches	27 to 32 minutes
Top Loin Steak, boneless	¾ inch	2 to 3 inches	9 to 11 minutes
	1 inch	3 to 4 inches	13 to 17 minutes
	1½ inches	3 to 4 inches	19 to 23 minutes
Tenderloin Steak	1 inch	2 to 3 inches	13 to 16 minutes
	1½ inches	3 to 4 inches	18 to 22 minutes
Top Sirloin Steak, boneless	¾ inch	2 to 3 inches	9 to 12 minutes
	1 inch	3 to 4 inches	16 to 21 minutes
*Turn occasionally as needed during cooking	1½ inches	3 to 4 inches	26 to 31 minutes
	2 inches	3 to 4 inches	34 to 39 minutes*
Flank Steak (marinate)	1½ to 2 pounds	2 to 3 inches	13 to 18 minutes
Top Round Steak (marinate) Recommend cooking to medium-rare (145°F) doneness only.	¾ inch	2 to 3 inches	12 to 13 minutes
	1 inch	2 to 3 inches	17 to 18 minutes
	1½ inches	3 to 4 inches	27 to 29 minutes
Bottom Round (Western Griller) Steak (marinate)	1¼ inches	3 to 4 inches	18 to 20 minutes
Chuck Shoulder Steak, boneless (marinate)	¾ inch	2 to 3 inches	10 to 13 minutes
	1 inch	3 to 4 inches	16 to 21 minutes
Ground Beef Patties USDA/FSIS recommends cooking ground beef to medium (160°F) doneness, until no longer pink in center.	½ × 4 inches (4 oz)	3 to 4 inches	10 to 12 minutes
	¾ × 4 inches (6 oz)	3 to 4 inches	12 to 14 minutes

All cook times are based on beef removed directly from refrigerator.

Three Easy Steps to Roasting

1. Heat oven to temperature specified in beef roasting chart.
2. Place roast, fat side up, on rack in shallow roasting pan. Season roast before cooking, if desired. Insert ovenproof meat thermometer so tip is centered in thickest part of roast, not resting in fat or touching bone. Do not add water or cover.
3. Roast according to chart on the next page. Transfer roast to carving

BEEF ROASTING

Beef Roast	Oven Temperature (preheated)	Weight	Approximate Total Cooking Time		Remove Roast from Oven When Internal Temperature Reaches
Shoulder Petite Tender	425°F	Varies	medium-rare:	20 to 25 minutes	145°F
			medium:	20 to 25 minutes	160°F
Tenderloin Roast	425°F	2 to 3 lbs (center-cut)	medium-rare:	35 to 40 minutes	135°F
			medium:	45 to 50 minutes	150°F
		4 to 5 lbs (whole)	medium-rare:	50 to 60 minutes	135°F
			medium:	60 to 70 minutes	150°F
Tri-Tip Roast	425°F	1½ to 2 lbs	medium-rare:	30 to 40 minutes	135°F
			medium:	40 to 45 minutes	150°F
Sirloin Tip Center Roast	325°F	2 to 2½ lbs	medium-rare:	1¼ to 1½ hours	140°F
Round Tip Roast	325°F	3 to 4 lbs	medium-rare:	1¾ to 2 hours	140°F
			medium:	2¼ to 2½ hours	155°F
		4 to 6 lbs	medium-rare:	2 to 2½ hours	140°F
			medium:	2½ to 3 hours	155°F
		6 to 8 lbs	medium-rare:	2½ to 3 hours	140°F
			medium:	3 to 3½ hours	155°F
Bottom Round Roast	325°F	3 to 4 lbs	medium-rare:	1½ to 2 hours	135°F
Eye Round Roast	325°F	2 to 3 lbs	medium-rare:	1½ to 1¾ hours	135°F
Meat Loaf	350°F	8 x 4 inches, 1½ lbs	medium:	1¼ hours	160°F

Medium-rare doneness: 145°F final meat temperature after 15 to 20 minutes standing time.
Medium doneness: 160°F final meat temperature after 15 to 20 minutes standing time.
All cook times are based on beef removed directly from refrigerator.

board; tent loosely with aluminum foil. Let roast stand 15 to 20 minutes. (Temperature will continue to rise 5°F to 10°F to reach desired doneness and roast will be easier to carve.)

Three Easy Steps to Braising

1. Slowly brown beef on all sides in small amount of oil in heavy pan. Pour off drippings. Season beef, as desired.
2. Add small amount (½ to 2 cups) of liquid (e.g., broth, water, juice, beer, or wine) to pan.
3. Cover tightly and simmer gently over low heat on top of the range or in

BEEF BRAISING

Beef Steak	Weight/ Thickness	Approximate Total Cooking Time (covered over low heat)
Chuck Shoulder Pot Roast, boneless	2½ to 4 pounds	2 to 3 hours
Bottom Round Roast, boneless	3 to 4 pounds	2½ to 3¼ hours
Chuck Shoulder Steak, boneless	¾ to 1 inch	1¼ to 1¾ hours
Brisket, flat half	2½ to 3½ pounds	2½ to 3 hours
Round Steak (Eye or Bottom), boneless	¾ to 1 inch 1 to 1½ inches	1¼ to 1¾ hours 1¾ to 2½ hours

All cook times are based on beef removed directly from refrigerator.

a preheated 325°F oven according to chart above or until beef is fork-tender. (It is not necessary to turn the beef cut over during cooking.) *The cooking liquid may be thickened or reduced for a sauce, as desired.*

Three Easy Steps to Cooking in Liquid (Stewing)

1. Coat beef lightly with seasoned flour, if desired. Slowly brown beef, in batches, on all sides in small amount of oil in heavy pan. Pour off drippings. *Omit browning step for corned beef brisket.*
2. Cover beef with liquid such as broth, water, juice, beer, or wine. Add seasoning, as desired. Bring liquid to broil; reduce heat to low.
3. Cover tightly and simmer gently over low heat on top of the range according to chart below or until beef is fork tender. *The cooking liquid may be reduced or thickened for a sauce, as desired.*

COOKING IN LIQUID (STEWING)

Beef Steak	Weight/ Thickness	Approximate Total Cooking Time (covered over low heat)
Beef for Stew (Boneless Round or Chuck Pieces for Stew)	1 to 1½ inches	1¾ to 2¼ hours
Shank Cross Cuts	1 to 1½ inches	2 to 3 hours
Brisket, flat half, fresh	2½ to 3½ pounds	2½ to 3 hours

All cook times are based on beef removed directly from refrigerator.

Guide to Using Alternate Cuts of Lean Beef in Recipes

You Can Also Use	Steaks: Grill, Broil, or Pan-Broil							Steaks: Marinate and Cook (Grill, Broil, or Pan-Broil)							Roasts: Grill or Roast in Oven				Roasts: Braise or Cook in Liquid			
	T-Bone Stk	Tenderloin Steak	Top Loin (Strip) Steak	Tri-Tip Stk	Sirloin Tip Center Steak	Ranch Steak	Top Sirloin Steak	Round Tip Steak	Eye Round Steak	Top Round Steak	Sirloin Tip Side Steak	Western Griller Steak	Chuck Shoulder Steak	Flank Steak	Tri-Tip Rst	Sirloin Tip Center Roast	Eye Round Roast	Round Tip Roast	Chuck Shoulder Roast	Brisket Flat Half	Shank Cross Cuts	Bottom Round Roast
Eye Round Roast															X	X	X					
Eye Round Steak				X				X			X	X										
Top Round Steak							X			X			X	X								
Bottom Round Roast																			X	X		
Sirloin Tip Center Roast																X	X					
Sirloin Tip Center Steak		X	X			X																
Sirloin Tip Side Steak									X		X	X										
Top Sirloin Steak										X			X	X								
Round Tip Roast															X	X		X				
Round Tip Steak									X	X			X	X								
Bottom Round (Western Griller) Steak									X		X											
Brisket, Flat Half																			X			X
Shank Cross Cuts																			X	X		X
Shoulder Center (Ranch) Steak		X	X	X	X																	
Chuck Shoulder Roast																				X		
Chuck Shoulder Steak														X								
Top Loin (Strip) Steak				X	X		X															
Flank Steak							X			X			X									
Tri-Tip Roast																	X	X				
Tri-Tip Steak	X	X		X	X																	
Tenderloin Steak	X	X		X	X	X																
T-Bone Steak	X	X		X																		

Quick Guide to Matching a Beef Cut with a Recipe

Beef Cut	Recipes
Chuck Shoulder Pot Roast or Steak *Also known as:* *Book Roast or Steak* *Center Cut Shoulder Pot Roast* *Clod Roast* *Chuck for Swissing* *Clod Steak Boneless*	• Summertime Steak Salad (61) • Slow Good BBQ Beef Sandwiches (66) • Beef and Vegetable Pizza (70) • Chipotle Pot Roast with Cheddar Mashed Potatoes (130) • Beef Pot Roast with Maple Sweet Potatoes and Cider Gravy (137) • Basic Beef Pot Roast (139) • Rustic Polenta with Beef Pot Roast Ragù (140) • Beef Portobello Bread Pudding (142) • Spring Vegetable and Beaujolais Beef Stew (164) • Southwest Beef Stew (174) • Provençal Beef Stew (178) • Tortilla Beef Soup (183) • Italian Pot Roast with Sweet Peppers, Olives, and Capers (212)
Shoulder Center Steak *Also known as:* *Ranch Steak* *Aspen Strip* *Summit Steak* *Santa Fe Strip*	• Beef Tostadas with Grilled Vegetable Salsa (28) • Steaks with Cowboy Coffee Rub and Spicy Pico de Gallo (32) • Beef and Heirloom Tomato Salad with Balsamic Syrup (38) • Southwest Beef and Warm Vegetable Salad (48) • Beef and Lemony Lentil Salad (52) • Ranch Steak Panini (76) • Beef Steak Gyros (80) • Szechuan Beef Stir-Fry (100) • Thai Noodles with Beef and Broccoli (112) • Ranch Steaks with Pepper Rub (114) • Cumin-Crusted Beef Steak with Orange-Olive Relish (117) • Asian Beef Steaks and Noodles (132) • Jamaican Jerk Ranch Steaks with Chipotle Island Relish (198)

Beef Cut	Recipes
Shank Cross Cuts *Also known as:* *Fore Shanks*	• Fennel, Beef, and Bean Soup (167)
Brisket, Flat Half *Also known as:* *Brisket First Cut*	• Mole Beef (146) • Braised Brisket with Fig and Onion Confit (200) • Smoked Texas Beef Brisket with Cabernet Barbecue Sauce (209) • Holiday Brisket with Red Cabbage and Creamy Mustard Sauce (220)

Flank Steak
Also known as:
  Flank Steak Filet
  London Broil
	• Curried Flank Steak with Fruit and Almond Basmati Rice (19)
	• Cracked Wheat and Beef Salad (55)
	• Balsamic Marinated Steak Sandwich (84)
	• Flank Steak with Creamy Poblano Chile Sauce (119)
	• Tandoori Beef Skewers with Pistachio Couscous (202)
	• Lemon, Parsley, and Pine Nut–Crusted Flank Steak with Sherry-Wilted Spinach (215)

Top Loin (Strip) Steak
Also known as:
  Strip Steak
  Kansas City Steak
  New York Strip Steak
	• Grilled Brazilian Beef with Chimichurri (33)
	• Beef and Spinach Salad with Roasted Tomato Vinaigrette (44)
	• Pizza on the Side Salad (45)
	• Ancho Chili–Rubbed Beef Steaks (103)
	• Bistro Beef Steak with Wild Mushroom Ragoût (109)
	• Peppered Strip Steaks with French Herb Cheese (195)

T-Bone Steak	• Spicy Five-Pepper T-Bone Steaks (11) • Southern Spiced T-Bone Steaks with Chili Mashed Potatoes (21)

Tenderloin
Also known as:
  Filet Mignon
  Short Tenderloin
  Butt Tenderloin
  Fillet de Boeuf
  Tender Steak
  Fillet Steak
	• Tenderloin Steaks with Arugula Salad and Sweet and Spicy Beets (7)
	• Tenderloin Steaks with Espresso-Bourbon Sauce (13)
	• Provençal Beef Salad (40)
	• Tenderloin, Cranberry, and Pear Salad with Honey Mustard Dressing (43)
	• Tenderloin Sandwich with Balsamic Caramelized Onions (81)
	• Easy Beef Tenderloin Steaks with Blue Cheese Sauce (97)
	• Tenderloin Steaks with Jalapeño Pepper Sauce (116)
	• Honey Mustard Beef Tenderloin with Tarragon Sauce (189)
	• Five-Spice Tenderloin Steaks with Creamy Polenta (207)
	• Garlic and Wine Tenderloin with Cremini Mushroom Risotto (217)
	• Marsala Roast Tenderloin with Shiitake-Leek Compote (222)

Top Sirloin Roast or Steak
Also known as:
  Boneless Sirloin Butt Steak
  Top Sirloin Butt Center Cut Steak
	• Beef Kabobs with Roasted Red Pepper Coulis (9)
	• Mojo Beef Kabobs (16)
	• Grilled Italian Steak and Pasta (25)
	• Beef Sirloin with Grilled Tomato Pesto (30)
	• Sirloin with Sugar Snap Pea and Pasta Salad with Gremolata Dressing (51)
	• Mixed Greens and Steak Salad with Creamy Peppercorn Dressing (62)
	• Sirloin Sandwich with Red Onion and Dried Fruit Marmalade (86)
	• Seasoned Steaks with Brown Rice and Vegetables (99)
	• Bistro Beef Kabobs with Broccoli Pilaf (102)

Beef Cut	Recipes
Top Sirloin Roast or Steak *(continued)*	• Beef Paprikash (105) • Barbecue Beef Stir-Fry with Couscous (106) • Middle Eastern Beef Brochettes with Couscous (107) • Beef Sirloin with Oven-Roasted Vegetables (127) • Spinach and Beef Skillet (135) • Curry Beef and Aromatic Rice (149) • Beef Fried Rice (150) • Bistro-Style Steak and Potatoes (155) • Grilled Beef Bruschetta with Feta Cheese (191)
Tri-Tip Roast *Also known as:* *Bottom Sirloin Roast* *Triangle Roast*	• Grilled Beef Tri-Tip Roast with Caramelized Three-Onion Sauce (14) • Beef, Mango, and Barley Salad (56) • Caribbean Jerk Tri-Tip with Basil Lime Salad (58) • Mexican Chili Beef Wrap (72) • Roasted Herb-Rubbed Beef Tri-Tip with Orange and Red Onion Salsa (219)
Sirloin Tip Side Steak	• Balsamic Dijon Steak with Asparagus (8)
Top Round Steak *Also known as:* *Top Round London Broil*	• Grilled Steak with Spicy Mango Salsa (22) • Steak with Ginger Plum Barbecue Sauce (35) • Thai Beef Noodle Salad (41) • Farmer's Market Vegetable, Beef, and Brown Rice Salad (46) • Beef and Wild Rice with Belgian Endive Salad (53) • Stir-Fry Orange Beef Lettuce Cups (69) • Beef and Broccoli with Noodles (125) • Beef Spanish Rice (126)
Bottom Round Roast *Also known as:* *Beef Bottom Rump Roast*	• Bistro Beef Stew (159) • Thai Curry Beef Stew (161) • Beef and Butternut Squash Soup with Chipotle Cream (169) • Cajun Beef Fricassee (171) • Indian Beef Stew (173)
Eye Round Steak	• Garlic-Yogurt Marinated Eye Round Steaks (20) • Pho Beef Noodle Soup (162)
Round Tip Roast or Steak *Also known as:* *Tip Sirloin Roast* *Crescent Roast* *Knuckle Roast* *Beef Sirloin Tip Roast* *Thin cut steak also known as:* *Sandwich Steak* *Breakfast Steak*	• Dijon-Wine Steak Kabobs with Mushroom Wild Rice (27) • Beef and Tomato Sauce with Pasta (98) • Spicy Beef and Spinach Stir-Fry (111) • Southwest Beef and Pasta Skillet (115) • Beef and Broccoli Soup (175) • Three-Mustard Beef Round Tip with Roasted Baby Carrots and Brussels Sprouts (186)

Beef Cut	Recipes
95% Lean Ground Beef	• Southwest Burgers with Corn Relish (24) • Chipotle Sloppy Joes with Crunchy Coleslaw (64) • Asian Express Beef Lettuce Wraps (67) • Caribbean Grilled Burgers with Chipotle Pepper Sauce (71) • Mediterranean Burgers with Hummus (74) • Mushroom Merlot Burgers (77) • Basic Lean Beef Burgers (88) • Asian Burgers with Ginger-Lemon Mayonnaise (92) • Blue Cheese and Caramelized Onion Burgers (93) • Taco Burgers (94) • Beef Enchiladas with Red and Green Sauces (122) • Beef, Arugula, and Spinach Lasagna (129) • Bow Tie Pasta with Beef and Beans (134) • Wine Country Meatloaf with Sun-Dried Tomatoes, Basil, and Parmesan (144) • Basic Beef Meatballs (151) • Ratatouille Meatball Pasta (152) • Beefy Mexican Lasagna (154) • Beef and Couscous with Butternut Squash (156) • Easy Beef Chili (160) • Tomato-Basil Meatball Soup (168) • Cowboy Beef and Black Bean Chili (177) • Bold Beef Chili with Queso Anejo (181) • Panhandle Beef Chili (184) • Triple-Ginger Beef Dumplings (193) • Beef Beggar's Purses (196) • Porcini Mushroom and Beef Bolognese (204)

Measurements and Equivalents

Volume Measure Equivalents

1 teaspoon	60 drops or ⅓ tablespoon	½ cup	8 tablespoons or 4 fluid ounces
3 teaspoons	1 tablespoon	⅔ cup	10 tablespoons plus 2 teaspoons
1 tablespoon	3 teaspoons or ½ fluid ounce	⅝ cup	½ cup plus 2 tablespoons
2 tablespoons	⅛ cup or 1 fluid ounce	¾ cup	12 tablespoons or 6 fluid ounces
4 tablespoons	¼ cup or 2 fluid ounces	⅞ cup	¾ cup plus 2 tablespoons
8 tablespoons	½ cup or 4 fluid ounces	1 cup	16 tablespoons or 8 fluid ounces or ½ pint
12 tablespoons	¾ cup or 6 fluid ounces	2 cups	1 pint or 16 fluid ounces
16 tablespoons	1 cup or 8 fluid ounces or ½ pint	1 pint	2 cups or 16 fluid ounces
⅛ cup	2 tablespoons or 1 fluid ounce	1 quart	2 pints or 4 cups or 32 fluid ounces
¼ cup	4 tablespoons or 2 fluid ounces	1 gallon	4 quarts or 8 pints or 16 cups or 128 fluid ounces
⅓ cup	5 tablespoons plus 1 teaspoon		
⅜ cup	¼ cup plus 2 tablespoons		

Metric Weight Equivalents

1 ounce	¹⁄₁₆ pound or 28.35 grams	12 ounces	¾ pound or 340.20 grams
4 ounces	¼ pound or 113.40 grams	16 ounces	1 pound or 453.60 grams
8 ounces	½ pound or 226.80 grams	1 pound	16 ounces or 453.60 grams

Notes

228   *"stearic acid is unique and does not raise blood cholesterol levels"*   Mensink RP, Zock PL, Kester ADM, Katan MB. Effects of dietary fatty acids and carbohydrates on the ratio of serum total to HDL cholesterol and on serum lipids and apolipoproteins: a meta-analysis of 60 controlled trials. *American Journal of Clinical Nutrition.* 2003;77:1146–1155; Kris-Etherton P, Mustad V, Derr JA. Effects of dietary stearic acid on plasma lipids and thrombosis. *Nutrition Today.* 1993;28:30–38.

228   *"naturally occurring trans fat holds promise"*   Field CJ, Schley PD. Evidence for potential mechanisms for the effect of conjugated linoleic acid on tumor metabolism and immune function: lessons from n-3 fatty acids. *American Journal of Clinical Nutrition.* June 2004; 79(6 suppl):1190S–1198S.

231   *"lean red meat as part of a diet designed to reduce the risk of heart disease"* Davidson, MH, Hunninghake D, Maki KC, Kwiterovich PO, Kafonek S. Comparison of the effects of lean red meat vs. lean white meat on serum lipid levels among free-living persons with hypercholesterolemia. *Archives of Internal Medicine.* 1999;159:1331–1338; Hunninghake DB, Maki KC, Kwiterovich PO Jr, Davidson MH, Dicklin MR, Kafonek SD. Incorporation of lean red meat into a National Cholesterol Education Program Step 1 Diet: A long-term, randomized clinical trial in free-living persons with hypercholesterolemia. *Journal of the American College of Nutrition.* 2000;19:351–360.

231   *"when you deprive yourself of favorite foods"*   Polivy J. Psychological consequences of food restriction. *Journal of the American Dietetic Association.* 1996;96:589–592.

232   *"more than twice as likely to meet 100 percent of the Daily Value for iron"* Waylett DK, Mohamedshah F, Murphy MM, Douglass JS, Heimbach JT. The role of beef as a source of vital nutrients in healthy diets. *ENVIRON.* July 1999.

232   *"mild, short-term iron deficiency can leave you feeling run-down and fatigued"* Haas JD, Brownlie T. Iron deficiency and reduced work capacity: a critical review of the research to determine a causal relationship. *Journal of Nutrition.* 2001;131(suppl 2):691–696.

232   *"children, adolescent girls, and women of childbearing age are the ones consuming the least"*   Looker AC, Dallman PR, Carroll MD, Gunter EW, Johnson CL. Prevalance of iron deficiency in the United States. *Journal of the American Medical Association.* 1997;277:973–976.

232   *"lower scores on math tests among older children and adolescents"*   Halterman JS, Kaczorowski JM, Aligne CA, Auinger P, Szilagyi PG. Iron deficiency and cognitive achievement among school-aged children and adolescents in the United States. *Pediatrics.* 2001;107:1381–1386.

232   *"greater risk for preterm and low-birthweight deliveries"*   Institute of Medicine,
Food and Nutrition Board. *Standing Committee on the Scientific Evaluation of
Dietary Reference Intakes for Vitamin A, Vitamin K, Arsenic, Boron, Chromium, Cop-
per, Iodine, Iron, Manganese, Molybdenum, Nickel, Silicon, Vanadium, and Zinc.*
Washington, DC: National Academy Press; 2001.

232   *"increase your body's ability to absorb iron by two to four times"*   Cook JD, Mon-
sen ER. Food iron absorption in human subjects. III Comparison of the effect of
animal proteins on nonheme iron absorption. *American Journal of Clinical Nutrition.* 1976;29:859–867.

234   *"effects of eating a moderately high protein diet"*   Layman D, Boileau R, Erick-
son D, Painter J, Shiue H, Sather C, Christou D. A reduced ratio of dietary carbohydrate to protein improves body composition and blood lipid profiles during
weight loss in adult women. *Journal of Nutrition.* 2003;133:411–417.

234   *"more likely to meet their daily needs for protein, iron, zinc, and
B-vitamins"*   Waylett DK, Mohamedshah F, Murphy MM, Douglass JS, Heimbach
JT. The role of beef as a source of vital nutrients in healthy diets. *ENVIRON.* July
1999.

About the Authors

Richard Chamberlain is the owner and executive chef of two renowned Dallas restaurants: Chamberlain's Steak and Chop House and Chamberlain's Fish Market Grill. Chef Chamberlain has a true passion for food, cooking both for business and for pleasure. He brings his love of food and good health home to his wife and two children. As a family, they enjoy cooking together and especially love tasting and trying new foods. Chef Chamberlain's philosophy is to start with the freshest and best ingredients available and treat them in the simplest way possible to create delicious dishes that also promote good health. His commitment to health is evident in his restaurants, where he offers a variety of choices, including smaller portion sizes of steaks and other entrees and the option to share a dish without a surcharge, and he gladly accepts special requests to meet the health needs of his guests. Chef Chamberlain serves on the board of the Dallas chapter of the American Heart Association.

Betsy Hornick is a registered dietitian specializing in nutrition education and communications. She has written and edited numerous nutrition and health education publications for both consumers and health professionals. As a busy mother of three active children, she faces the same daily dilemma that many Americans do—deciding what to prepare for dinner that will satisfy the taste and nutrition needs of all family members. Betsy tested many of the recipes on her family, with wonderful results. She discovered a variety of dinner solutions that satisfy even a dietitian-mother's standards for healthy meals while receiving thumbs-up from her family of recipe testers. Favorites included Chipotle Sloppy Joes with Crunchy Cole Slaw, Tomato Basil Meatball Soup, Thai Noodles with Beef and Broccoli, and Cowboy Beef and Black Bean Chili, to name just a few.

The National Cattlemen's Beef Association (NCBA), on behalf of the Cattlemen's Beef Board and the Beef Checkoff Program, coauthored this cookbook with ADA. The NCBA is a trade association of America's cattle farmers and ranchers, the largest segments of the nation's food and fiber industry. NCBA and State Beef Councils are sources of information about beef nutrition and beef recipes and cooking. For more information about beef, visit www.beefitswhatsfordinner.com.

With nearly 70,000 members, the Chicago-based **American Dietetic Association (ADA)** is the nation's largest organization of food and nutrition professionals. ADA serves the public by promoting optimal nutrition, health, and well-being. The ADA Foundation (ADAF) is the charitable arm of the ADA. The mission of the foundation is to improve the nutritional health of the public. The ADAF achieves this mission by supporting scholarships for dietetics students and professionals, food and nutrition research, and nutrition education programs. For more information, visit ADA's website, www.eatright.org.

Recipe Index

Page numbers in *italics* refer to illustrations.

Index

Page numbers in *italics* refer to illustrations.